# THE MERCEDES-BENZ BOOK

# THE
# MERCEDES-BENZ
# BOOK

Victor Boesen *and* Wendy Grad

DOUBLEDAY & COMPANY, INC., GARDEN CITY, NEW YORK
1981

*Library of Congress Cataloging in Publication Data*
Boesen, Victor.
The Mercedes-Benz book.

1. Mercedes automobile. I. Grad, Wendy,
joint author. II. Title.
TL215.M4B63      629.2′222

ISBN 0-385-12554-2
Library of Congress Catalog Card Number 77-15145

iv

# PREFACE

The Speedway was just a few miles beyond the woods and fields from our house on the Allisonville Pike. During the big race on Decoration Day (when people put flowers on the graves of Civil War soldiers), it took only a little help from our imaginations to hear the howling of the cars, rising and falling on the wind, as the begoggled demons at the wheel drove them around the track.

"Ralph De Pawl-ma won in the Mercy-dees," my brother Richard said next day after the mailman had brought the Indianapolis *News*. "He drove eighty miles an hour."

Eighty miles an hour!" This was not possible. Why, it was forty miles to our new farm, and when Mr. Burkett drove the family there in his Model T, the trip took all day. He didn't loaf along, either. Sometimes, where the stretch between chuckholes was long enough, he got the car up to fifteen miles an hour. The fence posts went by so fast it was hard to count them—much faster than when we rode in the surrey behind old Jewel. Eighty miles an hour meant that Ralph De Palma in his Mercedes—with a little better road, of course—could have gotten there in a half hour. The fence posts would have been a

blur. Clearly, Richard was having sport with his kid brother.

But Richard told the truth, as time would reveal. Actually, he was a little conservative in his figure. Ralph De Palma, in that historic race of 1915, averaged not eighty but nearly ninety miles an hour for the five-hundred miles: 89.84. In those early days, this speed for that distance has never been matched.

For all that, though, if De Palma's racer had been flesh and blood, it likely would have yawned. The Mercedes car was used to being first. From its very beginning, as a Daimler, it had been the one to beat, not only on the race course but on the drawing board as well. And this was fitting, for it was Gottlieb Daimler—along with Carl Benz, though not as partners, each going his own way as if the other did not exist—who founded the institution of the motor car. They were first.

Thus, the story of Mercedes-Benz is the story of the automobile. In distinction from other books on the subject, we have tried to tell it with as little of nuts-and-bolts as needed to hold things together, hoping to attract not just the reader who owns a Mercedes-Benz, but the less fortunate fellow who doesn't have one.

# ACKNOWLEDGMENTS

Many people in many ways gave to this work: Estelle and Charles Grad, Richard Boesen, Moana Tregaskis, Henry Austin Clark, Jr., the Wiedmann family, Dr. Alfred Gleiss, Helmut Schmidt, Gunther Molter, Bernd Harling, Heidi Rausch, Hyazintha Jurak, Ruth Witzel, Peter Viererbl, Max-Gerrit von Pein, Claus-Peter Schulze, Eva Maria Francke-Neu, Dr. Grube-Bannasch, Dr. Otto Nübel, Burkhard Huelsen, Rudolf Maier, Rainer Karnovski, Thomas A. Weisshaar, Emil Kern, Helmut Pless, Hans Hemsen, Karl-Martin Schroth, A. B. Shuman, Gerhild Drücker, Ghislaine E. J. Kaes; Carl, Gertrud and Jutta Benz, Paul Gottlieb and Ira Daimler, Guy Jellinek-Mercédès, Hans Polack, Walter Gotschke, Martin Schroeder, Gerhard von Raffay, Tassilo von Grolman, Jeffrey S. Miles, Prince zu Hohenlohe-Langenburg, Hans Otto Neubauer, Berthold Rückwarth, Brigitte Heling-Hagelstein, Deutsche Durst, Libby Turnock, Judith Karfiol, Strother MacMinn, Duane Law, Martha Urann, Willy Helmerding, Michel Pyrozowski, Harry S. Morrow, Jane Jordan Browne, Paula Goeptert, Judith Kalmus, Hal Bloom, Peter Praed, the authors of a dozen books and numberless magazine articles, the host of those who gave of their time and knowledge for interviews.

To those and to the many more who lent a hand along the way—for their generosity and patience—we gratefully dedicate this book.

# CONTENTS

# COLOR PLATES

*For notes on the color plates, see page 197*

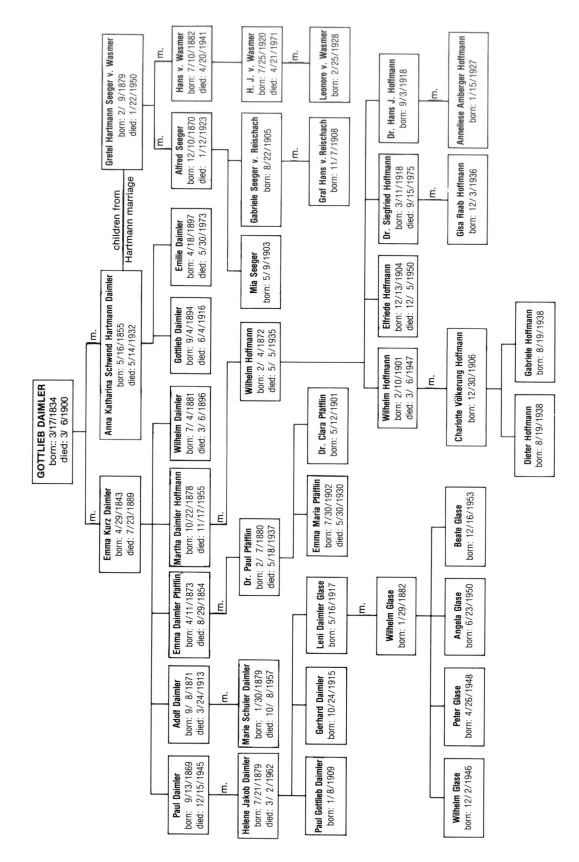

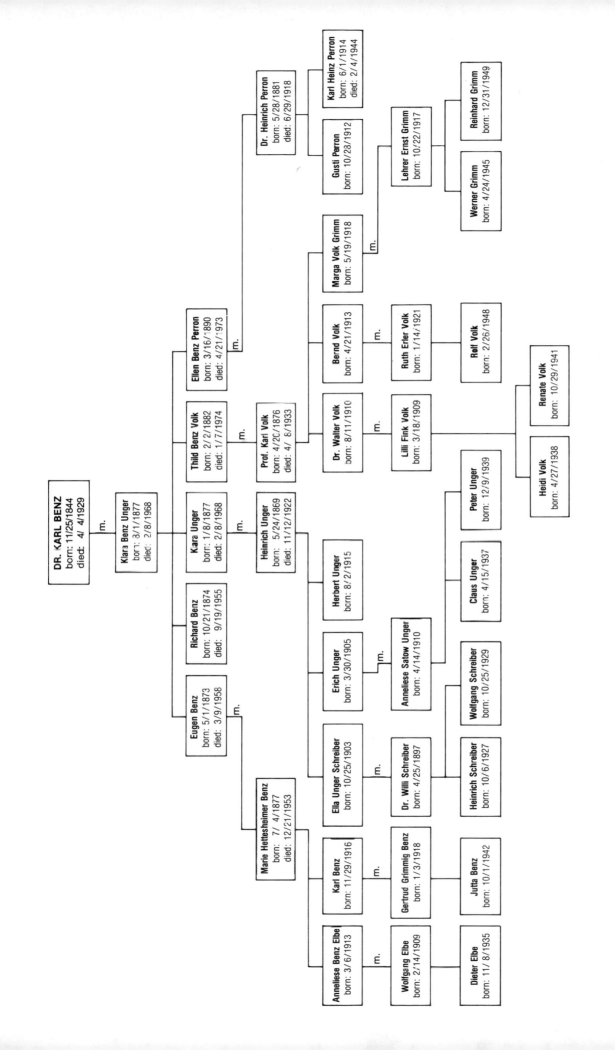

GOTTLIEB DAIMLER

(1834–1900)

Gottlieb Daimler was born in Schorndorf, Württemberg, March 17, 1834, the first of his family in four generations not to become a baker. In 1883, at Cannstatt, Daimler and Wilhelm Maybach built the world's first light-weight, high-speed engine, an indispensable prerequisite to motorized transportation. The engine, with one horizontal cylinder and burning a gasoline-type mixture, reached nine hundred revolutions a minute, compared to a top of 180 for conventional engines, which weighed up to a ton per horsepower.

In 1885, about the time Carl Benz was test-driving his three-wheeler some sixty miles away (the two men never met or communicated), Daimler mounted a half-horsepower engine on a two-wheel vehicle: the first motorcycle. In 1886, the year Benz patented his three-wheeler, Daimler installed an engine in a carriage. Three years later, in 1889, Daimler and Maybach introduced the "steel-wheeler," the first four-wheel vehicle designed for an engine rather than a horse.

Daimler died in 1900, one year before the appearance of the first "Mercedes," named for the daughter of a business associate and, radically advanced over all others, considered the first modern automobile.

CARL BENZ
(1844–1929)

Carl Benz (born Karl, he himself used Carl) was born near Karlsruhe, Germany, in the remote Black Forest village of Pfaffenrot, on November 25, 1844, to a long line of blacksmiths and burgomasters. He built the first vehicle in history powered by a gasoline engine. Patented on January 29, 1886, the machine was a tricycle and incorporated features that have remained basic to the automobile down to the present time: differential gearing, sparking ignition, carburetor.

With a single, horizontal cylinder, Benz's engine developed .8 horsepower at 250–300 revolutions a minute—it would do 450—and weighed just over 200 pounds. This was roughly twice the speed and a fraction the weight of the stationary coal-gas engine of the era.

In 1893, Benz patented the guidance system by which, with refinements, every automobile is still steered. His Vclo, of 1894, was the first car ever produced by mass-production methods. By 1900, Benz & Company, Mannheim, had built nearly three thousand machines and led the world in the manufacture of automobiles. Benz died in 1929.

# THE MERCEDES-BENZ BOOK

# CHAPTER ONE

# We Are 850,000 Orders Behind

The blue pennants with their three-pointed star over the entrance to CAR DELIVERY snapped in the springtime breeze. The attendant finished briefing the new car's owners, an elderly couple who intently studied the dashboard. He shook their hands. "Good-bye and good luck!"

The pair drove cautiously forward to the fuel pumps—two rows marked Diesel, two marked Super—and received fourteen gallons of fuel on top of the one gallon already in the tank, courtesy of the house. The fueling went fast. With six-hundred cars a day clearing through the station, there was little time for ceremony.

If the red-carpet treatment ended at the gas pumps, no one minded. Most had waited four years for this moment: the opportunity to drive away in a new Mercedes-Benz. Those who make the pilgrimage to the Daimler-Benz assembly plant at Sindelfingen to take personal delivery on their cars come from all parts of the world, but chiefly Europe. Buyers in the United States, where ownership of a Mercedes-Benz is coming to be a condition of social acceptance, are less patient.

"Americans won't wait that long," said Waldemar Bubeck, boss of the thirty-four thousand workers at Sindelfingen, a half-hour bus ride from the main Daimler-Benz works, at Untertürkheim, on the edge of Stuttgart. "They want the car at once," added Bubeck, a sun-tanned, square-shouldered man with a crisp, direct manner.

The United States, therefore, gets the lion's share of the one thousand other cars in the day's output at Sindelfingen which are held back for export. In 1977, these amounted to fifty thousand machines, give or take a few hundred—not a large figure by Detroit standards, but impressive considering that until a dozen or so years ago the Mercedes-Benz in the United States was still a curiosity. No longer ago than 1952, the first year of the car's distribution in this country, only thirty-six were sold.

It was the same story around the world: more and more people everywhere were able to persuade themselves that they could afford the fifteen to thirty thousand dollar Mercedes price tag. To keep up with the demand, the company has increased production each year since World War II. The sixteen hundred it now turns out daily at Sindelfingen is as many as it built in the whole of 1947. By the spring of 1978, the company had produced five million cars since it rose from the rubble and got going again after the shooting had stopped.

All the same, the firm was losing ground. "We are 850,000 orders behind," Bubeck said.

To its partisans, there is scant mystery why seemingly everybody wants a Mercedes-Benz, the most imitated car of the age. At Jenkintown, Pennsylvania, industrialist Stephen Pitcairn had owned "a smattering of all the Mercedes models," including his current fleet of four. He recalled some of them as he drove his new 450 SL along the road that wound through the woods from his office to his estate, a few miles away. How did the Mercedes compare with other cars he had owned?

The question seemed to jar him. "Why, there is no comparison," he retorted. "In my opinion the reason the car is popular is its quality and the way it handles." He thought a moment, then turned and looked his passenger in the eye. "There is no question in my mind," he said, "that it's the finest car in the world."

While there may be those with other ideas, there are good reasons why aficionados like Pitcairn rank the Mercedes-Benz among the front runners for excellence. In most automobile plants, basic decisions having to do with design, styling, power, release dates for new models, and so forth are made by the business end of the operation. At Daimler-Benz all such matters are decided by the engineering department.

Then there is the factor of technical precision. To see that rigidly exacting standards are maintained, one employee in ten is an inspector. "This is the highest inspector-to-worker ratio maintained by any standard automobile manufacturer," wrote the late American authority Ken Purdy.

The workers are painstakingly schooled in their tasks, each plant having its own training setup, more or less autonomous but with policy fixed at headquarters in Unterturkheim. Before a worker so much as turns a lathe on his own, he puts in a long apprenticeship—three years if he's quick to learn, three and a half if he's like most of us. Again, "one of the most detailed in the world," Ken Purdy wrote of the Daimler-Benz apprenticeship program.

Some sixty-five hundred workers, coming from many nations—Italy, Greece, Spain, Yugoslavia, Turkey, Portugal, as well as West Germany and even the United States—are in training at any one time, at a yearly cost to the company of about twenty thousand deutschemarks, or ten thousand dollars for each student. The program includes the handicapped: At the moment, six with mental disabilities were taking a two-year course for metal-working. "If a big firm doesn't do something about this, nobody else will," said Heinz Brennenstuhl, assistant director of the technical training program at Unterturkheim, obvious pride in his voice.

Once the apprentices graduate, more

than 75 percent stay with the company, as members of the "Daimler-Benz family." They are paid 2,000 to 2,500 deutsche-marks a month (approximately $1,200), with a few earning nearly twice that figure. In addition, each is privileged to buy a new Mercedes-Benz from the company every year at a substantial discount. All that's necessary, once the worker is "in the system," is to put 10,000 kilometers (6,242 miles) on the car during the year. The employe's name is in the computer and his eligibility for the new one comes up automatically. With the company upward of a million orders behind, the workers have little trouble finding someone to buy last year's car, often at more than they paid for it.

At Daimler-Benz, "worker wretchedness" gains nothing from the parking lots, which are a sea of Mercedes-Benz automobiles.

Carl Benz— he spelled his name with a "C" for reasons unknown to his descendants—would be pleased to know that the blood children of his 1885 three-wheeler are proving worthy to bear his name. It should also give him satisfaction that his idea caught on as it did: the notion that there was a future for a vehicle that ran by itself, rather than being pulled by a horse. The results might even overwhelm him, except that Benz seems to have been a quiet, introspective man, not given to emotion.

In the world today there are nearly 330 million automobiles. It has been suggested that a visitor from outer space, swinging in close for a better look and seeing the automobiles speeding along the roads, would conclude that the planet was inhabited by beetles.

Parked bumper to bumper (as indeed many are much of the time), the world's cars would make a traffic jam nearly one and a quarter million miles long, circling the earth almost fifty times. We Americans, who own nearly half of the total, could load our entire population, of 225 million, into our automobiles at one time without using the back seat. Each day, we drive them the equal of nearly three round trips to the sun, 93 million miles away.

In our country, one in every six workers makes his living by the automobile, not counting those in the trade of stealing it. Nor does this include its contributions to the hospital and burial industries. In the United States, since 1900, more people have been killed by automobiles than by guns in all the nation's wars.

Nor does the employment created by the automobile take in the bureaucracies that have proliferated in recent years to nurture its place in the public mind as the chief scapegoat for air pollution. Nor must one forget the devoted servants of our legislative halls, who seem bent on making as many laws governing its use as there are automobiles. The Lord gave the Law to Moses in ten crisp sentences. The State of California, for one, gives the law to the driver of a motor car in 547 pages, with the number of pages going up each year. Count in the several thousand more laws of jealous local jurisdictions, many overlapping or contradicting one another, and motorists become as minnows to the policeman's barracuda, the cop, flowing along with traffic, having only to decide which minnow to pounce on under what law—or how many of them. The automobile is undoubtedly man's most regulated artifact.

Also, starting at the very first and continuing to this day, the automobile has been an unfailing boon to the doomsayers. "It is clear that in the laboratories of nature you can only have oil being formed at about one ten-thousandth or millionth the rate at which it is being consumed," warned a Professor Leslie in Pittsburgh, the first to be heard from. Soon, he said, it would be necessary to find a substitute for gasoline. That was in 1886, the very same year that Carl Benz patented his little, three-wheel *Motorwagen* and only twenty-seven years after "Colonel" Edward Laurentine Drake brought in the world's first oil well, at Titusville, Pennsylvania, in 1859.

By 1909, with the automobile looking as if it might be here to stay, the widely read *Harper's Weekly* took alarm. "With 100,000 automobiles, boats, and combustion engines to be built in 1909 with gasoline the main fuel . . . and this number likely to increase for several years to come," cried

Carl Benz, a student at the Polytechnical School, in Karlsruhe, in 1865.

the periodical in its issue for July 31, "we will have to start using alcohol as a substitute."

No rush to alcohol having developed by 1913, the prestigious *Scientific American* joined in the concern, warning somberly, "[The] question of the possible exhaustion of the world's oil supply deserves the gravest consideration. There is every indication we are face to face with this possibility . . . ."

Running out of oil became a headline staple through the years. ONLY SIX YEARS' SUPPLY LEFT—OIL FAMINE CLOSER—OIL SHORTAGE GROWING WORSE—LAST TRAFFIC JAM. . . .

Nothing has changed except that now it's "energy" we're running out of.

These worries might have been deferred but for a printer friend of Carl Benz, back there a century ago, who suffered from a foot ailment and bought a velocipede to help him get around. It proved useless to him, though, and he gave it to Benz, who had often remarked about the coming vehicle that would run under its own power. Benz put a seat on the velocipede and made other changes, as the late St. John Nixon tells it, but saw that there was no way he could adapt it to self-propulsion without completely changing the design.

Benz threw the tricycle away but hung onto some ideas it gave him. They blended with ideas he had picked up a few years before in polytechnic school in Karlsruhe, as he listened to Ferdinand Echtenbacher, a cerebral trail-blazer who spoke of such esoterica as atomic physics and who had written books about the construction of engines. Professor Echtenbacher, much beloved by his students, predicted that the steam engine, a cumbersome, inefficient affair but all there was at the time, one day would be displaced by something better. The key, he said, lay in a better understanding of how heat worked, "so that engines can be kept down to a reasonable size."

Benz, born near Karlsruhe in 1844 into a family of blacksmiths, began thinking about internal combustion. He went on thinking about it after he graduated, at twenty-one, and as he went about getting experience as an engineer—in Karlsruhe building and repairing locomotives, working in half-darkness twelve hours a day; in Mannheim making scales, and in Pforzheim building bridges.

At Pforzheim he found something besides bridges to interest him. This was Bertha Ringer, the bright and spirited daughter of a well-known contractor. Benz flung over his job and went looking for a way to make more money. He returned to Mannheim, bought a shed, and opened a machine shop. He was soon at odds with his partner over the question of fixing the place up, the partner feeling that capital improvements should await a more stable cash flow.

Bertha Ringer resolved the issue by arranging with her father for the pre-wedding transfer of her dowry to Benz. Carl bought out the partner, and he and Bertha were married, July 20, 1872.

But then came a stock-market crash. Disaster threatened Carl Benz's Iron Foundry and Machine Shop when a court ordered Benz to pay back a 2,500-mark loan. All that saved the shop from being auctioned was that the value of the property had gone up. The bank, however, required that Benz pledge the shop's entire contents as security.

But adversity would have its uses. Benz and Bertha searched their minds for something new to make that was badly needed—some item of machinery with significant industrial potential. Freshly to Benz's mind came the replacement for the steam engine that his old teacher Professor Echtenbacher had foretold. He immersed himself in a study of the internal-combustion engine.

There was a great deal of new material on the subject at this time, the autumn of 1877, for the internal-combustion engine had come into the limelight. The idea of harnessing explosions for motive power had begun, so far as the record tells, with Christian Huygens, the Dutch mathematician, astronomer, and physicist, toward the end of the seventeenth century. Genghis Khan had demonstrated the utility of gunpowder in propelling missiles at one's enemies five hundred years earlier, but it proved too unmanageable for engines.

In a pioneer version of the gas engine built in the 1860s, the explosion of the gas drove the piston upward. Atmospheric pressure (14.7 pounds to the square inch at sea-level) pushed it back down, helped

Bertha Ringer, circa 1869.

along by gravity and the vacuum left under the piston by the explosion. At about the time that the atmospheric engine was being designed, Étienne Lenoir, of France, built a gas engine that functioned more or less on the order of the steam engine—and wasn't much better. The Lenoir engine used copious amounts of oil and water and was prone to overheat, although for a brief time Lenoir's gas engine was excitedly hailed as the engine everybody was looking for.

It was another Frenchman, Beau de Rochas, of Paris, who laid out the rudiments of how to make internal combustion work. First, the fuel mixture should be compressed. This made for a bigger and hotter explosion, improving efficiency. There should be four strokes of the piston. The first stroke drew the fuel mixture into the cylinder. The next stroke compressed the mixture. At the third the

Nikolaus August Otto (1832–91), the self-taught engineer who, in 1876, built the first four-stroke engine.

fuel was ignited. On the fourth the exhaust was expelled, clearing the cylinder to repeat the cycle.

While De Rochas had now told how it should be done, it fell to Nikolaus August Otto, a traveling salesman in the Rhineland and self-taught engineer, to put De Rochas's prescription into practice. Fourteen years after De Rochas, Otto built an actual four-stroke engine, and the age of internal-combustion power was on its way. The year was 1876.

A century and several hundred million engines later, the internal-combustion engine still works just the way Beau de Rochas said it would: fuel in—compress—explode—exhaust, the cycle being repeated thousands of times a minute. How fortunate that the inventors didn't know this was impossible!

For his four-stroke engine, Otto was issued patent Number 532, on August 4, 1877. This was bad news for Carl Benz, hoping to invent himself out of the crisis brought to a head just a month before by the court's order to pay his debts. Benz—and everyone else, for that matter—would have to limit his efforts to a two-stroke engine, a far trickier machine, or pay a license fee to Otto.

Dugald Clerk, of Glasgow, was working on a two-stroke engine at the time and received a British patent on it in 1878. Clerk's engine, however, had the flaw that the fuel mixture tended to go off inside the pump, before it reached the cylinder. Benz now demonstrated his inventive colors by making Clerk's engine better, improving both fuel pump and air pump so that pre-explosion was eliminated. Benz's two-cylinder engine ran for the first time on New Year's Eve, 1879. The engine was still being balky as the long twilight began at day's end. "After supper my wife said, 'Let's go over to the

6

French woodcut of the De Dion-Bouton-Trépardoux steam-driven quadricycle, invented in 1883. Count Albert de Dion hired mechanical toy builders Georges Bouton and his brother-in-law Trépardoux in 1881. The firm, which became De Dion-Bouton, continued to manufacture automobiles until 1932.

shop and try our luck once more,' " Benz wrote in *Memories of an 80-Year-Old Man,* written with the help of his son-in-law, Dr. Karl Volk, a professor at a junior college, which may account for the oddly lyrical tone of the text: "Something tells me to go and it will not let me be.

"So there we were, back again, standing in front of the engine as if it were a great mystery that was impossible to solve. My heart was pounding. I turned the crank. The engine started to go 'put-put,' and music of the future sounded with regular rhythm. We both listened to it run for a full hour, fascinated, never tiring of the single tone of its song. The two-cycle engine was performing as no magic flute in the world ever had."

Benz (or Volk) seems to have been carried away as he continues: "The longer it played its note, the more sorrow and anxiety it conjured away from the heart. It was the truth that if sorrow had been our companion on the way over there, joy walked beside us on the way back. For this New Year's Eve we could well dispense with congratulations of friends and neighbors, for we had known the heartiest kind of happiness that evening in our poor little workshop, which now had become the birthplace of a new engine. We stood around in the courtyard listening for quite a while, and through the still of the night we could still hear the 'put-put-put.'

"Suddenly the bells began to ring— New Year's Eve bells. We felt they were not only ringing in a new year, but a new era, which was to take on a new heartbeat from the all-important instrumentality of the engine."

But the world at large seems to have heard rather less than Benz did that New Year's Eve, for it bought no engines from him. The backers he had hoped to attract failed to materialize. The future that had looked so promising was turning to despair when salvation appeared one day in the person of Emil Buhler, the court photographer, who needed a polished steel plate for a glazing machine. "I've been all over town trying to have one made," Buhler complained. "Can you do it?"

Buhler was impressed by how quickly and expertly Benz turned out what he needed. Looking around the shop, the visitor was further moved by the preparations Benz had made for the commercial manufacture of his engine. The upshot was that Buhler advanced Benz money each week to keep him going. Buhler found Benz another backer, Otto Schmuck, a businessman, and on October 14, 1882, Gasmotorenfabrik Mannheim was incorporated.

In three months, however, one of the directors fell into the error of injecting himself into technical matters. Benz was quick to find two new partners, Max Kaspar Rose, another businessman; and

Friedrich Wilhelm Esslinger, who had strong commercial connections along with a good technical background. On October 1, 1883, the three men founded what would live to become a historic name: Benz & Co., Rheinische Gasmotoren-Fabrik, whose business was "building combustion engines according to the designs of Carl Benz."

Meanwhile, Benz went on inventing things to make the engines work better. One was a throttle control device, the basic idea of which has remained unchanged to the present day. He followed this with patents for improving ignition and simplifying the engine, these likewise fundamental steps in the evolution of the internal-combustion power plant.

All the while, in the back of his mind lurked the thought of designing a vehicle that moved under its own power. He said little about it for fear of making his partners nervous. "Once the business is making enough money from solid turnover to assure its continuation, then we can think about taking a jump into the future," Max Rose said.

The "solid turnover" Max Rose spoke of soon developed. Within a year of the company's founding, Benz & Co. was being flooded with letters from customers telling of their pleasure with Benz engines, which delivered from one to ten horsepower. In 1885 a Benz engine gained international notice by winning an award at the Exposition Universelle at Antwerp. The company soon needed more space and bought forty thousand additional square feet in the Waldhofstrasse.

Benz decided to go ahead with his long-stored-up plans to build a vehicle that propelled itself, needing no horse. The time was opportune. He had learned that August Otto's patent on the four-cycle engine was being canceled for technical reasons, clearing the way for others to pursue the development of four-cycle engines.

Rose and Esslinger turned no cartwheels at the news of Benz's plans, but neither did they make an issue of it. Perhaps, as good businessmen, they reflected that Carl Benz might be onto something.

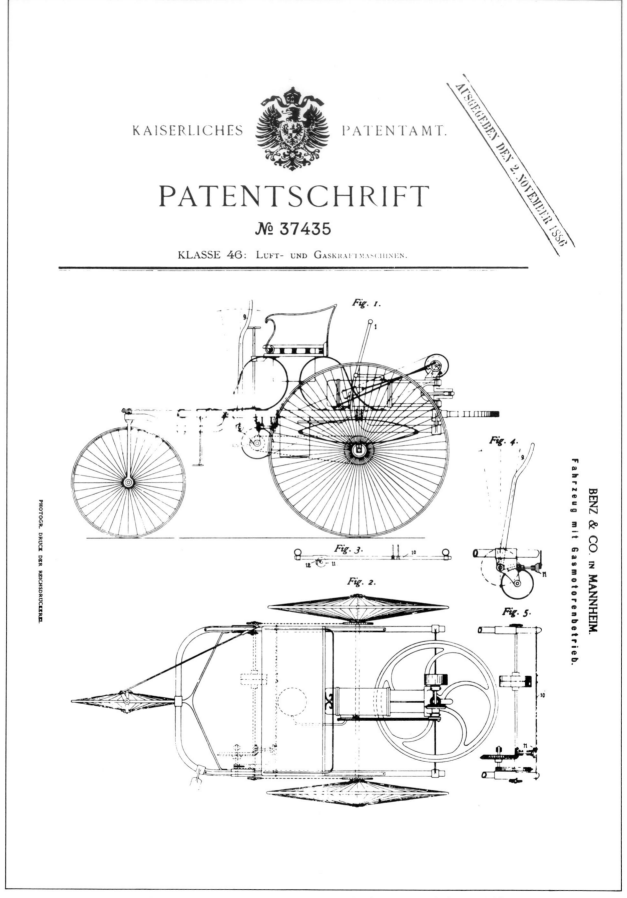

KAISERLICHES PATENTAMT.

# PATENTSCHRIFT

№ 37435

KLASSE 46: Luft- und Gaskraftmaschinen.

AUSGEGEBEN DEN 2. NOVEMBER 1886.

BENZ & CO. IN MANNHEIM.

Fahrzeug mit Gasmotorenbetrieb.

PHOTOGR. DRUCK DER REICHSDRUCKEREI.

Fig. 1.

Fig. 4.

Fig. 3.

Fig. 2.

Fig. 5.

Carl Benz's patent drawing of the world's first automobile, in 1886.

# CHAPTER TWO

# A Complete Substitute for Horses

As he set out to build what was to become known as the automobile, Carl Benz realized that the greatest problem before him was an engine. He would have to make his own, just as the Wright Brothers would have to tailor an engine to the special needs of their airplane at Kitty Hawk not many years later.

The customary engine, built to drive pumps, lathes, and other stationary apparatus, was much too big and heavy, weighing up to a ton for each horsepower it turned out as it slogged along at 120 to 130 revolutions a minute. Moreover, the gas engine was tied to the source of its fuel supply, unable to travel.

What Benz needed was an engine that was smaller, lighter, and independent of the gashouse, while at the same time mustering at least the same power as the gas engine. In short, Benz needed an engine that, so to speak, reconciled the irreconcilable.

It occurred to him that power could be raised if the engine ran faster, and that this additional speed could be attained if the fuel used was benzine, derived from petroleum. He knew the explosive force of benzine from having read about a blast that killed several people after a housewife using the substance to clean gloves set the container too close to the kitchen stove. The benzine, of course, could be carried aboard the vehicle. The umbilicus with the powerhouse could be cut.

Benz's completed benzine engine, with a single, horizontal cylinder, weighed only 200 pounds, a flyweight compared to its gas-driven counterparts. His engine raced along at 250 to 300 revolutions a minute—and could actually do 450. This was roughly twice the speed of the gas engine, and at just under one horsepower, the benzine engine developed proportionally far more power, just as he had calculated. Benz mounted the flywheel to

Benz drove this car for the first time in public on July 3, 1886. (Fritz Held, an employee, pointing forward; photographed in Mannheim, circa 1893.)

turn horizontally because he was afraid the gyroscopic effect of the usual, vertical wheel would cause steering problems on the corners.

With the engine built, Benz next took up the problem of the vehicle to go with it. How should it be designed? He had nothing whatever to go on. No one had gone before him to leave the hint of a path to follow. He was on his own, a techno-logical Magellan on a sea without charts.

He chose a three-wheel base over four, with the single wheel in front, because it was easier to devise a way to steer one wheel than two. And what influence might the velocipede have had which his printer friend had given him years before? Benz arranged with a bicycle builder to make the wheels. He ordered special drive chains, since no stock chains were rugged enough.

The chains worked from a shaft turned by a pulley connected to the engine by belt, as was done in factories. The shaft also carried an idling, or neutral, pulley, next to the fixed pulley. To go or to stop,

Benz installed a lever to nudge the belt from pulley to pulley. He controlled the engine by a second lever, working through the throttle regulator he had developed and patented earlier. He equipped the engine with electric igni-tion, using a battery and a spark plug of his own design. There were differential gears, a carburetor, and a cooling system whereby water was circulated through coiled tubing, augmenting the water jacket around the engine. All these fea-tures were to remain basic to the nature of every automobile to come. He executed his plans remarkably close to the drawings he submitted with his application for a patent.

On a spring day in 1885, Benz was ready to try out his creation for the first time. He poured benzine into the carbu-retor and water into the little tank over the engine. A mechanic put a spot of oil on the cylinder where it was exposed at the rear. Several hands laid hold of the fly-wheel, whose diameter nearly spanned the width of the car, and gave it a whirl. The engine coughed to life.

Benz took his seat at the tiller and edged the belt onto the drive pulley. At the sud-den load, the engine choked and died. The car was pushed to get the belt back on the idling pulley, and the engine was re-started. Benz resumed his seat. This time, before he nudged the belt over to the drive pulley—put the car in gear, as it were—his men gave the machine a shove, reducing inertia as the engine again re-ceived the load. The car rolled out the door and into the yard. For the first time, a vehicle had moved under the power of an internal-combustion engine.

Around and around the yard Benz drove, Bertha running along beside him, clapping her hands. On the fourth circuit, an ignition wire broke and the engine stopped. Repairs were made and the driving continued. Then one of the drive chains parted. The day's tests were over, but Carl Benz was a happy man. He would always say that this was the day the horse was through on the highway.

Benz installed stronger chains. He took the engine down, scrutinized each part, and put the engine back together. He designed a better mounting for the battery and had a carriage builder make a seat to take the place of the box he had first used. He painted the machine a gleaming white. He now felt he was ready to show his work to the public, putting an end to the rumors about the goings-on at the shop, most of them wrong. He announced that on a certain day he would drive his machine on the road that passed the shop, in full view of everybody who cared to see. He invited friends and relatives, including his two sons, Eugen, twelve, and Richard, ten, to be his witnesses. Mrs. Benz would be on the car with him.

On the appointed day, after giving a short talk to the guests assembled inside the gate, Benz helped Bertha aboard and took his place as the driver. The flywheel was spun—and spun again, without results. After several mortifying minutes, the belt was worked over to the drive pulley and the car given a push. Concentrating on keeping the engine running as the machine began to move, Benz crashed into the brick wall that enclosed the shop, scoring another first. The impact nearly catapulted him and Mrs. Benz over the front wheel, which was driven back, out of alignment, and broken. The frame was bent.

Benz abashedly helped his crew manhandle the machine back into the shop, where it was found that the damage was not as disastrous as first thought. The broken parts were replaced, the bent ones straightened, and within the week Benz was ready to try again.

This time he prudently told no one of his plans, but the word somehow got out, and a large crowd gaped in disbelief as Benz trundled through the gate, Bertha again at his side, the two of them speeding off down the road with nothing visible impelling the carriage. The scene became more credible to the watchers as the engine suddenly raced out of control and Benz brought the car to a halt. Something had gone wrong with the drive belt.

Benz helped Bertha to the ground, and together they pushed the car back to the shop, assisted by a sympathetic onlooker who didn't mind the jeering and laughter of the rest of the crowd.

On his next effort, Benz covered nearly a half mile, at about ten miles an hour. Thereafter, each time out, he extended his distance but was discomfited by the growing size of the throng that swirled around him each time he stopped. Worried about the police, he took to driving at night, protected by darkness. In due time, he achieved his goal of two loops of the city—the second loop wider than the first—without a breakdown.

On January 29, 1886, the state ratified the validity of his invention by granting him Patent No. 37435.

Benz's fellow townsmen, however, shook their heads. Why would a man of his talents waste them on something so clearly useless? What was the need for a horseless carriage when there were so many horses around?

The newspapers ignored him until they could no longer do so. "A velocipede driven by ligroin gas, built by the Rheinische Gasmotoren-Fabrik of Benz et Cie. . . . was tested this morning early on the Ringstrasse, during which it operated satisfactorily," reported the *Neue Badische Landeszeitung* on July 3, 1886.

Some weeks later, under the headline ROAD VEHICLE WITH GAS-ENGINE DRIVE, the

Mannheim *Generalanzeiger* ran a detailed account of Benz's invention, referring to previous coverage they had given the subject and bringing the reader up to date.

"We saw this first vehicle being put together, and we saw it run months ago," the story read. "The very first time we saw it tested we were certain that Benz's invention had solved the problem of building a road vehicle driven by a basic power source." The machine needed improvement, but "the difficult task of inventing it may now be considered over and done with. . . .

"This motor vehicle is not meant to have the same purpose and characteristics as a velocipede, which one could take for a pleasurable spin over a smooth, well-kept country road. Rather, it is conceived as a cart or peasant's wagon, suitable not only for traveling fairly good roads but also for carrying heavy loads up steep inclines. For example, it would enable a commercial traveler to take his samples from one place to another without any difficulty."

The account concluded, "We believe this wagon has a good future because it can be put in use without much trouble, and because when the speed is made sufficient, it will be the most inexpensive promotional tool for traveling salesmen, as well as a way for tourists to get around."

As Benz continued to drive his *"Patent Motorwagen"* on the streets of Mannheim, perhaps feeling some security in the recognition his work was beginning to get, the thing happened that he had long feared: the police moved. The chief himself summoned Benz to headquarters. Did Benz realize it was against the law to drive a self-propelled vehicle in the province of Baden?

Benz did, he admitted, but he argued that there was such an important future for the horseless carriage that if he were barred from using the streets to test his machine, other countries than Germany would take the lead in the *Motorwagen's* development. "I have taken every precaution on the side of safety," he said. "Any of my mechanics who drives too fast I confine to the workbench for two weeks."

The chief magnanimously agreed to let him drive in town but said Benz would need a permit from the Minister of Baden to venture outside the city. This privilege was granted on August 1, 1888. The document read: "This is to authorize Mr. Benz, owner of Rheinische Gasmotorenfabrik, to drive for the time being for purposes of testing the motor vehicle that he has produced and patented, on the streets and lanes leading through the communities of Mannheim, Sandofen [and so forth], with the express provision that the driver will be responsible for any damage that may be caused to others as a result of using the motor vehicle."

Six weeks later, apparently feeling, upon reflection, that it had been too casual with Benz, the government followed up with further hobbles on him. "With reference to the permit issued on August 1 of this year . . . to the Rheinische Gasmotorenfabrik to engage in driving the Patent Motorcar," began this newest word from Olympus, "we impose the condition that whenever the Patent Motorcar encounters horse carriages, it must in time and in such a fashion that there will be no danger of the horse shying, reduce its speed.

"At a point 15 steps from the carriage being encountered, it is not permitted to drive faster than a man walking," the decree continued. "In the same fashion the driver must reduce his speed when he passes the horse carriage from behind. Violation of these conditions will be punished according to [the laws of the highway]."

In taking this supplemental action, the

authorities may have been prompted by an episode that, nearly a century afterward, is still celebrated by aficionados of autodom. This was the famous drive by Bertha Benz to her hometown of Pforzheim and back with sons Eugen and Richard, history's first cross-country trip by automobile.

It annoyed Mrs. Benz that her husband kept tinkering and changing, seemingly never satisfied that his machine was ready for more exalted performance than little jaunts around the block. One August morning in 1888, she and the two boys rose at five o'clock and tiptoed from the house, careful not to awaken Benz. Stealthily they pushed the *Motorwagen* from the garage, started the engine, and were off, Eugen at the tiller, his mother at his side, Richard on the jump seat.

The journey was not uneventful, though the tourists proved equal to all emergencies. The first came near Heidelberg, when something went wrong with the ignition. The boys fixed it with a garter borrowed from their mother.

Next came a carburetor failure. Again Eugen and Richard found the answer in a personal item from their mother—this time a hairpin. The leather on the brake shoes wore out, calling for a cobbler to nail on new leather. And there wasn't always a drugstore in sight to supply ligroin, the petroleum-derived solvent used by the *Motorwagen* as fuel.

Hills were the worst problem. At each little rise in the road, Mrs. Benz took the tiller while Eugen and Richard pushed, nimbly vaulting back aboard as the car topped the summit and began gathering speed on the downgrade.

The travelers reached Pforzheim in safety, arriving just as night closed in; they had no lights. After visiting relatives a few days, they drove back to Mannheim, filled with suggestions for improving the *Patent Motorwagen*. Most

important was a lower gear for the hills, which meant any stretch of road where water ran the other way. Benz put their suggestions into effect and showed the car, his second model, at the Munich Engine Show the following month.

If Carl Benz theretofore had been a

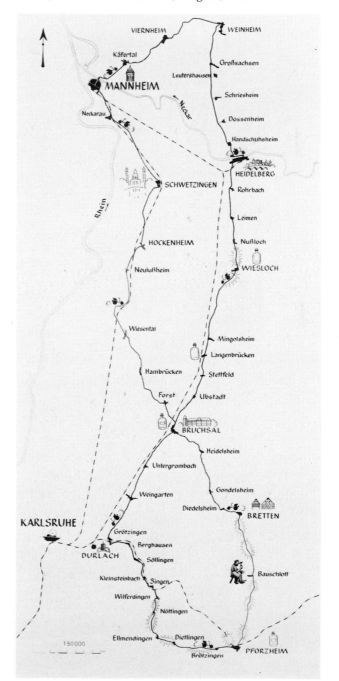

The route followed by Bertha Benz and sons Eugen, fifteen, and Richard, thirteen, on the first long-distance journey ever undertaken by automobile. They covered a round-trip distance of almost one hundred and twelve miles, unbeknownst to Carl, August, 1888.

stranger to Munich, he was a stranger no more. "Seldom, if ever, have passersby in the streets of our city seen a more startling sight than on Saturday afternoon when a one-horse chaise came from the Senlingerstrasse over Senlingertorplatz and down Herzog Wilhelmstrasse at a good clip without any horse or thill [shaft of a carriage], a gentleman sitting under a surrey top, riding on three wheels—one in front and two behind—speeding on his way toward the center of town," one newspaper wrote.

"The amazement of everyone on the street who saw him was such that they seemed unable to grasp what they had before their eyes, and the astonishment was general and widespread."

The press beyond Bavaria likewise took notice. The influential *Leipziger Illustrierte Zeitung* published an account, illustrated with woodcuts, was picked up by *The Scientific American*, January 5, 1889, carrying the word of Benz's wonderful machine to the United States—where, it was said, forty thousand mechanics at once became unhappy with bicycles and wanted to build automobiles:

"Complete substitute for carriage and horses," heralded the caption over a picture depicting a couple driving gaily along a tree-lined street, the gentleman in a derby and his lady with a parasol laid back on her shoulder. In the background, symbolically, a team of horses is drawn up, the driver respectfully waiting, whip poised. Spectators lining the curb surge into the street as the car passes.

"At the exhibition of machinery which was held in Munich during the past year, the attention of the visitor was attracted to a vehicle with a motor constructed by the Rhine Gas Motor Works, Benz & Company of Mannheim," the account began. "This motor is driven by gas which it generates from benzine or analogous material. As can be seen from the accompanying cut, this new vehicle is well-shaped compared with others of the same class.

"The motor, which is not visible from the outside, is placed in the rear of the three-wheeled carriage over the main axle, and the benzine used in its propulsion is carried in a closed copper receptacle secured under the seat, from which it passes drop by drop to the generator, and which holds enough benzine for a journey of about 75 miles. The gas mixture is ignited in a closed cylinder by means of an electric spark—a very safe and reliable arrangement. After regulating the admission of the gas, the motor can be started by simply turning a hand lever.

"The operator climbs upon the seat and, by pressing the lever at his left, sets the motor into operation, and it starts the vehicle, being connected with the back wheels. The speed of the motor can be increased or diminished at will by turning the lever backward or forward, and it can be stopped by pulling on the lever. The vehicle is steered in the same manner as a tricycle, by a small front wheel.

"It can attain a speed of about ten miles an hour, but in crowded streets it can be made to move as slowly as an ordinary vehicle. A quart of benzine is sufficient for an hour's trip, making the cost of the motive power about seven cents per hour, and the experiments with the vehicle in the streets of Munich during the exhibition proved the practicability of substituting this kind of motive power for the more expensive horse power in many cases."

For all the good words, though, there was no rush to buy Carl Benz's "complete substitute for horses." The popular consensus seemed to go along with the *German Yearbook of Natural Science* for 1888, which loftily noted that while Benz's ma-

Benz et Cie. was founded in Mannheim in 1883, sixty miles from what became the Daimler-Motoren-Gesellschaft, founded in 1890. These employees helped Carl Benz to produce his first passenger cars and, in 1894, the first bus.

chine had "caused some stir at Munich . . . this employment of the petroleum engine will probably be no more promising for the future than the use of the steam engine was for road travel."

Up to this point, Benz had sold but one car. This sale was to Émile Roger, his agent in Paris, who kept the car at the plant of Panhard-Levassor, builders of Benz's stationary engines in France. Benz visited Paris in the hope that he might induce Messrs. Panhard and Levassor to build his *Motorwagen* as well as his engines. He took the two Frenchmen for demonstration rides in the countryside, but they remained strangely noncommittal, showing only a polite interest in his

car. What Benz did not know was that Panhard-Levassor were closely involved with Gottlieb Daimler, who was drawing increasing attention to a petroleum engine he was developing at Cannstatt, sixty miles or so to the southeast of Benz's shop at Mannheim.

But for the fact that Émile Roger agreed to handle the sales of his car in France, Benz returned home from Paris empty-handed. It was perplexed disappointment for him once more when he displayed his *Motorwagen* at the 1889 Paris World's Fair, expecting to repeat his Munich success of the year before, in particular since Parisians were showing an unusual interest in things technical at the time.

The directors of Benz et Cie. pose aboard Benz's eight-seat phaeton. Named after the horse-drawn vehicle, the term phaeton refers to the double benches. Seated from left to right they are Herr Kupterschmidt, Herr Mitachle, Richard Benz, Herr Brecht, Herr Strasser, V. Fischer, Carl Benz and Herr Ganss. Circa 1895.

This interest clearly did not extend to horseless carriages. The fairgoers drifted up to the platform holding Benz's car, looked briefly, and moved on.

None of this scored Benz any points with partners Rose and Esslinger, who had frowned on his preoccupation with his motor-driven vehicle. The business of Benz et Cie., after all, was the manufacture of stationary gas engines, not the pursuit of visions.

"Herr Benz, we've now made a nice pile of money, but you had best keep your fingers out of that motorcar or you'll lose everything!" Rose cautioned one day, as recalled long afterward by Eugen Benz. "My god, my god!" Rose cried in despair, "where is this all going to end?"

For Max Kaspar Rose and Friedrich Wilhelm Esslinger, it ended on May 1, 1890, when both withdrew from the firm. Benz replaced them with Friedrich von Fischer and Julius Ganss, both more sympathetic to Benz's ambitions. He was now free to go ahead with his automobile, unfettered of hand or mind in what he was doing.

He worked harder not only to improve the car but also, apparently, to sell it. He wrote a letter to the postmaster in Speyer, dated January 1, 1891, suggesting that the postal service use his *Motorwagen* to deliver the mail. The postmaster wrote back with some ideas to improve the new model in general and to suit it to the special needs of the Post Office in particular.

For the first time, the builder of an automobile was hearing the voice of the consumer. ". . . In your new four-wheel model [still in the future] could you not have a sort of coachman's seat up front so that the enclosed room could be all at the disposal of the passengers?" the postmaster wrote. "Could you not put under the driver's seat, or in the rear, two closable compartments, a large one and a small one, where letters and money for postal transfer could be safely kept?"

One thing above all troubled the postmaster. "Why are there no controls for going backward?" he asked. "The fact that you cannot go backward is really something to puzzle at." Also, he suggested a "more powerful engine so that swampy sections of the road and deep snow could easily be traversed." He threw in some ideas for navigating on ice and going down hills. "If you are able to include these improvements in your car, indispensable for a safe and sure road performance," he wrote, "then I am positive that your ingenious and most practical invention will be crowned with success."

The postmaster added that he was thinking of the machine's use to country doctors, too. "Not every doctor in a small village has box stalls, horses, and a farm to maintain them, yet some kind of a cart is essential for a doctor who has to make calls in a number of places distant from each other," he wrote.

"How often is a doctor called on during the night, and how else is he meant to get where he has to go? Before he has roused the sleep-drunk peasant out of his bed and gotten him to put the bridle and harness on the horse, a lot of valuable time has been lost."

As if Benz might not be fully aware of what he had wrought, the postmaster listed some of the advantages of his machine over a horse-drawn outfit. "It doesn't need any feed, or any groom, no blacksmith, no danger of having a horse shy; it just moves along as if a ghostly hand were pushing it, and one stroke of the brakes and it stops. That is what makes it so inexpensive to operate. Even the stupidest blockhead must be able to see such an immense advantage as this."

There was one further small criticism. "The vehicle in motion does have something comical in its appearance from the aesthetic point of view, and someone who did not know what it was might think it was a runaway chaise he was looking at," the postmaster wrote. "That is because we have not yet grown used to it. But here also, in my opinion, a lot of minor changes and adjustments can be artfully made to improve its appearance. . . . If this were done, the lack of an animal in front . . . would not be so striking."

The letter concluded, "You must forgive me for making known my views at such length, but I know that men in special fields often want to know how a layman feels. I am curious to see how the first four-wheel vehicle works out, and I wish you success with your most excellent invention, which cannot be wanting once you get it started."

Benz did know that his invention was wanting as long as it lacked two wheels in front, and in the spring he actively began work on a four-wheeler, having by now gotten some ideas for steering it. Yet it was nearly two years before he received Patent No. 73515, on February 28, 1893, for "a steering mechanism for a car with steering circles set on a tangent to the wheels." This meant that instead of the whole axle being pivoted right or left to make a turn, as with a carriage or wagon, each front wheel swung on a vertical spindle, the axle remaining fixed. Again, Benz had it right the first time; this is still the way an automobile is steered.

Benz now followed his famous three-wheeled *Patent Motorwagen* with the Viktoria, an elegant four-wheeler incorporating the new steering system. It was the first time a woman's name had been given to an automobile. There was another automobile with a woman's name on the way, as Carl Benz would learn soon enough.

The Viktoria embodied a number of innovations besides the four wheels. It had a three-horsepower, one-cylinder engine, a vertical rather than a horizontal flywheel, and an accelerator. The drive belt was slipped back and forth among pulleys of differing ratios, according to speed and power requirements, and there were other improvements as well.

In the autumn, Émile Roger, Benz's enterprising French distributor, opened an American headquarters for Benz in the Astor Building, 10 Wall Street, New York, and put a Viktoria on display, making sure the public knew about it. "The new propelling power that has come out of poetic Germany!" excitedly headlined the

New York *Sun*, October 29, 1893, over the first public-relations release for an automobile ever to appear in an American newspaper. "It is independent of rails, and can fly over country roads at thirty miles an hour—The Ride of Emperor William—No noise, no smoke, no steam, no odor—Anyone can handle it—To be seen in the city immediately.

"In no branch of applied science has greater progress been made in the direction of locomotion. The past few years have brought about the beginning of a mighty change. Horse traction is falling into disuse . . . improvement follows improvement. . . . The efforts of inventors have been largely turned toward safe, steady, and swift methods of conveying people and goods from place to place. . . .

"After years of experiment this problem has been solved by Germany. Though now for the first time brought to America, the Benz motorwagen is not by any manner of means in the first flush of success. It has been tested, experimented with,

Bertha and Carl Benz pose, center, on Benz's second model, the Viktoria. As the first of the grand touring cars, it was high in performance, comfort, and reliability. Thus began the era of discovering the countryside by means of the automobile. On either side of the Viktoria are Velo production cars. Circa 1895.

A 3½-horsepower Benz Velo being demonstrated at the Agricultural Hall Show, in England, 1900.

improved, and remodelled, always with betterment, since it was first shown at the Munich Exposition in 1888."

The Viktoria had won a number of gold medals, the account continued, and in September Kaiser Wilhelm had driven it fifteen miles in thirty-five minutes. "The carriage in which this notable imperial run was made has arrived here, together with Instructor Fred Haas, who will operate it and show off its running quality. . . ."

With the Viktoria solidly launched, Benz added a modified version that he called the Vis-à-Vis; and in April 1894 he began turning out the Velo, from "velocipede," the name reflecting the popularity of bicycling at the time. Stealing a march on Henry Ford, who had yet to be heard

from, Benz designed the Velo with the poor man in mind, making it light and cheap, and building one after another in identical models. The Benz Velo was thus the first car to be produced on mass-production principles.

The first Velo was driven by an engine of one and a half horsepower, later boosted to three horsepower. There were two speeds, then three, plus reverse. The car weighed six hundred pounds and could do about twelve miles an hour, rolling on wire wheels with pneumatic tires. Of the 135 machines Benz built in 1895—including a couple of eight-seaters and his first bus—sixty-two were Velos.

The Benz Velo, known as the "doctors' car" because so many doctors used it, became the car American builders tried to

21

A Benz Velo at the start of the fifty-three-mile Emancipation Run, from London to Brighton, November 14, 1896. Of the thirty-three entries in the event, beginning at the Metropole Hotel, four were Benz automobiles. Some others were Daimler cars.

emulate. Charles and J. Frank Duryea, who kept abreast of European automobile development through *Scientific American* and the *Patent Office Gazette* and were first to produce a car commercially in the United States, freely acknowledged that they were especially influenced by the work of Carl Benz and Gottlieb Daimler. Others likewise took their cues from Benz. The Winton, wrote a French authority, was "a Benz copy," as was the Detroit-built King "a variation of the Benz machine."

All in all, 1895 was a good year for Carl Benz. The same issue of *Scientific American* that recorded Kaiser William's tour in the Viktoria also told of a man who for some time had been routinely commuting in Benz cars. Director Wilhelm Eiswein, of the Bavarian Railroads, owned two, one with a top, the other without. Eiswein drove sixty miles a day between his home and office at Ludwigshafen, fifteen miles away, coming home for lunch. He averaged two minutes and forty seconds a mile, and he had been making these daily runs for eighteen months.

Finally that year, a Benz car won the first automobile race to be held in the United States. Inspired by the first race in Europe, from Paris to Bordeaux in June, publisher Hermann Kohltsaat of the Chicago *Times-Herald* posted five thousand dollars to be paid the first man to complete the ninety-two-mile round trip between Chicago and Waukegan within thirteen hours. The date was set for November 2.

"There is no doubt but that America is limping behind Europe in this field," the *Times-Herald* editorialized in announcing the contest on July 9. The horseless carriage had arrived, the paper later commented, "but its usability on American roads is viewed with some skepticism. If bad roads should obstruct their general introduction, the people will decide such public matters as usual and will do away with those bad roads. . . ."

A side issue to be settled at the same time was to find another name than "horseless carriage" for the carriage that ran without a horse. An early suggestion was "motocycle." The term "automobile" was still a long way down the road.

The prize was to be based on six considerations involving the machine: general utility, speed, cost, economy of operation, general appearance, and excellence of design. Each car must be equipped with a horn, two headlights, and a tail light, and was required to carry an "umpire" in addition to the driver.

Excitement over the event was fanned

by the arrival in New York of Carl Benz's man Émile Roger with three gleaming new Velos, which presently appeared in the windows of the city's three leading department stores: Macy's, Gimbel's, and Hilton, Hughes & Company (later Wanamaker's). "Now for horseless wagons," proclaimed Hilton, Hughes, as if it hadn't read the papers when the Viktoria was in town, two years before. "Paris is going wild over them. All the world is watching. Up hill, down hill, twist, turn—at a snail's pace or up to 15 miles an hour, they say.

"No steam, no electricity, just a little petroleum air engine—simple, cheap, almost noiseless. Have they solved the runabout wagon problem? Judge for yourselves. We have the first Horseless Wagon ever brought to America. . . . At 11 A.M. today it shall have the first trial on the streets of New York."

Something of what happened when the Velo took to the pavement was described by the New York *Evening Post*, August 29, 1895. "The crowd surged about in the wake of the Benz wagon, yelled with pleasure as it put on speed, and crowded as near as it could to peep in at the engine and shower questions on the Frenchman in control. . . ."

The paper added, "Monsieur Roger thinks that his wagon is now so far perfected that its use by commercial firms in the United States would result in a saving in expenses as well as in better service . . ."

Eighty-three machines were entered in the Chicago-Waukegan derby, but as the starting date neared, the list shrank to thirty-four. These included twenty-one with gasoline engines, four steamers, seven electrics, one driven by compressed air, and one propelled by a spring mech-

Carl Benz with his children and the Velo. From left to right are Richard, Thilda, Ellen, Carl, Klara, and Eugen Benz. Circa 1893.

anism. On starting day, only two machines showed up, a Benz, owned and driven by Hieronymus Mueller, of Decatur, Illinois, who only recently had brought the car over from Mannheim with plans to manufacture it, and a Duryea driven by Frank Duryea. To give the others more time to get ready, the race was postponed to Thanksgiving Day, November 28.

For the sake of the thousands of spectators who had gathered along the route, it was decided by the organizing committee, named by President Grover Cleveland, to have the two lone machines that made it to the starting line make the run as a sort of warm-up for the main event at the end of the month. The winner of this preliminary run was to get five hundred dollars. As the "representative of American automobile construction," Duryea was the favorite.

The two cars wheeled away from Jackson Park at 8:15 in the morning, running a gauntlet of spectators pressing so close that there was barely room to pass. Mueller reached Waukegan at 2:40 in the afternoon, six and one half hours later, with nearly everyone in town on hand to greet him. His car was "replenished"; ice was dumped into the cooling box above the engine, and in seven and a half minutes he was on his way back to Chicago. He completed the return lap at 6:43, having covered the 92 miles in the gross time of 10 hours, 22.5 minutes, well within the allotted 13 hours.

One minute was deducted for each of seven stops at railway crossings. Forty-six more minutes came off for other delays, including trouble with the "sparking machine," a lost tire, getting lost, and taking on supplies at Winnetka. Mueller's net running time came out at 8 hours and 44 minutes.

Duryea failed to finish, though this was hardly the fault of his car. Tooling along the road near Prairie View—whether coming or going isn't clear—Duryea came on a cart with a load of hay. Duryea sounded his horn, but the farmer in his confusion swung his team "Haw" instead of "Gee," forcing Duryea's car into the ditch and out of the race.

Unhappily, by Thanksgiving, the new date for the official race, winter had come with four inches of snow on the ground and a polar wind blowing off Lake Michigan. The course was shortened to Evanston, Chicago's nearest neighbor to the north, reducing the round trip distance to 55 miles. Only six cars appeared for the start, three of them Benz machines, among them Mueller's. The winner this time was Duryea, who had been first away, at eight fifty-five in the morning. Mueller, although last to leave because of a broken drive belt, came in second, twenty-four minutes behind Duryea. Another Benz finished third. With two Benz machines finishing in the money in a field of six, the event was considered a Benz victory.

Among those who missed the race was Henry Ford, who had built a car of his own a couple of years before, working on it in his spare time as an employee of the Detroit Edison Company. Ford desperately wanted to attend the event but was too broke to make the trip to Chicago—a fiscal condition he later remedied.

In the spring, Mueller took his Benz on an exhibition tour to Indianapolis, where the car seems to have aroused the same kind of awe as Lindbergh's *Spirit of St. Louis* after Lindbergh's solo flight to Paris a generation later. Throngs jostled for position to see the machine. A torchlight parade was described by one newspaper as "a comet on its path, with its long, fiery tail of bicycle lamps." William Jennings Bryan used Mueller's Benz on his

Under the Red Flag Law, this Benz Velo was required to trail behind the outrunner who bears the warning flag. The law was abolished in 1896, and the speed limit was raised to twelve miles per hour.

campaign through Illinois for the 1896 presidential nomination, the car drawing more attention than Bryan's famous oratory. The Benz was still enough of a curiosity after another year to be a main attraction with the Barnum & Bailey Circus.

It looked as if P. E. Studebaker, builder of wagons and carriages, had been right when he enthusiastically wrote to Benz after the Benz car won the warm-up run to Waukegan, "Your action has hastened the development of the motocycle several years and what is more important, it has had the effect of transferring the manufacture of the motocycle from Europe to America."

This would prove to be extravagant prophecy. At about the time Studebaker was writing his letter, attorney George Selden, of Rochester, New York, was

granted a patent, applied for in 1879, to build a road vehicle powered by a gasoline engine. Selden produced nothing, but, for years, by shoving everyone else aside through his patent monopoly, including five hundred who applied for patents in one year, 1895, he hampered development of the automobile in the United States, until Henry Ford put an end to his mischief via the courts in 1912.

The Selden patent also affected Carl Benz, since Selden's licensing company threatened the buyers of imported cars with lawsuits. Émile Roger, with plans to distribute Benz cars throughout the United States, died in 1897. Hieronymus Mueller fell victim to a gasoline explosion while he was working on a 10-horsepower car in 1901

The gray outlook in the United States

An outing on the Viktoria. In the foreground, from left to right, are Klara, Bertha, and Carl Benz.

was balanced by good news from England. This was the repeal by Parliament of the archaic Locomotives on Highways Act, which in effect had denied the roads to motorcars, holding back development of the automobile there much as the Selden patent in the States. This ancient legislation, called the Red Flag Law, had been passed to rid the roads of steam vehicles, which frightened horses and were given to blowing up. Under its provisions, a man carrying a red flag by day and a red lantern by night was required to precede the oncoming "road locomotive" by at least fifty yards, with the additional duty of helping to control excited horses. He was one of a crew of three that the law demanded for each vehicle. The second

man steered, and the third stoked the boiler. Speed was set at four miles an hour in the country, two in town.

In 1878, the distance the outrunner with the flag and lantern must keep ahead was grudgingly reduced from fifty yards to fifteen, but that was as far as the lawgivers could bring themselves to go in amending the Red Flag Law. It was eighteen more years before it began to come through for the solons that the growing numbers of self-propelled vehicles seen on the roads—on the Continent, not in England—were not really "locomotives" but something different. Hence Parliament's passage of the "Emancipation Act"—after a great deal of prodding.

A goodly measure of the prodding came

from Evelyn Ellis, himself a member of Parliament but also a car enthusiast. How Ellis felt on the issue of horses versus machines, in which it was often argued that horses were cleaner, Ellis indicated in an exchange with his father, Lord Howard de Walden, as Ellis arrived in his car for a visit.

"If you must bring that infernal thing here, kindly bring a little pan to put under it to catch the filthy oil it drips," the elder man objected caustically.

"Certainly, father, if you'll bring a big pan for your carriage horses when you visit me," Ellis retorted.

While the Emancipation Act, given royal assent on August 14 and taking effect on November 14, 1896, eased restraints on the automobile, the new law did so just barely. It abolished the crew-of-three rule and advanced the speed limit to fourteen miles an hour, but at the same time gave local authorities the right to cut speed to twelve, the pace of a good trotter. This, of course, local authorities promptly did. Nobody liked automobiles—or their drivers—except those who owned cars. Police were quick to invent the speed trap, and judges all but threw the whole courtroom at accused motorists, levying the heaviest fines allowable against them. One justice of the peace, when he wasn't on the bench dealing out punishment to drivers, hid behind a wall bordering the road and hurled garden refuse after them.

To celebrate the new freedom for drivers—such as it was—the British Motorcar Club organized an "Emancipation Run" from London to Brighton, an ancient sea-side resort fifty miles south of London. Since the first excursion, on the day the law became effective, only war has been suffered to interrupt the annual drive between the two points by the old-timers, who rally for the occasion from all parts of the world.

Meanwhile, Carl Benz went on growing as an automobile manufacturer. Thanks to the aggressive sales organization of partner Julius Ganss, Benz cars were being seen universally. There were models for a wide range of tastes and uses. The Comfortable, a three-horsepower semi-luxury car for two, added to the Benz reputation in the *Daily Mail*'s 100-mile reliability run from London to Oxford and back. The Comfortable averaged 13.5 miles an hour for the distance and came through without a breakdown. "The Benz wagon, although built in Germany, and cheap, functioned excellently," commented the *Daily Mail*, presumably meaning no offense.

By the end of 1901, sixteen years after he first drove his three-wheeled *Patent Motorwagen*, Carl Benz had built and sold 2,702 machines. His peak year had been 1900, when he produced 603 vehicles. He was the leading automobile manufacturer of all nations, the General Motors of his day, and Mannheim was the Detroit.

Then, in 1901, the bottom fell out. Benz sold only half as many cars as he had the year before. In 1902, the figure dropped to 226; then, in 1903, to 172.

What had happened?

There was a one-word answer: *Mercedes.*

Mercedes Jellinek (1889–1929). Her father, Emil, renamed the Daimler cars he sold after this favorite daughter.

# CHAPTER THREE

# We Are in the Era of the Mercedes

The time was early 1901 and the place Nice, on the Mediterranean coast of France, a favorite winter watering place of Europe's mandarins. Nice Week, featuring the growing sport of motor racing, was approaching, and the excitement this year ran higher than usual because of a new and very different car entered in the lists. The machine had the striking name of Mercedes, and it came from the Daimler-Motoren-Gesellschaft, of Cannstatt, Germany, a hundred kilometers or so down the Neckar River from Carl Benz's place in Mannheim.

"Innovations in the field of automobilism don't appear today in Paris but in Nice," chided *L'Automobil Revue du Littoral,* official organ of the Nice Automobile Club. "The first Mercedes car of the Cannstatt Works has arrived in Nice and the agents of Mercedes have invited all drivers who are interested to inspect the new model.

"It is not our business to make a comparison between French cars and those produced in a foreign country," the journal commented. "We have praised the first so much that we cannot be held under suspicion for an exaggerated leaning towards the latter. But we want to say frankly: the Mercedes car is very, very interesting.

"We have no longer the 2000 kg Daimler, with its high center of gravity, which is a danger to stability on bends at high speeds. The Mercedes is low, long and does not differ very much outwardly from the Panhard and Mors. . . . It is most thoughtfully designed. Strength, perfection, easy and safe hand governing, steering and braking, everything is there. And then there is the most interesting engine. . . ." With four cylinders, the engine of the Mercedes developed 35 horsepower at 1,000 revolutions a minute, making it the most powerful engine ever mounted in a car, while at the same time being compact and light. It weighed only 15 pounds per horsepower, far less than any other engine yet built.

"This remarkable car will be a dangerous rival to the 28-horsepower Panhard and the 35-horsepower Mors in the races this year," the account ended.

The writer of the piece should not have been surprised, however, for Paul Meyan, general secretary of the French Automobile Club, had visited the Daimler factory at Cannstatt in July and warned, in *La France Automobile*, of what was coming.

"Every previous production is far surpassed by this new car," Meyan wrote. "The chief advantage lies in its lightness. The metal used is an alloy of magnesium and aluminum termed magnalium. Further advantages are the long wheel-base, mechanically operated inlet valves, low tension electric ignition . . . a new and improved type of carburetor and improvement in the cooling system. . . . These pretty rumors are not pretty rumors any longer but established facts. The French factories would do well to get busy extremely quickly in order that Daimler shall not set the fashion in Paris." He urged French designers to take heed of "this engine which bears the name Mercedes" and to look ahead "before it is too late and Daimler becomes the fashion of the day."

*The Autocar*, founded in 1896 by the British Motor Syndicate to lend a hand in getting the Emancipation Act passed, took up Meyan's call to action, lest the Germans with their Mercedes put everyone else hopelessly behind: "The entire workmanship, design, and performance of this car have struck terror into the heart of a capable critic like Paul Meyan."

If anyone thought Paul Meyan was unduly worried about the German threat, he was quickly disabused as the Nice Week races got underway, on March 25. The exotic maverick from Cannstatt, standing as low as a dachshund to a wolfhound in comparison to the other cars, took charge from the start. It won the lead-off event: the distance run from Nice to Aix, Sénas, Salon, and back to Nice, covering the 244 miles at 36.1 miles an hour. The driver was Wilhelm Werner, one of a beginning stable of Mercedes drivers who would soon be giving rival drivers reason to consider other careers.

Three days later, Werner won two big events on the Promenade des Anglais: the one-mile race from a standing start, and the one-kilometer dash from a flying start, hitting 53.5 miles an hour, a speed thought impossible. The following day, Werner took his Cannstatt mount up La Turbie Hill in 18 minutes, 7 seconds, only a little over half the time it had taken a Daimler car the year before. Nearly neck and neck with him came another Mercedes, in second place.

At the finish of Nice Week 1901, everyone agreed that the car from Germany had made all others obsolete. "We are now," Paul Meyan wrote, "in the era of the Mercedes."

Gottlieb Daimler was not at Nice to see his star ascend. He had died the year before, at sixty-six.

Daimler had entered the world ten years ahead of his competitor, Carl Benz, on March 17, 1834, at Schorndorf, Württemberg. He was the first Daimler in four generations who was not a baker. What genetic caprice inclined him toward nuts and bolts instead of loaves of bread, only nature knows. To head off what he saw as deviant behavior, his father, Johannes Däumler (as the family name was then spelled), who ran a bake shop and wine bar in the Höllgasse, took Gottlieb out of the town's elementary school and sent him off to Latin school, sure that Latin would soon make the bakery trade look better to the boy. This move only made matters worse.

Young Gottlieb came out of Latin school with a report card attesting that he had "successfully gone through plane and solid geometry, as well as algebra and trigonometry, and is able to solve practical problems by means of these disciplines." Moreover, the lad had shown a keen interest in animals, both exotic and domestic, and in the fashion of a naturalist had drawn sketches of various specimens, in full anatomical detail, identifying the animals by their Latin names and telling where they were found.

Since war with France was in the wind, the precocious young Gottlieb was ap-

prenticed to a carbine manufacturer. Here he distinguished himself by making a double-barreled pistol of such excellence in design and craftsmanship that he forthwith was elevated to full journeyman status. But Daimler had little taste for gun making. Through industrialist Ferdinand Steinbeis, who sponsored gifted young men in further study and experience, he found a place at the "Factory College," in Grafenstaden, near Strasbourg. This establishment was so named because Friedrich Messmer, the plant manager, had once taught at the Karlsruhe Institute of Technology and continued to teach at the factory.

The plant built railway cars, vans, tenders, bridge parts, and machines. When it added locomotives to its output, Daim-

Gottlieb Daimler and Emma Kurz, who were married in 1867. Emma bore him three sons and two daughters. She died in 1889.

ler, age twenty-two, was made foreman. He soon saw that he needed to know more about science and engineering and enrolled as a special student at the Stuttgart Polytechnic Institute. Returning to his job after graduation, as he had promised, Daimler confessed to Messmer that his heart was not in steam engines.

What did interest Daimler was an engine that would be fast-starting and economical to operate for the many small industries that couldn't afford a steam engine. He had come across something in print, written in 1826 by an Englishman named Cheverton, that discussed the theory of such an engine, and had heard that current investigations showed it to have promise. Daimler asked Messmer to let him use the plant's facilities to build parts and run experiments of his own in pursuit of this bird in the bush. Messmer refused, believing there was still wide room for improvement in steam power.

After a decent interval, Daimler asked and was granted Messmer's permission to resign, June 10, 1861. He went to Paris and, by some accounts, had a look at Etienne Lenoir's gas engine, then at the height of its notoriety, but didn't think much of it, telling Lenoir so. While in Paris he turned down a job with a struggling little factory that made band saws and woodworking tools, an outfit which one day would grow up to become Panhard-Levassor, pioneer leader of the French automobile industry and heavily involved in Daimler's own lifework.

After Paris, Daimler became a sort of vagabond engineer. He traveled to England, where he worked in a number of cities—in Leeds for Smith, Peacock and Tannet, builders of an advanced engine; in Manchester for Roberts and Company, makers of textile machines and machine tools for building ships, steam engines, and locomotives; in Coventry for Whit-

worth, famous for its precision machine tools and at the time a builder of breech-loading cannon for the Confederacy in the American Civil War.

Back in Germany, having polished his English as well as broadened his engineering and intellectual horizons, Daimler became manager of the Bruderhaus Engineering Works in Reutlingen, which used its profits to support a kindergarten and vocational school for orphans. One of the former orphans, living in Reutlingen, would exert a profound influence on the fortunes of Gottlieb Daimler and, through Daimler, on the world at large. His name was Wilhelm Maybach.

In 1921, Maybach recorded something of himself and his days in Reutlingen. "I was born on the ninth of February, 1846,"

Wilhelm Maybach (1846–1929).

he began. "After the untimely deaths of my father and mother when I was ten years old, I went to that well-known friend of orphan children, Father Werner, in the Bruderhaus in Reutlingen.

"Both at home and at the Bruderhaus I had to work, as well as study and play, and I had to go to bed early and get up early. When I was fifteen, I went into apprenticeship, and because I was good at drawing, my job was in the drafting room of the Bruderhaus Engineering Works. During my five years of apprenticeship, I went to evening classes in the town high school, where I learned physics and free-hand drawing, and in the latter class I got to draw three-dimensional representations in perspective. At the end of my apprenticeship, I was allowed to take the mathematical courses of the city's technical college, which made it possible for me to study for myself. . . .

"An employee of the business office of the factory taught my friends and me foreign languages," Maybach wrote. "We used to have to wake him up early for this. I began inventing things during my last year of study. Among other things I fitted the gold leaf stamping press of a book bindery with oil heat. During my period of study, I was allowed to follow out the execution of all the things I designed in the drafting room in the factory, and they let me take half a year of practical work. . . ."

Maybach's talents impressed Gottlieb Daimler, who, after two years at the Bruderhaus, moved on to larger undertakings, becoming director of all factories under Maschinenbau Gesellschaft, in Karlsruhe. One of his first acts was to hire Wilhelm Maybach, putting him to work in the design department. So began an association that lasted to the end of Daimler's life, thirty-one years later.

Meanwhile, Nikolaus August Otto and his partner, Eugen Langen, organized Gasmotoren-Fabrik Deutz, near Cologne, to produce an improved atmospheric engine. To manage the factory, they hired Gottlieb Daimler, who brought along Wilhelm Maybach as chief designer. The company prospered, getting up to an output of more than six hundred engines a year.

But the atmospheric engine, limited by the law of atmospheric pressure, was a dead end in the evolution of the internal-combustion engine. Three horsepower was about the most that could be had from it, and its ponderous size foreclosed the engine for many uses. Even the two-horsepower version called for a ten-foot ceiling, to accommodate the piston. The three-horsepower engine needed at least thirteen feet of head room. It was necessary to look in other directions.

With sales of the atmospheric engine now approaching zero, the Deutz board of directors, on January 12, 1875, authorized plant manager Daimler to concentrate on the development of an engine that ran on petroleum, making it independent of the gas works for its fuel supply. Daimler appears to have worked fast, for just a year later, January 5, 1876, there was another directive from on high, ordering tests of the petrol engine for safety from explosions.

Under pressure of the sales crisis, however, the firm chose to hold development of the petrol engine in abeyance, and instead tried to improve the more familiar gas engine, moving on from the atmospheric design. "Otto must get on his hind legs and Daimler on his front legs," warned an academic friend of Langen who served as unofficial technical adviser to the company.

For his part, Otto was already on his hind legs, having gotten some new ideas for making the four-stroke engine work.

He had given it up in 1862 as hopeless after experimenting with a model of the Lenoir engine that he had had a mechanic build for him after reading about it in a newspaper. The key problem had been to cushion the shock of the explosions, keeping the engine from wrecking itself.

Still working with gas, Otto now tried again—and again. Finally, in his entry in his research diary for May 9, 1876, Deutz chief engineer Franz Ring was able to include a diagram of a four-stroke engine— said to be the first time such an engine had been depicted in actual outline.

A production model was built, and by September and October, Otto's four-stroke gas engine—the "Silent Otto"— was being tested, all this happening with the speed of light as engineering tempo goes. Types ranging from one half to eight horsepower were designed and produced. The engine proved to have the flexibility for a wide range of forms.

What now remained was to reduce the weight, which was about a ton per horsepower, and boost the speed to increase power—controlling characteristics in any engine driving a vehicle. The answers to these two imperatives were to come from Gottlieb Daimler, but not as a Deutz employe.

Daimler and Otto, both strong-minded, clashed until it began to interfere with plant operations. To ease tensions, Daimler was sent to Russia to see what was happening there in the way of industrial development. Returning in ten weeks, he enthusiastically reported that "everything is crying to be brought to life by technical progress." The Deutz directors decided to set up a plant in St. Petersburg and offered Daimler the post of running it, at the same time canceling his contract. Daimler said no, thereby ending his Deutz connection.

At last on his own after years of subor-

dination to others, Daimler again invited Wilhelm Maybach to join him, this time in developing a light, high-speed internal-combustion engine for the express purpose of driving vehicles. Maybach accepted, and the two drew up a contract between them, dated April 18, 1882.

In July, Daimler moved to Cannstatt with his wife and five children. The new family home was a spacious villa on an estate that today is a public park. His workplace was a fifteen-by-forty-foot brick tool shed with a greenhouse adjoining. He converted the front part of the little building into an office and the rest into a shop. At forty-eight, he savored the long-deferred freedom to do things his own way.

The visitor to the site today, turning in from busy Taubenheimstrasse, quickly comes upon a bronze plaque amid the shrubs bearing Daimler's likeness in bas relief. At the base are a laurel wreath, the dates of his birth and death, and the information that the memorial was erected by "Württembergischer Ingenieur-Verein," a local engineering society, in 1902.

A few steps farther on, screened from the street by the trees and bushes, sits "Gottlieb Daimler's erste WERKSTÄTTE." Inside, cheerful under a large skylight, the shop looks much as Daimler must have left it each evening at the end of the day's work.

In the corner stands the forge, with the anvil resting on a log stump conveniently alongside. On the wall are racked the tools of the forge: tongs for taking the white-hot metal from the fire and holding it on the anvil, hammers for beating it into shape. The bellows are a fan underneath the grate, enclosed by brick on the sides and back, turned by a pulley connected by belt to a treadle. Assorted tools, including a scoop for removing ashes from

Daimler's workshop, on the edge of a park, at 13 Taubenheimstrasse, Cannstatt (a suburb of Stuttgart).

the fire chamber, lie at either side of the forge, ready for use.

Arrayed on the workbench are hacksaws and files, hammers, an oil can, and a metal tray containing wrenches, pliers, and screwdrivers. Two vises are clamped to the edge of the bench, a large one in the middle, a smaller one at the end. Nearby stands a hand-turned grindstone. There are metal-cutting tools, threading tools, calipers, a pair of flywheels mounted on wooden blocks. Nothing seems to be lacking that Daimler would need should he return and start all over again.

As Daimler and Maybach—just the two of them here in this little shop in the garden—started to work on a high-speed engine, they knew that they had first to improve on the ignition developed by Nikolaus August Otto for his gas engine. Otto's was an ingeniously complicated system which, in getting the fire from an outside standing flame into the cylinder, worked somewhat like the locks in a

canal. At the firing point, a slide valve opened a slot to the cylinder, admitting the fire, an instant after the key behind closed to the outside. When the flame set off the mixture in the cylinder, the key opened again, admitting new fire for the next stroke.

This rigmarole would never do for the engine Daimler and Maybach had in mind, which would run several times faster than Otto's. The answer proved to be as simple as Otto's had been complicated. It consisted of a gas-filled tube, closed at the outer end and kept red-hot by a Bunsen burner, which projected into the cylinder. That was all—there were no moving parts. Firing timed itself according to the position of the piston in the cylinder.

The main barrier to a fast-running engine was now out of the way. For his "hot-tube" ignition, Daimler was issued Patent No. 28022, on December 16, 1883.

"Thus, the first practical ignition sys-

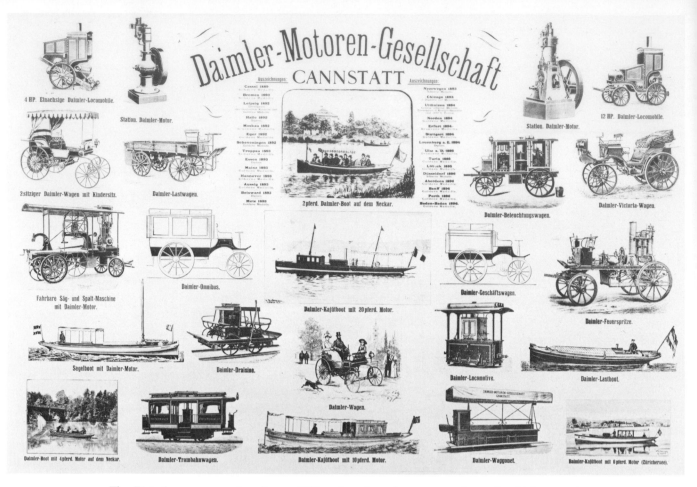

The Daimler company brochure, 1894, advertises the great variety of vehicles run by Daimler engines.

tem for the gas engine came into being, once and forever relegating to the scrap heap all the impractical slide door, 'flame-thrower' type of ignitions used heretofore," wrote Alexander E. Ulmann, the well-known American authority and alumnus of the Massachusetts Institute of Technology, in 1948. "Now full compression could be maintained on the top of the stroke and a violent explosion could be had just at the right time. . . . Engine speeds increased from a measly 200 revolutions per minute to 1000 and more [a Daimler-Benz authority places the figure at 700 to 900]. Power rose ten or more fold. Weight per horsepower came comparatively down to nothing, and once and for all the cumbersome gas engine threw off its stationary cast iron foundation and

shackles and jumped into the field of self-propelled vehicles that had been waiting for a light, efficient, prime mover for over one hundred years. The era of the automobile had been born."

The simple answer that laid open this wide new world, like most simple answers, had not been easy to come by. "It was a long road, requiring endless tests and unremitting pursuit of the objective . . . to move ahead from the initially quite hopeless results of work with free ignition," Daimler wrote. "Premature firing of the mixture occurred again and again when the engine was being started and during compression, before reaching dead center, when the flywheel was suddenly and unexpectedly thrown backwards instead of forward and the crank

36

would be ripped right out of the . . . hand like a bolt of lightning. . . ."

One who understood only too well what Daimler meant was Carl Benz, who wrote, "For me the problem of problems was ignition. If the spark does not work, then all is in vain, and the most brilliant engineering designs do not help at all."

While Daimler's hot-tube ignition was a long step forward, the flame was not too steadfast in wet or windy weather. It was well into the 1890s before Robert Bosch, the Swabian peasant genius, came up with the magneto, which made use of Michael Faraday's discovery in 1831 that when a conductor is passed between the poles of a magnet, electricity is generated. With the magneto supplying the fire for the fuel in the cylinders, the parting felicity "Good ignition!" soon was heard no more.

Backfiring was not the only trouble faced by Daimler and Maybach in working out the firing problem. The closed doors and curtained windows of the shop brought rumors among the neighbors that they were counterfeiters. The whoomph—whoomph—whoomph of the engine could be nothing else but the sound of the machine stamping out the bills.

One night as they worked late, there came a loud rap at the door, followed by an imperious, "Open up, in the name of the law!"

The commissioner of police, in person, backed by a large, armed retinue, had come to investigate. When he saw what was going on, the chief proved to have a sense of humor. He laughed and apologetically withdrew his forces.

Though Daimler and Maybach had now achieved their goal of a high-revolution internal-combustion engine, there was still much to be done, as there would yet be room for improvement a hundred years later. They changed the air cooling system for the single cylinder to water cooling. They altered the design from horizontal to

Daimler's motorized bicycle, which was patented on August 29, 1885.

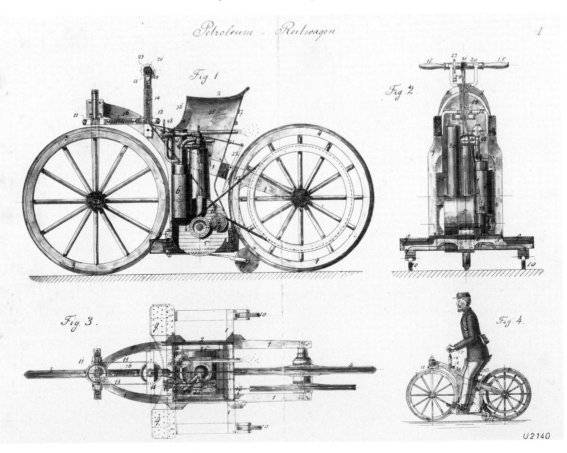

As inventor of the motorboat, Daimler did not at first inform the passengers of his unheard-of power source during cruises on the Neckar River. Circa 1887.

upright, and enclosed the whole, including the flywheel, in a dustproof, oiltight housing. This model, Daimler's first engine suitable for driving a vehicle, was patented April 3, 1885—about the time Carl Benz was putting the finishing touches on his three-wheeler down the Neckar River at Mannheim.

Gottlieb Daimler had in mind motorizing not only the carriage but all conveyances contrived by man to carry himself and his goods, on land or water (and in the air, too, when the time came). He and Maybach, therefore, made it a guiding principle to aim for an engine that combined the highest power with the least weight and size, to save room for payload. They epitomized the idea with a one-half-

horsepower engine, patented August 29, 1885, which they put to work in what was to be the first motorcycle.

In 1886, some months after Carl Benz patented his three-wheeler, Daimler installed an engine in a carriage—the first time four wheels on the road had been made to turn by an internal-combustion engine. Because he wanted no one to know what he was doing, Daimler told the builders of the coach, Wimpff and Son, in Stuttgart, that it was to be a birthday present for his wife. He asked only that it be "handsome but very solidly built." When the carriage was ready, for lack of room at his own little shop in Cannstatt, Daimler sent it to the nearby Esslingen Engineering Works for the ad-

Daimler fire engine at the Tunbridge Exhibition, England, 1895.

Maybach and Daimler (standing to the right) brought their second truck to the Paris Exhibition of 1898, where it roused great interest. With an engine of two cylinders and ten horsepower, the truck had a capacity of five tons. Two years earlier, Daimler had built the world's first truck for the British Motor Syndicate.

Daimler display trolleys, Bremer, 1889.

dition of the engine, making the delivery under cover of darkness.

The engine turned out 1.1 horsepower at 650 revolutions a minute. As on Benz's *Motorwagen*, the power was carried to the rear wheels by belt. Unlike Benz, Daimler had no differential to help on the corners, but instead used slip couplings, which allowed slippage under extra load, at each end of the transmission shaft. The radiator was at the back of the carriage.

A familiar photograph of this equipage

Gottlieb Daimler's elder son, Paul, is driven by Wilhelm Maybach, 1889. The "steel-wheeler" was the first all-metal four-wheel automobile.

converted from horsepower to engine power shows Gottlieb Daimler reclining paunchily in the rear seat, derby-hatted and with cane resting against the floor, his son Adolf, likewise in derby, at the tiller in front. Even the whip socket is there, at the right-hand side of the dashboard. All that's missing is the horses. Indeed, it was a "horseless carriage."

Next, Daimler bolted an engine into a boat. Since people knew that gasoline was highly explosive, he arranged large, important-looking insulators on the sides of the craft, interconnected with wire, to suggest that the boat was run by electricity.

Even the newspapers were baffled. "Recently a boat has been circulating on the Neckar with about eight persons aboard," one paper reported. "It appears to be propelled by some unseen power up and downstream with great speed, causing astonishment on the part of the bystanders. The little ship has been outfitted with a special propelling mechanism by engineer Daimler. The first test run was made at the beginning of August. Since then, many outstanding engineers have been on these trips. The man at the tiller needs only to press in one direction or another to have the boat go anywhere he wants, either fast or slow."

To those who asked what drove the boat, Daimler quoted a complicated pun whereby he neither lied nor answered the question.

The garden workshop became too small. More space was found in a building at 67 Ludwigstrasse, on a hill called the Seelberg, not far away. With more room came more projects. Among other things, they installed more engines in more boats, put an engine in a maintenance car of the Stuttgart street railway, and motorized a fire engine.

Daimler read of a Leipzig book dealer named Wölfert who had made a flight in a balloon. He invited Wölfert to bring his balloon to Cannstatt for some experiments together. The result was a powered balloon—the first motorized aircraft?—driven by a specially developed two-horsepower engine spinning two propellers, one taking the balloon forward, the other down. On August 2, 1888, Daimler and Wölfert took off from the Seelberg, returning to earth, necks intact, about two and a half miles away. For the first time, a

Karl Wölfert in the gondola of his balloon powered by a 4-cylinder, 2-horsepower Daimler engine in 1888. Its first flight took him and Daimler two and a half miles.

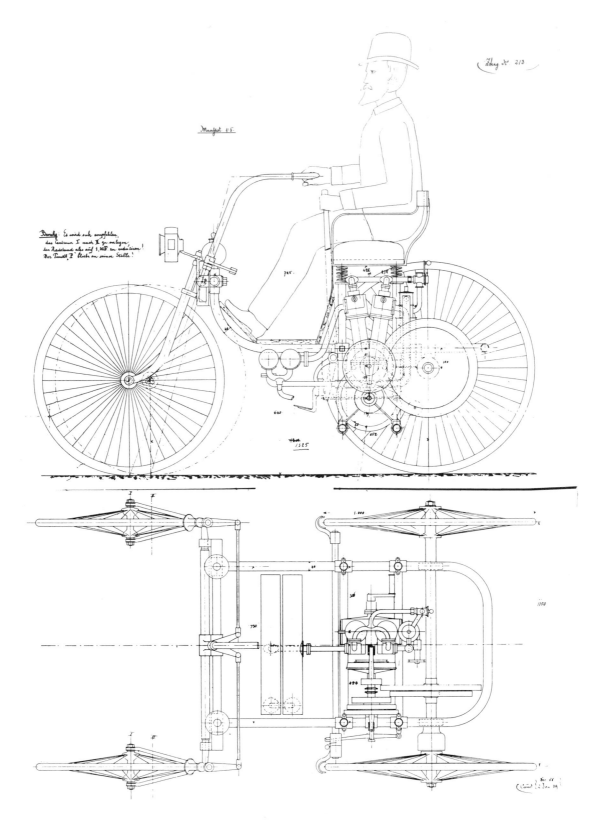

Patent drawing of Daimler's steel-wheeler, 1889.

Replica of Daimler's motorized bicycle, photographed inside Daimler's workshop, 1978. Daimler and Maybach mounted a 0.4-horsepower engine in a wooden bicycle, naming in *Reitwagen,* or Straddlecar. Maybach rode it three kilometers for the first time publicly, from Cannstatt to Untertürkheim, in November 1885.

Daimler engine had driven an aircraft. One day it would be the chief power plant for the wings of Germany.

In addition to these diverse activities, Daimler and Maybach found time to design an engine that doubled power at no increase in weight—an unprecedented jump forward in power-to-weight ratio. The engine comprised two cylinders, set to form a "V." Appropriately for its first task, they installed the new engine in the "steel-wheeler," designed by Maybach as the first four-wheel vehicle built specifically to be driven by an engine, rather than a horse. With all suggestion of a horse-drawn carriage gone and looking like siamese-twin bicycles, the steel-wheeler had a four-speed transmission and could do between ten and eleven miles an hour.

Daimler welcomed the chance to show the car at the 1889 Paris World's Fair, fea-turing Alexandre Gustave Eiffel's 984-foot tower, but the crowds seemed to care no more about Daimler's steel-wheeler than about Carl Benz's *Patent Motorwagen,* also on display. They watched bemusedly, however, as Daimler's son Adolf took one fairgoer on repeated rides up and down the banks of the Seine in the steel-wheeler. They likewise clustered at a dock where two Daimler motorboats, *Violette* and *Passe-Partout,* piloted by Gottlieb Daimler and Wilhelm Maybach in person, interminably came and went on voyages to St. Cloud and Suresnes, the passengers invariably including a certain lady and gentleman.

Observing these goings-on, journalist Pierre Giffard wrote that few at the fair could have known that "off in this hidden corner of the Exposition was germinating the seed of the modern technological revolution."

Two motorists aboard a Panhard et Levassor of 1895 fitted with a Daimler engine.

# CHAPTER FOUR

# Wealthy Featherheads

The man Adolf Daimler took on rides up and down the banks of the Seine aboard the steel-wheeler was René Panhard, of the Panhard-Levassor woodworking firm, in Paris, where Adolf's father had once refused a job and which had gone on to a more exalted place in French industry.

The couple whom the elder Daimler and Maybach meanwhile were treating to cruises in the motorboat were Émile Levassor, Panhard's partner, and Madame Édouard Sarazin, whose late husband had been French representative for Daimler's old outfit Gasmotoren-Fabrik Deutz. When he died, Sarazin had been working on a program with Panhard-Levassor to build Daimler engines in Paris. Shortly before his death, December 24, 1887, Sarazin had advised his wife to keep up the business relationship with Daimler. "That which he is working on is unquestionably worthy of confidence and has a future beyond anything we can imagine today," Sarazin said.

Hence, all those motorboat rides were not simply to indulge a fascination with the water; there was business to discuss. Before he returned home to Cannstatt, Daimler gave Madame Sarazin a written agreement assigning her the right to exploit his "French and Belgian patents on gas and petroleum engines. . . ."

Madame Sarazin later visited Cannstatt to formalize the agreement with Daimler, who at the same time made her his new agent in Paris. He also gave her a Daimler car to drive home in.

As for Émile Levassor, his interest in the widow Sarazin went beyond simple business concerns. On May 17, 1890, he married her, and together the two played a key role in getting Daimler's products established in France, Panhard-Levassor becoming the first company to build

The New York Daimler Manufacturing Company, Steinway Avenue, Long Island City, circa 1893.

Daimler engines for ships and other heavy-duty uses there. With Daimler's approval, the French firm transferred to Peugeot the rights to use Daimler engines in the manufacture of motor vehicles.

The Peugeot company were pioneers of the industrial revolution, having converted the family textile business into a foundry after the brothers Jean-Pierre and Jean-Frédéric invented the cold-roll process for making steel, in 1810. The company made all sorts of things to improve the human condition—corset stays, hoop-skirt frames, coffee mills, umbrella ribs, the "pince-nez" part of eyeglasses, workmen's tools, springs for clocks and watches. They added bicycles in 1885.

Peugeot did so well building cars that Panhard-Levassor themselves decided to make cars, starting in 1891. Thus, with two leading companies—Peugeot and Panhard-Levassor—turning out motor cars with Daimler engines, the firm of Daimler-Motoren-Gesellschaft of Germany, founded November 28, 1890, became the parent of the French automobile industry.

With France in his pocket, Daimler looked to the other side of the Atlantic for further expansion. The origin of his contacts with the United States arose from a trip to New York in 1876 by Maybach to visit his brother, who worked for Steinway & Sons, the piano makers. Through his brother, Maybach met William Steinway, senior member of the firm and a man of many interests. Steinway listened closely as Maybach described the Otto four-cycle engine, which had come into being that year.

Steinway kept in touch with Maybach and Daimler, intently following their work, and in 1888 he visited them in Cannstatt. Out of Steinway's visit came an agreement that gave Steinway the rights for all Daimler patents in the United States. The Daimler Motor Company of New York was founded on September 29 of that year, with its main office on Steinway Street, in Long Island City, and a branch office in Manhattan, actual production to be handled by the National Machine Company, of Hartford, Connecticut. The first American-built Daimler engine issued from there in 1891.

The Daimler Motor Company published its first prospectus in the United States the same year, showing the diverse uses of the Daimler engine—in "street railroad cars, pleasure boats, carriages, quadricycles, fire engines as well as stationary manufacturing or other purposes." The firm maintained a continuous exhibit of Daimler products from the Daimler-Motoren-Gesellschaft, in Cannstatt.

When the World's Columbian Exposition opened in Chicago in the summer of 1893, celebrating the four hundredth anniversary of Columbus' discovery of America, the Daimler home firm sent over a long line of products to be shown at the fair by its American branch. They included an illumination truck and accessories, with a ten-horsepower gasoline motor, for fire-fighting uses; three "wagonnets" and accessories, with two-horsepower motors; a fire engine with six-horsepower engine and all replacement parts; one boat made of pine, with a ten-horsepower engine; one complete track installation with turntable and miniature trolley; a two-horsepower Daimler gas motor; and one three-horsepower gasoline engine.

The German displays, notably the automobiles, caused a great deal of excitement, and at the end of June, when the exposition was two months old, Steinway wrote to Daimler suggesting that Daimler himself come to Chicago so that he personally could explain details of design and engineering to the fairgoers. Daimler had just remarried, his first wife having died four years earlier, and he accepted Steinway's invitation, combining the journey with a honeymoon.

Soon after he stepped from the train in Chicago, Daimler joined with Steinway in arranging for an additional car to be sent over from Cannstatt to add to the exhibit. This was an advanced version of the steel-wheeler, with heavy-spoked wheels in place of wire wheels, twin headlamps, fenders, armrests, and other amenities and refinements. A few days before the fair closed, on October 31, Yankee interest aroused by Daimler's cars at the Chicago fair was fanned anew by the arrival in New York of the headline-stealing Benz Viktoria, described earlier.

Between them, Daimler and Benz had ensured that the United States would never again be quite the same.

"The events of 1893—Daimler at the World's Fair in Chicago and the first public demonstration of a Benz car in New York—must be considered to be the most significant stimulation of the work done by the new publicly emerging pioneers of the American automobile industry," wrote automobile historian Dr. Friedrich Schildberger.

So far as Daimler's plans in the United States were concerned, however, not much came of them. William Steinway died in 1896, losing the enterprise its strong guiding hand. Some Daimler cars were eventually produced, but by that time the car made by the parent company in Germany was so far advanced that its U.S. offspring could never catch up. Who wanted a Yankee-built German car, anyway? The notorious Selden patent, which held up development of American cars, had played its part, and in 1913 fire leveled most of the factory. This brought down the final curtain on the Daimler enterprise in the United States.

There were few mourners that things hadn't worked out for Daimler in the States. The horseless carriage was widely viewed here as an evil, horse breeders and carriage makers in particular seeing it as a menace to the commonweal. No less an abomination than automobiles were their drivers, who tended to be rich.

"Wealthy featherheads," the New York *Times* fulminated in an editorial against speeders on April 21, 1903. "Is it possible that the men in this city who can afford to own an automobile are as a class so stupid that they do not see that the law should be obeyed?" Unless something was done to control these violators, who were like the "ignorant, rough, tough, semi-criminals" of Hell's Kitchen, the public might take things into its own hands and "avenge what the law does not prevent," the *Times* warned. "In such a case, do these respectable gentlemen realize that the sentiment of a great body of the public would be with the man who used a pistol and not with him who fell by the bullet?" If a vote could be taken, the paper concluded, automobiles would be banished from the highway.

Elsewhere, the paper carried the news that "Lorillard Spencer" had been arrested for speeding, making it clear that the miscreant was a "member of the Lorillard family": "Bicycle policeman Mallon stopped young Spencer at 99th Street [and Central Park West] and said the machine had been speeded at the rate of 15 miles an hour." At the station, the malefactor found a new enemy in the person of G. L. Brower, chairman of the Grievance Committee of the West End Association, who showed up to see that Lorillard was pointed for court.

"The driving of automobiles by rich men at the furious rate is outrageous," Brower said. "Again and again I have timed automobiles going a block in eight or ten seconds, or from 18 to 24 miles an hour."

Laws were passed that threatened to hamstring car development in the United States, as the Locomotives on Highways Act had done in England. As the legislative harassment grew, the car builders threw up defenses in the form of the National Association of Automobile Manufacturers, while the owners of cars gathered themselves into their own associations. "This bill, on account of the way it is forcing the automobilists to get together and work for its defeat, is almost worth all the trouble it is causing," said a member of the Albany (New York) Automobile Club, referring to the latest bedevilment against motorists pending in the capital, at Albany. He noted that the bill had already caused the formation of the New York State Association of Automobile Clubs, comprising the clubs of a half dozen cities.

Among other things, the proposed law would require the driver of an automobile to stop for horses and other domestic animals whether the animals were coming or going. Since the streets in 1903 were filled with horses—there were 20 million horses and mules in the country at the time—this of course would prevent cars from moving at all.

So matters stood with the automobile in the United States in the early days of the century—not much different from the way it had been in Europe, where, as the old century faded, a more sophisticated attitude already was setting in. It was in Europe that the idea of a race among engine-powered vehicles was first conceived—an event, incidentally, that would do much to make known the name Daimler. Promoted by the sports-minded *Le Petit Journal*, of Paris, the race lay between Paris and Rouen, a distance of 78.5 miles, and it was designated a "reliability" run because the machines were to be judged on safety, comfort, and economy, in addition to speed.

Everything on wheels more or less ca-

A 5-horsepower Benz Viktoria makes good time in the 745-mile Paris–Bordeaux–Paris race in June 1895.

pable of self-propulsion was entered in the contest. There were 102 vehicles all told, although in the end, on July 22, 1894, only twenty-one were qualified to start.

Paul Daimler, Gottlieb's eldest son, described the scene. "Father and I were near Porte Maillot in Paris. A great crowd gathered to see what in those days must have been a unique sight: cars getting ready for a race. The cars in this race differed widely in shape, size and character. Heavy, massive, steam-driven cars with trailers and powerful engines competed with the lightest model of steam tricycles, and these in turn competed with the gasoline-driven automobiles. They were all there for the same reason—to be first to Rouen and first back to Porte Maillot in Paris. Both of us . . . followed the racers in our car.

"The variety of types made an odd impression. In the heavy steamer we saw the fireman, his face running with sweat and covered with soot, working like mad

to get fuel on the fire. We saw the driver of the little steam tricycle constantly looking at the water-level and pressure gauges on the small, cleverly built tubular boiler and reaching in to regulate the oil flame. In sharp contrast, the drivers of the benzine and petroleum burning cars were leaning back, relaxed in their seats, adjusting this or that lever occasionally, and driving as if they were just doing it for fun. This was a remarkable sight, one I shall never forget."

Of the twenty-one starters, fifteen finished. The best all-round performers were judged to be the Peugeot and Panhard-Levassor cars, both powered by Daimler's two-cylinder "V" engines. The two were awarded first place jointly.

The winners averaged 10.5 miles an hour. While this was slower than a man on a bicycle could have done it against a medium head wind, the public marveled that these horseless wonders had made it at all. The French Society of Engineers

49

honored Daimler for his work and issued a bulletin: "Races will be the right solution to the problem of speeding the progress of mechanized road travel."

The world's first full-fledged, long-distance automobile race was not long in following, in June 1895. This was a punishing, 745-mile dash from Paris to Bordeaux and back to Paris. Again the Daimler engines triumphed, bringing in a Peugeot and a Panhard in the top places. Levassor, who had done much on his own to advance auto design after he first saw Daimler's work in Stuttgart, drove his own car, covering the distance in 48 hours, 48 minutes, at 15 miles an hour, without relief.

In this very first authentic automobile race, one driver adventurously tried out pneumatic tires in place of the customary solid rubber ones. André Michelin, whose family in France had been making rubber goods since 1832, fitted them on his Peugeot l'Éclair, but the results were not encouraging. Michelin had so many punctures, mostly from horseshoe nails, that he was the last man into Bordeaux. On the way back to Paris, spending more time fixing tires than driving, he made it only as far as Orléans before the allotted one hundred hours was up, putting him out of the race.

Émile Levassor, seeing how they had done for Michelin, predicted that pneumatic tires would never have the slightest use. This proved Levassor to be a better driver than prophet, for only a year later most cars rolled on air—however uncertainly. As long as a half dozen years after the Paris-Bordeaux race, Alfred Harmsworth, the British newspaper tycoon, complained that he was spending thirty-five hundred pounds sterling annually to keep each of his four cars in tires. One George Lanchester had twenty-one "bursts" in delivering a car two hundred miles to Rudyard Kipling.

Air tires first appeared in 1845, as "patented aerial wheels" for carriages. They died out after a couple of years—nobody seems to know why—then came back at the advent of the bicycle craze in the 1880s. The era of the modern pneumatic tire began with John Boyd Dunlop, a Belfast veterinarian, who patented one for

Levassor, who met his competitors coming the other way, arrived first at Porte Maillot with entry number 5, his 4-horsepower standard-production-model Panhard.

his son's tricycle in 1888. By the time of the Paris-Bordeaux event, the unreliability of air tires notwithstanding, Dunlop already had a $25 million tire-making corporation going.

The success of the Paris-Bordeaux race inspired a greater one: from Paris to Marseille to Paris, 1,080 miles. Once again the Daimler engine prevailed, and again under the hood of Émile Levassor's Panhard. Tragically, however, Levassor was hurt in an accident along the way—not seriously, it was thought at the time—and died soon afterward.

Then came a third race, this one between Marseille and Nice, in 1897. The Daimler-powered Panhard machines made it a clean sweep, capturing the first three places.

While their products were being proved on the road, Daimler and Maybach went on laboring to make them better. To be free to do so, unfettered by Daimler's partners, who doubted whether developing a high-speed engine was the right thing to be doing from a profits standpoint, Daimler and Maybach moved their experimental work to the big summer hall of the vacant Hotel Hermann, in Cannstatt. From there came the Maybach spray carburetor, which adjusted the mixture of fuel and air automatically, as needed, a great step forward. There were a new belt-driven car, with improved transmission, cooling, and springs—although Daimler and Maybach would return to gear transmission—and a milestone two-cylinder in-line engine to go with the new car. The Panhard-Levassor firm, building the engine on license, called it the "Phoenix," equipping their own cars with it.

The accomplishments of Daimler and Maybach at the Hermann did not escape the notice of Daimler-Motoren-Gesellschaft, who wanted to get the talents of these two back under the DMG roof. They

succeeded with the assistance of Frederick Richard Simms, an Englishman born in Hamburg, who had been trying to introduce Daimler's engines and motorboats into England. Simms additionally had wanted to get an automobile factory started in Britain, ever since the Daimler engine won the day in the Paris-Rouen Dependability Run, in 1894.

Simms approached his friends of the British Motor Syndicate, Ltd., to form a consortium to buy the patent rights to build Daimler products in the British Empire. The syndicate agreed, offering more cash for the Daimler patents than Daimler-Motoren-Gesellschaft itself had been asking—with the proviso that Gottlieb Daimler be called back to head the Cannstatt factory. The contract was signed November 1, 1895. And of course, along with Daimler came Maybach. Simms became a member of the DMG board of directors, serving until 1902.

While the Daimler Motor Company, Ltd., tooled up to build cars at Coventry, the British Motor Syndicate (to make it all worthwhile) went after the stultifying Red Flag Law—with results you know if you've been paying attention.

With Daimler and Maybach once more in authority at DMG, ideas proliferated. There were assorted new chassis, fresh designs in trucks and buses, improved stationary engines. There was a new system for cooling the automobile engine, a problem that had never really been conquered. The "honeycomb" radiator incorporated a mass of 8,070 tiny tubes with air blown past them by a fan built into the flywheel. This reduced the water needed to two gallons and was a major step toward high-performance engines.

The honeycomb radiator struck down a barrier to automobile development much as new, heat-resistant alloys, at a later time, made possible high-thrust jet engines, unleashing the airplane.

Emil Jellinek (1853–1918).

# CHAPTER FIVE

# Make Stronger Engines!

Baron Arthur Rothschild disliked being overtaken as he coaxed his eight-horse-power Panhard up La Turbie Hill, outside Nice. On a morning in 1899, as the story was told some years later by his nephew, Baron Henri Rothschild, who was riding with his uncle at the time, this indignity was visited upon Baron Arthur by a mammoth machine that plunged by him on La Turbie much as if there were no hill there at all.

At the summit, Rothschild walked over to the driver of the behemoth, who said his name was Mercedes, and without ado wrote him a check for the car. It was a German make, Mercedes explained, built by the Daimler works in Cannstatt, at the edge of Stuttgart. A couple of weeks later, it happened again—same hill, same man at the wheel, same make of car—and once again Baron Arthur produced his checkbook and bought the source of his annoyance.

"Mercedes" was Emil Jellinek, honorary consul-general to the Austro-Hungarian Empire in Nice and head of the Crédit Lyonnais, a large French banking house. For the past two years, since 1897, he had added the sale of Daimler cars to his activities. When he drove, he used the name of his favorite daughter, just as Baron Henri Rothschild called himself "Dr. Pascal," his identity as an oculist, in line with the practice of "gentlemen drivers" of assuming noms de guerre at the wheel. This helped to conceal their driving from their families and it stressed their amateur status, setting them aseptically apart from those uncouth fellows who drove for a livelihood.

As the two men became better acquainted, Jellinek asked Rothschild, "How would you like to own a car with twenty-four horsepower? That would put the two cars you have in the shade on La Turbie."

Rothschild could hardly wait. To hurry matters along at Cannstatt, he wrote to Jellinek, October 22, 1899, ostensibly to acknowledge a letter from Jellinek acknowledging the check Rothschild had already sent him in payment for the new car. "I am very pleased to hear that it will be ready on time," Rothschild wrote. "The earlier the car is delivered, the more bottles of brandy you will get. I am sending you today two hares and two pheasants. . . ."

Born in Vienna, Emil Jellinek was the blacksheep son of Adolf Jellinek, well-known classical scholar, described as "probably the greatest synagogue orator of the 19th century." Emil Jellinek was an impatient, irascible man with reddish hair and chin whiskers, who wore a pith helmet for safety from what he considered the pernicious effects of sun and cold on the brain.

His interest in automobiles awakened by the Paris-Rouen run in 1894, Jellinek had been among the first customers to show up at Cannstatt after Daimler and Maybach returned to the company. From the first, he had harried them to put more power into their cars. He had no complaints against the machine except that it was too slow. It cruised at only 20 kilometers (12.4 miles) an hour. He wanted one that would do 40, at least.

The company objected that no vehicle not on rails would be safe at such speeds. How could they know the car wouldn't be safe if they hadn't tried it? Jellinek demanded.

"Don't wrack my brains! Make stronger engines! How you achieve it is your affair. I herewith order four cars and will pay for them. You don't risk anything. The 40 kilometers per hour is my business."

The machines were duly delivered and Jellinek exultantly reported to Daimler and Maybach that he had driven them 42 kilometers an hour and that he was "still in one piece." But he disapproved of the engine placement. "The engine should be in front, because that was where the horse used to be," he wrote. "The engine replaces the horse; therefore it should be in front."

Moreover, Jellinek wanted engines with four cylinders. The Daimler company tactfully replied that at high speeds, their calculations showed, the weight of the engine in front could cause steering troubles. With four cylinders, weighing still more, the problem would be worse.

Jellinek retorted that four cylinders were not twice two cylinders—meaning, one surmises, that he had in mind the four cylinders integrated into a single unit. He called the manufacturers "asses" and ordered six four-cylinder cars with the engines in front. The machines were delivered as ordered. They gave Jellinek the doubled speed he demanded—and he reported no steering problems.

It must have been a pair of these cars that Jellinek sold to Baron Rothschild on the La Turbie summit in 1899. Ten-horsepower was the highest power yet reached as Daimler gradually began the transition to four-cylinder engines—and higher power—in 1898.

By the following year, engines at the Cannstatt plant were up to twenty-three horsepower. It was now time to see what could be done at La Turbie, as Jellinek saw it. For the hill-climb of March 30, 1900, under Jellinek's badgering, the company reluctantly produced a twenty-three-horsepower racing car, driven by Wilhelm Bauer, a foreman at the Daimler works. Bauer pushed hard, knowing he was expected to win. At the first turn, he lost control and crashed into a cliff. He died next day.

Jellinek blamed the machine. The factory blamed the course—and Jellinek, reminding him that it was he who had ordered a racer. But the car wasn't designed right, Jellinek countered. It must have a much lower center of gravity and a longer wheelbase. Above all, Jellinek argued, the engine must be still more powerful, not less.

If they would build him exactly the kind of machine he wanted, Jellinek wrote, he would take thirty-six of them, in return for the exclusive sales rights for the Daimler car in Austria-Hungary, France, Belgium, and the United States. The car would be sold in these countries, Jellinek stipulated, under the name "Mercedes." Elsewhere, the machine would be known as the "New Daimler."

Mercedes Adrenne Manuela Ramona, born in 1889, was Jellinek's daughter by his first wife, who died of cancer in 1893. Her full first name was "María de las Mercedes." Jellinek gave Spanish names to all the children of his two marriages, according to his son Guy, who is constrained to add in his book about the family that his father, who lived in North Africa as a young man, admired all things Spanish.

Jellinek was unencumbered by any trace of technical knowledge—indeed, lacked the capacity to acquire it, Guy wrote. It gave Jellinek no pause, therefore, that what he was asking of the Daimler company called for breaking entirely new engineering ground. He blandly demanded that the revolutionary new cars

The carnival float of Jellinek with his Mercedes during Nice Week. Circa 1903.

Vintage photograph of the first "Mercedes" racer, 1901. The vehicle was distinguished by its honeycomb radiator and 5.9-liter, 35-horsepower engine with mechanically operated valves.

be delivered by October 15, only months away.

When he was told that it would be a miracle if such a radically new car could be completed in the time allowed, by a man even of Maybach's talent, Jellinek snapped back that miracles were expected of those capable of them. The gentle Maybach, the only man in the Daimler organization who enjoyed Jellinek's full approval, came close. The car was shipped on December 22, 1900, arriving in good time for Nice Week of the new year—the first car known as "Mercedes."

One of those in the United States who evidently followed the historic Nice Week events of 1901, noting the performance of the Mercedes, was millionaire William K. Vanderbilt, who forthwith ordered one for himself. "The first Mercedes make of automobile built in Germany for W. K. Vanderbilt, Jr., is expected here in a few days," reported the New York *Times*, June 9, 1901. The newspaper pointed out that the machine "is considered one of the largest built in Germany this year. It is very low in front, with accommodations for four persons for carriage traveling. But two seats are to be used when the machine is in racing trim"—which would be its configuration most of the time.

From 1901 onward, Nice Week belonged largely to the Mercedes, the name being registered as the trademark of the car in 1902 as "Daimler" faded from use. In Nice Week of that year, with horsepower up to 40, a Mercedes made a clean sweep of it, winning all contests. In the one-mile race, it hit 51.1 miles an hour from a standing start. It covered the flying kilometer at 75 miles an hour, and it stormed up La Turbie at 34.73 miles an hour.

The engine of the 1902 car, though more powerful, weighed substantially less than its 35-horsepower predecessor, dropping the power-to-weight ratio from 14.9:1 to 10.1:1. The fan was done away with, the discovery having been made that at high speeds it wasn't needed, the air blowing through the radiator serving the purpose of cooling the water.

"The first thing that strikes one is their wonderfully quiet running," admiringly observed *The Autocar*, April 19, 1902. "When the vehicle is standing, a rapid rhythmical beat is only just audible, scarcely more than a low hum, and there is absolutely no vibration. It is generally supposed that the motor is then turning at not more than 150 rpm, but Herr Daimler assured us that it was still running at 500 rpm.

"It is difficult to imagine how elasticity of engine power and economy of effort can be brought to a higher stage of development in an autocar," the account continued, "but it is nevertheless certain that finality has not been reached, and we may now confidently look to the time when the petrol car will become as quiet and docile as the electric vehicle."

At the Fifth International Automobile and Cycle Exhibition, at the Grand Palais, in Paris, in December 1902, the Mercedes "constituted the main theme in a great symphony of automobile design," as one writer put it. Most leading car builders thereafter copied the honeycomb radiator along with the overall changes in layout and design that the new radiator influenced.

One of the more zealous motoring fans among the spectators at the Paris show was King Leopold of Belgium, who owned one of the new 40-horsepower Mercedes touring cars. In a long discussion with Wilhelm Maybach, described by the Paris edition of the New York *Herald* as "the leading automobile designer of the day," the king said he needed a car that was the fastest on the road. "Unless I can touch 130 kilometers [about 80 miles] an hour, it's no use to me."

Not to keep His Highness in want, Maybach added the design of a 90-horsepower car to that of the 60-horsepower machine already in the works for 1903. In the latter car, yet a further cut in power-to-weight ratio was had, and radiator efficiency was improved with the addition of more tubes. The 60-horsepower Mercedes posted new records at Nice Week, averaging 74.3 miles an hour; but the sport this year was darkened by the death of Count Eliot Zborowski, in a Mercedes. The count, who was well liked and known for his knack of somehow coming through the dustiest race still looking clean and fresh, was going for a record when his car struck a rock. The machine turned over and he died instantly.

Count Zborowski's death foreshadowed a great deal worse to come in the growing sport of motor racing. This was the disaster of the Paris-Madrid event in May, which ended city-to-city contests and put a chill on the development of the automobile.

Daimler, while entering their cars in the race, hesitated to expose their own men to the danger of accidents inherent in a run of that distance—837 miles—at the speeds then being reached. "The advantage which we would *perhaps* achieve, would be more than outweighed by the loss of manpower in the workshop," the company wrote Jellinek. "In addition, we are not certain that our people can stand up to the French drivers," who, they argued, had more experience because of the popularity of racing in France.

Jellinek said he would drive, himself, if he weren't "a bundle of nerves" and were younger. The problem of finding drivers was complicated by the fact that, in Germany, title counted more than experience, and experience was hard to get in any case because the German Automobile Club excluded men of common clay from

Jellinek's salon at Villa Mercedes in Nice, 1900.

membership. Hence, many drivers rated among the best but who had red blood instead of blue in their veins were barred as "unsuitable personalities."

There weren't many like Baron Pierre de Caters, who met both the blood test and driver qualifications, not to mention Jellinek's description of the "genuine fools" he wrote the company he was looking for. De Caters readily signed up to chauffeur the 90-horsepower Mercedes, on which development had proceeded apace after the spectacular successes of the 60-horsepower machine at Nice Week.

As part of the arrangement, ceremoniously negotiated at Jellinek's Villa Mercedes, in Nice, Baron de Caters agreed to lend his personal 60-horsepower machine to Camille Jenatzy to drive as a second Mercedes in the race, which would be run in three stages—Bordeaux the first day, Vitoria the second, Madrid the third.

The race began at Versailles on May 24, with seemingly half of France lining the road. There were two hundred and thirty contestants, give or take a few—no exact count was ever made—and they included every species on wheels with an engine to run it. The lineup began with the big machines and tapered down through diminishing sizes to a tail of some fifty motorcycles. The first machine left at dawn "with a tremendous rush, disappearing in a cloud of dust." The last got away three hours and forty-five minutes later.

Nobody got farther than Bordeaux. As

each of the ninety-four machines to reach there wheeled into the city—the first arriving just after noon and the last at 3 o'clock the next morning—it was impounded and placed under military guard by order of the French Government. No engines would be started again. The drivers could have their cars back only on condition that they have them towed to the railway station by horse and shipped home by train.

The Spanish Government joined with the French in calling an end to the contest. Anyone who wanted to drive on into Spain was free to do so, the government said, but he would have to proceed at the leisurely pace of an ordinary tourist. The fast stuff was over.

Rumors of death and injury were heard well before the last machine left Versailles, passed by word of mouth in both directions by spectators at each point of mishap. At an arched bridge, a car surfboarded into the crowd at more than seventy miles an hour when the "mechanician" grabbed the arm of the driver to hang on. Three people were killed, six injured. Another machine sommersaulted and exploded after hitting a dog, burning the mechanic to death.

Marcel Renault, one of France's most popular drivers, died when his car smashed into a tree after a wheel caught in a ditch as he was passing another machine at full throttle.

All told, ten were killed in the race. Many more were hurt, some to carry the marks for life.

A near victim was the automobile itself. Its enemies cackled righteously that this was what they had been saying all along: that the automobile was but a dangerous plaything of the rich, without promise for the common good. In the Chamber of Deputies, Premier Émile Combes lamely told the house that the government hadn't expected such speeds when it sanctioned the race. But he blamed the roads and the drivers, rather than the lack of precautions by the organizers, and he advised the chamber against action that might inflame public opinion against the automobile, bringing a demand for measures that would retard the growth of the industry.

The New York *Times* had some things to say too. "The frightful results of the attempted race of automobiles from Paris to Madrid are not most to be deplored on account of the loss of life among the contestants," the paper began in an editorial, "Massacre by Automobile," May 26, 1903. "When a man projects himself along a public highway at the rate of nearly ninety miles an hour, he deliberately risks his life. If he did not know of this risk intuitively, there have been already accidents enough in the automobiling business to bring the risk to his notice. It is the innocent persons who are passing along the same highway upon their lawful occasions who are entitled to be protected against the risk which the racing automobilist deliberately incurs for himself."

The newspaper had hard words for William K. Vanderbilt, at the same time getting in a swipe at France as well. It recalled that Vanderbilt had recently complained "that automobiling had been 'practically killed' in this country by what he regarded as absurd legal restrictions. It seems that he would have stood a very good chance of being 'practically killed' in person if the disablement of his machine had not put him out of this latest competition in the country of his choice. Most Americans, upon reading the record of slaughter in France, will be inclined to congratulate themselves upon living in a country which in one essential point is so clearly more civilized. . . ."

For a while, in reaction to what the *Times* called "the awful run" in France, it

Christian Werner driving a 125-horsepower Mercedes in the last of the James Gordon-Bennett races, Circuit d'Auvergne, July 5, 1905. The car placed fifth. Photographed by Jacques-Henri Lartigue, France.

looked as if the James Gordon Bennett Race, coming up on July 2, might be canceled. These international automobile contests were founded in 1899 by James Gordon Bennett, owner of the New York *Herald-Tribune*, to be held annually under a strict set of rules. The winning country each year arranged the next year's event.

The race must be run on a course at least 550 kilometers, or 341 miles, in length, but no longer than 650 kilometers. Each car was required to have two drivers, seated side by side, who between them weighed 120 kilograms, or just over 132 pounds each. If they weighed less, the deficit must be made up with dead weight placed aboard the car. The prize, made up by Tiffany's on Bennett's order, was a 70-pound likeness of an automobile with a winged woman standing on the seat and a smaller figure perched on the dash holding a torch.

The host country in 1903 was England, which got around the illegality of road racing at home by finding a site in Ireland, centered at Ballyshannon, near Dublin. The matter of keeping the crowds safely back from the course would be met by stringing up ropes and lining the road on either side with automobiles and donkey carts, backed by nine thousand police and soldiers.

Proponents pointed out that in addition to these precautions, the James Gordon Bennett Race was a very different thing from the Paris-Madrid affair: The cars would all be going at more or less the same speed; there would be little or none of the passing and repassing that went on in the other event. Finally, there were only twelve cars in the race.

In the midst of Daimler's preparations for Ireland, catastrophe struck. On June 10, twenty-two days before the race, fire leveled the Cannstatt factory, wiping out the three 90-horsepower machines being honed for the occasion—along with one hundred other cars, finished and unfinished. Up with the flames seemed to go the only hope of bringing the coveted James Gordon Bennett trophy to Germany.

But despair lasted little longer than the smoke that drifted out over the vineyard-covered hills. At the suggestion of driver Baron de Caters, the company rounded up three 60-horsepower cars from their owners, procuring the first by telegraph. One of the machines was that of the American Clarence Gray Dinsmore, who demurred at first, explaining that because of his health—he was partly paralyzed—he needed the car to get around in. This obstacle was overcome by lending Dinsmore the use of a 40-horsepower machine.

One other difficulty remained. Under the rules, all cars of each competing country had to be made in the home country, down to the last nut and bolt. The Mercedes cars used Michelin tires; these were made in Germany, as required, but the valves were made in France. So the Ger-

Spectators at the start of the 1903 Gordon-Bennett race in Ireland. The white, privately owned, 60-horsepower Mercedes was driven to the first major international victory for Mercedes and for Germany by the Belgian Camille Jenatzy.

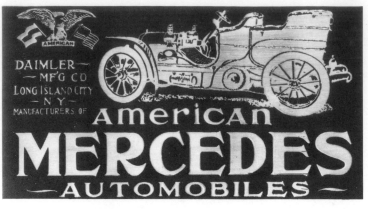

Vintage brass plate.

three 40-horsepower Napiers, but the brawny French cars were the favorites. The Mercedes would need a lot of luck.

To save time—and perhaps to show their contempt for the French titans, picking up some publicity in the bargain—the Germans got the cars to Ireland under their own power, to the extent that the map allowed. They drove the machines from Cannstatt to Paris and then to Le Havre, on the Channel coast, where they necessarily yielded to boats for the passage to England. Again taking the wheel, they drove the machines through Wales to the Irish Sea and, after another water crossing, piloted the cars directly to the scene of the action, roaring in not much before starting time.

The cars of the other contestants arrived by rail, carefully packed in cotton wool, and in ample time for the drivers to get in some preparation. The English and Americans practiced for weeks. The French gave themselves several days to look over the course, which was enriched by a wealth of twists and turns.

man cars were forced to use year-old Continental tires, made in Hannover—valves and all.

There were those who wondered if the detail of the tires might not be academic. The odds faced by the 60-horsepower Mercedes cars were fearful. Could they beat the 80-horsepower Morsmachinès and the 100-horsepower Panhards? The Americans had a Peerless and a pair of Wintons in the race, one driven by Alexander Winton in person, each with an 80-horsepower engine; and the English,

1906. Mercedes 70-horsepower, chain-drive touring car. The body was custom designed by Rothschild of Paris with three sets of seats for seven passengers. The Armour family, of Chicago, had the car built for their summer holiday in France.

One of the Mercedes entries at the Automobile Club de France, Sarthe Circuit, June 1906.
Photographed by Jacques-Henri Lartigue, France.

By the outcome of the race, in the view of all Germany, the Mercedes cars could have been driven home on the water. Camille Jenatzy, known as "The Red Devil" for his flaming beard and disdain of headgear, won in the borrowed car of Henry Gray Dinsmore. He put the 370 miles behind him in the astonishing time of 6 hours and 39 minutes, averaging 55 miles an hour and finishing 11 minutes ahead of the runner-up. (Jenatzy, who had been the first man in history to exceed 65 miles an hour, doing so in a cigar-shaped, aluminum body electromobile, the Jamais Contente, in 1899, had been approved to drive the Dinsmore car after Wilhelm Werner, Dinsmore's chauffeur, had been ruled out as not "a gentleman driver." Jenatzy would be a man to reckon with many times before he was finally

disposed of in the Ardennes Forest by a fellow hunter who mistook him for a wild boar and shot him to death, in 1913.)

Largely through the efforts of Wilhelm Maybach, and despite the company's preoccupation with plans to move to Untertürkheim, hastened by the fire, the 90-horsepower Mercedes was resurrected from the ashes and was being tested in the field by the end of 1903. First to demonstrate the machine publicly was the New York *Times*'s favorite motorist, William K. Vanderbilt. Driving a car that had been on the high seas on its way to the United States at the time of the fire, Vanderbilt traversed a mile in 39 seconds at Daytona Beach, Florida, on January 27, 1904. This meant a speed of 92 miles an hour, far faster than anyone had ever moved before.

Doctors shook their heads, saying no man could live at that speed. What they said when Baron de Caters, some months later, covered the same distance at 97.25 miles an hour, at Ostend, is not recorded.

Meanwhile, things had not gone as well elsewhere for Daimler as they might have. In the James Gordon Bennett classic of 1904, attended by the elite of several continents, including Kaiser Wilhelm II, Camille Jenatzy had lost the Bennett trophy back to France. Jenatzy put on a memorable battle with the top drivers of a half dozen countries, again at the wheel of a Mercedes belonging to Clarence Gray Dinsmore, this time a 90-horsepower machine, but tire troubles did him in. Also, a train held him up. The best he could do was to come in second.

But this was comparatively good con-sidering what happened at the next James Gordon Bennett event, July 5, 1905. Far from winning the trophy back, the Mercedes cars were plagued by technical problems and tire troubles, making sixty-five tire changes during the race. They lost badly.

Daimler-Motoren-Gesellschaft was very quick to hear from Jellinek, their man in Nice. "The only good thing which this heavy defeat may have is that the engineers of DMG will have their arrogance and overweening opinion of themselves somewhat damped," he wrote wrathfully next day. "If you don't want the DMG to become fourth or fifth rate after their present second rate position, the racing cars of 1906 will have to be constructed now!"

Whatever Jellinek may have thought

Factory workers illustrate the careful attention given to the construction of each Mercedes in the new Untertürkheim factory, 1908.

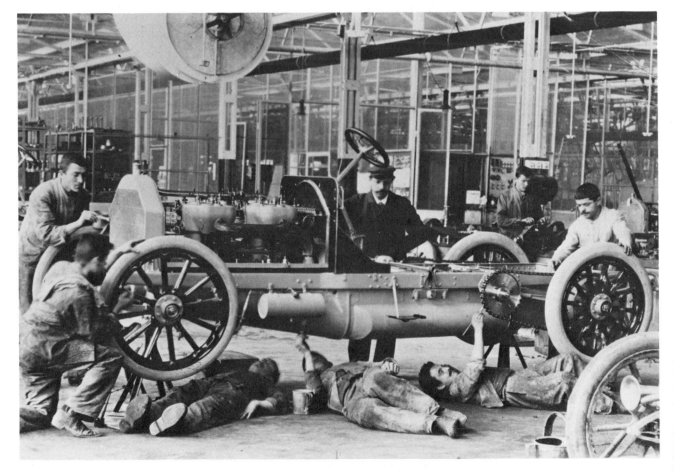

The Zeppelin LZ1, powered by two Daimler 4-cylinder, 16-horsepower motors, designed by Maybach, on its maiden flight, July 2, 1900.

privately of the next model, when it came along it was at least good enough that after the *Allgemeine Automobil-Zeitung* published a long, laudatory pamphlet about the 1906 Mercedes and the Daimler company without mentioning Jellinek, he speedily let the publication know of its error. "The whole lot would not exist if I had not appeared on the scene," wrote Jellinek, who was not given to excessive modesty. "Not only the whole business, but also the whole construction of the Mercedes car, was and still is, entirely built on my plans, and . . . all the faults that do creep in are caused by the unwillingness of the DMG to listen to me in the first place. . . ."

This unusual document brought a reply from the author of the offending pamphlet which, as an expert in the field of invective, Jellinek must have inwardly admired. The publication had been "able to draw the public's attention to various novelties as well as improvements" in the 1906 Mercedes, the author wrote. "Unfortunately," he went on, "we cannot say that of yourself. . . . You have remained as you were, if anything you have gotten worse. . . . You are quite transparent to me, and what I see inside is quite horrible. Once upon a time, when you pretended to have money, you were a charming person. . . . Now that you are really rich, you are becoming a bore. . . ."

Unhappily, however, the 1906 Mercedes fell short of expectations. There was a new kind of race that year, called the Grand Prix, after Grand Prix de Paris, a horse-racing classic founded in 1834. The James Gordon Bennett event, "the race of races," had been ended and the trophy returned to its donor, on the initiative of

65

Adolf Daimler in Wilhelm Maybach's office, Cannstatt, circa 1901.

the French, who objected to the rule limiting the entrants of each country to three makes of cars. That was hardly enough for France, by now spilling over with automobile manufacturers.

In the Grand Prix, it was car against car, rather than country against country. And all cars from a given nation bore the same colors: the British, green; French, blue; Italian, red; and the German, white.

But the white hope of the Daimler company came home far behind, straggling in tenth and eleventh, and the honors went to Italy and France.

As company fortunes persisted at a low ebb, Jellinek became steadily more abusive. "You continually demand that your cars should be driven by experienced drivers," he wrote, adding sarcastically, "I would suggest therefore that you open next to your motor car factory one for the production of drivers. With all other makes one does not need to be a scholar to be able to drive. It is only with a Mercedes car that one needs a certificated engineer. . . ."

Another time: "You just don't understand anything about the automobile business. . . . The public wants direct drive, no matter if such cars are better or worse than those with a change-speed gear. If you are not capable of producing a change gear with direct drive which is noiseless, you should learn from the French, whose cars run now as silently as electrical cars."

Jellinek seemed beyond appeasement. When the company telegraphed him of plans for certain mechanical improvements, he replied that the telegram "documents your complete inability" and that "the moment has now come when you will soon have shown that all my prophecies about the steady decline of your factory have come true."

With that, the worm at last began to turn. As the hapless year of 1906 waned, the company took steps to alleviate the problem of Mr. Mercedes-Jellinek, who had adopted the name of his daughter. It notified him that as of January 1 they would no longer supply him spare parts free. Jellinek's response, while presuming to have beat Daimler to the draw, could only have been the rainbow news of the year for the company. "Your attitude strengthens my decision, which is now irrevocable." But Jellinek's departure went slowly, in the manner of a military occupation. "I give up the ceaseless battle with you," he wrote with mock weariness. "If you want to ruin yourselves completely, do so. . . . You will surely destroy yourselves with the miserable construction of your cars, but mainly it will be with your swollen heads."

Full disengagement came finally in 1908. In a literal way, Jellinek flowered anew when he was made honorary vice-consul to Monaco, a post created for him with the help of Archduke Franz Ferdinand, heir to the throne of Austria, an old Mercedes customer. Bedecked in the military regalia of his office—blouse festooned with medals, epaulets the size of floor mops, sword at his side, all topped with a tall, dome-like headgear capped with ostrich plumes—he became a human bird of paradise.

For Emil Mercedes-Jellinek, the paths of glory ended with the shot that killed Archduke Franz Ferdinand, at Sarajevo, Bosnia, June 28, 1914, igniting World War I. Jellinek was suspected of being a spy. There followed flight, hiding, jail—and death, January 21, 1918.

As for Jellinek's daughter, Mercedes, with the peasants up and the aristocrats down, she was reduced to begging for herself and her two children. She died obscurely on February 23, 1929, in a small flat in Vienna, at the age of forty.

Paul Daimler sits next to Maybach (right) at the wheel of a 1903 Mercedes in the courtyard of the Cannstatt factory.

The Untertürkheim factory, on the Neckar River, 1908.

While the Jellinek withdrawal was evolving, another prominent divorcement from Daimler was taking place. Wilhelm Maybach, who had been pushed aside after the death, in 1903, of Max Duttonhofer, cofounder of the company and chairman of the board, found himself further demoted when he returned from "a long rest."

He wrote to his employers about the shortcomings of the 1906 car, which had done so poorly in the Grand Prix. He blamed the problem on "undue haste in changing the design" after he came home. "Designs and drawings which were shown to me by mistake are sufficient proof of how inexperienced is the work being done at this moment in the DMG," Maybach wrote. "It is therefore understandable that I wish to leave the company. I cannot see any hope for the future of the DMG under the present conditions . . . either [they] are changed so that all new designs will again come exclusively under my direction, or I shall leave the DMG for good."

Maybach refused the sop of a place in management. The "King of Designers," the man who had done so much to set motordom on course in the faltering days of its beginnings, left the company on April 1, 1907. Now sixty-one, Maybach made a new career for himself by joining Count Ferdinand von Zeppelin, who had gotten ideas about balloon travel when he made an ascent as a Union volunteer in the American Civil War and who at Friedrichshafen, had for some years been building airships powered by Daimler engines. Count Zeppelin provided Maybach with a small factory and put him to work designing engines for his "Zeppelins." The hand of Wilhelm Maybach, as well as that of his son, Karl, may be seen in the little-known fact that by the time of the First World War, five Zeppelin air-

68

ships with Maybach engines had carried 34,000 passengers 107,180 miles without a fatality or injury to passengers or crew.

At Daimler-Motoren-Gesellschaft, Maybach's old post was given to Gottlieb Daimler's eldest son, Paul, who was considered to have won his spurs by developing a four-wheel-drive vehicle at Wiener-Neustadt, the Austrian branch of the company. Paul Daimler had his work cut out for him. It was a period when it looked as if the dark predictions of Jellinek and Maybach might be coming true. The company was losing money. Mercedes cars were still losing races. There were other problems.

There was a deep nostalgia for the splendid day in Ireland when the flame-bearded Jenatzy snatched the James Gordon Bennett trophy from cars with nearly twice the horsepower of his borrowed Mercedes. Daimler desperately needed to win another big one.

Then came 1908.

Prince Henry of Prussia drives a 40-horsepower Benz in the International Touring Car Competition for the Herkomer trophy of 1906. The race, covering the five hundred miles from Frankfurt am Main to Innsbruck, included a hill-climb at Semmering and a speed trial at the finish.

# CHAPTER SIX

# The Watch on the Rhine

The old town of Dieppe, on the coast of Normandy, was swollen to many times its normal size as it played host to three hundred thousand strangers drawn by the well-conducted heraldry of the French Automobile Club for an international battle of automobiles: the Grand Prix of France, on June 7, 1908. Every nation that made them was represented in the contest: France, Germany, England, Italy, and the United States.

For Paul Daimler, preparing a machine for the occasion was his first major test in the shoes of the departed Maybach. He skillfully incorporated a number of innovations in his design, based on a distillation of all that had been learned in the company's pioneering experience with racing cars. The final result was a white juggernaut of 135 horsepower at 1,400 revolutions a minute. But there was no reason to expect that the big Mercedes would have things to itself among the forty-six entries.

Perhaps the most formidable rival was the Benz. With automobile technology moving rapidly forward, paced by Daimler, there had been some changes at Benz et Cie. Carl Benz, who believed that thirty miles an hour was fast enough for anyone to travel and that racing was frivolous, resigned from the board of directors in 1903 in disagreement with partner Julius Ganss over remedies to the company crisis brought on by the introduction of the Mercedes, in 1901. The trouble began when Ganss went over Benz's head and called in Marius Barbarou, well-known French design engineer, to update the Benz cars. Barbarou began by designing a race car with a 60-horsepower, 4-cylinder engine, to challenge the Mercedes racer.

Barbarou's speedster only added embarrassment to Benz's other problems by

The Mercedes race team gathers after the Dieppe French Grand Prix. Christian Lautenschlager is at the wheel of the car on the far left (number 9), with Otto Salzer at his side.

disgracing itself at the La Turbie hill-climb on April 1 of Nice Week, 1903. The car failed to finish, while Mercedes machines romped merrily up the hill in the first three places. Benz left the company three weeks later, on April 21.

Although Benz returned in 1904, guidance of the firm rested with his sons, Eugen and Richard, and a new board of directors. Ganss quit the company at about the time Benz rejoined it—as did Barbarou, some of whose work was salvaged in the design of the Parsifal, a machine said to have more than a surface resemblance to the Mercedes. Barbarou was succeeded by the brilliant young engineer Hans Nibel, who would leave a lasting mark on Benz cars, beginning with the machine he designed for the 1908 Grand Prix at Dieppe. This car developed 150

horsepower, fifteen more than Paul Daimler's Mercedes entry for the event.

For a time, as the dust began to rise over the 48-mile triangular course, the Fiat and the Renault put on a good show, but the race soon settled down to a duel between the Mercedes and the Benz, driven respectively by Christian Lautenschlager and Victor Héméry, Benz's top driver. Each man had more power at his disposal than he dared to use (in consideration of his tires) except as he was pressed by the other. Under the rules, the drivers did their own changing. There could be no help from the dugouts, or ''pits,'' scooped out near the grandstands.

There came the point when, with two laps to go and having changed tires ten times, Lautenschlager in his Mercedes was down to his last set. One more punc-

72

ture and it would be all over. Still leading, but with Hémery hanging on behind like a shadow, Lautenschlager decided to throw caution to the winds and go for broke. He cleaned up the last of the 477 miles of hills and turns and flashed across the finish line the winner, at an average speed of sixty-nine miles an hour.

Hémery came in second, ten minutes later. Another Benz arrived third. To the disgust of the band, not to mention the feelings of several thousand Frenchmen, the musicians were obliged to strike up not the "Marseillaise," as expected, but "The Watch on the Rhine."

Nor was defeat any easier for the discovery that Lautenschlager was the rawest of rookies. This was his first race. The closest he had come to a contestant's role before was as riding mechanic for Otto Salzer in the Mercedes team of the two preceding years.

For Daimler it was Ireland, 1903, all over again—the big one they had needed —and it was not lost on the company that the gods had ridden with them and that a blowout for their man would have sent the Benz across the line as the winner, followed by yet another Benz in second place. With two winners, Benz would have had a greater victory than Daimler. Dieppe was a taste of what was coming from Benz for the next several years. There was now a second great German contender in the field. In 1913, Benz counted twenty-nine victories, to thirteen for Mercedes. In the years from 1909 to 1912, two of the best-known American drivers, cigar-chomping Barney Oldfield and Bob Burman, between them posted twenty-three U.S. and world speed records in Benz machines.

The fabled Blitzen Benz, of 1909, wiped out all records with new ones that stood for years. Shaped like a bullet, this machine was based on the Benz Dieppe

Barney Oldfield, 1914.

Christian Lautenschlager, French Grand Prix, 1914.

cars. Designer Nibel bored out the four cylinders to near the size of beer kegs, achieving a Baron Munchausen-sized total displacement of 1,312 inches and 200 horsepower at 1,600 rpm.

On its first trial, at the Brooklands Track, in England, the Blitzen Benz reached a sensational new mark of 127 miles an hour. A little later, at Daytona Beach, Florida, the American ace, Bob Burman got the car up to 141.7 miles an hour, a record that endured for fifteen years.

After Dieppe 1908, the disgruntled French found economic reasons to work for an end to Grand Prix racing, and for a time there was a lull in the sport. As the bruises of defeat healed, however, the French decided to hold the grandest

Grand Prix of all, at Lyon, July 4, 1914. It was a decision that would bring them recurring melancholy.

For the new French Grand Prix, Paul Daimler set out to create a car that was all his own—unlike the Dieppe machine, which basically belonged to Maybach. The result was a car that, some have said, was as radically new as the first Mercedes, back in 1901. In designing the engine, Daimler drew heavily on the company's experience with aircraft engines, begun with its designs for Count Zeppelin in Maybach's time. As he worked, Daimler no doubt had it keenly in mind that by now Benz, too, had the benefit of such experience. Just the year before, in 1913, Benz won the Emperor's competition for the best aircraft engine among forty-four

74

designs submitted by twenty-six contestants.

Among the features of Daimler's Grand Prix car were four spark plugs per cylinder, with each cylinder built separately and enclosed by its own sheet-metal water jacket, welded on. The engine could run indefinitely at 3,200 rpm, rare if not unique in 1914, developing 115 horsepower.

In profile, Paul Daimler's car for the new Grand Prix was as far ahead of its Dieppe ancestor as the engine, the driver sitting lower by a foot than in the Dieppe Mercedes. The "V" radiator was seen for the first time, adorned on either side by the three-pointed star, adopted as the Mercedes symbol in 1908. What the car had in common with the other Grand Prix racers, as prescribed under the formula for the event, was a piston displacement only about one third the size of the old.

Gear ratios and wheelbases were adjusted to the characteristics of the track after visits to the course by teams of drivers and engineers well before the race. For days, starting at five in the morning, they roared around the twenty-three-mile circuit in half-finished cars, learning where to shift gears and cut the power for the corners—all under the cold eye of an authoritarian racing manager.

Once again favored to win were the French, who had done some re-engineering of their own since Dieppe. Peugeot had won the five hundred-mile race at Indianapolis the year before, to say nothing of several events in Europe. The Peugeot had four-wheel brakes, affording an advantage on the corners supposed to be worth one minute per lap. The Germans hadn't bothered about extra brakes, staying with the two on the rear wheels.

Brakes, on the whole, lagged behind other aspects of automobile development, the controlling idea being to go, rather

Tire change for Louis Wagner at the French Grand Prix.

Wagner on the course.

Communist terrorists riding a 1918 Mercedes military truck in front of the Brandenburg Gate, Berlin, 1919.

than stop. On the first crossing of the Alps by car, in 1901, the driver informally met the problem of disabled brakes by tying a tree trunk to the back of the machine and dragging it along behind. In England, it was wryly said of one car that on wet days the driver needed to apply his brakes before leaving Surrey in order to avoid running into the sea at the Sussex coast. Daimler offered four-wheel brakes optionally on passenger cars as early as 1903, but such brakes remained out of general use for another twenty years or so.

The Frenchman to beat in the Grand Prix was Georges Boillot, a showman as well as an expert at the wheel, and the man expected to redress the shame of Dieppe. The Mercedes men were ready for him.

They plotted a strategy in which the drivers functioned as a team, under strict control of the pits. Max Sailer, whose car was counted as expendable, was assigned the role of rabbit ahead of the hounds, leading Boillot at a pace calculated to wreck the Frenchman's car—even at the cost of his own. When Sailer had done his work, Lautenschlager, hero of Dieppe, would move into the opening made by Sailer. Louis Wagner and Otto Salzer were to take it easy, saving fuel, and await signals from the pits.

Boillot's four-wheel brakes worked as expected, enabling him to hold his speed longer as he went into the turns, but Sailer, with faster acceleration from his quasi-aircraft engine, outgunned him on the straightaways. Sailer finished the first lap eighteen seconds ahead of Boillot.

Gordon Watney stands beside the Jenatzy 60-horsepower 1903 Gordon Bennett race car that he modified with a streamlined cowl and tail in 1911. Lord Vernon drove the car to victory at Brooklands in the same year. Watney's collection of seven individually modified Mercedes cars won a number of trophies at Brookland, some of which are shown in the foreground. Weybridge, England, 1911.

At the end of the second lap, he had stretched his lead to forty-six seconds. On the fifth time around, Sailer led by two minutes and forty-four seconds.

Then, on the sixth lap, Sailer's engine blew up—as not unexpected, putting Boillot in front. Signals went out from the Mercedes pit. Lautenschlager moved up to take on the scrambling Frenchman. Wagner edged forward to challenge for second place. Salzer advanced to sixth position. Boillot clung to his lead, driving like a man fleeing from demons; but the Germans came inexorably closer.

"At the end of the seventeenth lap [with three to go]," as told by St. John Nixon, who was there, "[Lautenschlager] was only 14 seconds behind Boillot, and when the scoreboard announced this fact, the grandstand positively rocked with excitement . . . a sudden hush came over the crowd when the scoreboard announced that Lautenschlager had wrested the lead from Boillot. . . ."

At the nineteenth lap, Lautenschlager had broadened his lead to one minute, seven seconds. Wagner trailed Boillot by sixteen seconds, followed a breath behind by Salzer. Boillot pressed his machine to its outer limits. In the final lap, he passed those limits. Some chroniclers say his axle broke, others that the valves failed. Whatever the trouble, there was no argument about what followed. Lautenschlager, Wagner, and Salzer crossed the finish line in that order: one, two, three. All three averaged about sixty-five miles an hour for the 467 miles, less than a mile separating first from third.

France's disappointment was soon smothered by a far more somber contest between her and Germany. Archduke Franz Ferdinand had been assassinated during a visit to Sarajevo, Serbia, on June 28, six days before the Grand Prix at Lyon, and a month later to the day, Europe was aflame with World War I. The man chauffeuring the car bearing the Archduke at the time of his death was Otto Merz, a former Mercedes driver.

Somehow, by chance or plan, two of the winning Mercedes cars in the Grand Prix were held up in France, preventing their return home to Germany. This seemingly incidental circumstance in the wake of a sports event would have a crucial bearing on the fortunes of battle.

As the story is recounted by Alexander Ulmann, one of the cars came into the hands of the famous American race driver Ralph De Palma, who shipped it to the United States, where he drove it to victory in the Indianapolis 500 of 1915, averaging 89.84 miles an hour, a mark unbeaten for seven years.

De Palma's Mercedes, believed to have been the second-place winner at Lyon, wound up at the plant of the Packard Motor Company in Detroit. There, by stages, the engine inspired the design of the legendary Liberty motor, which powered American bombing planes. "Basically, [the Liberty] was an enlarged version of the Packard Model 3 that stemmed from the 1914 Lyon Grand Prix winner imported by De Palma," Ulmann writes.

By the time the war to "make the world safe for democracy" was over, on November 11, 1918, Detroit assembly lines had spilled out 15,131 Liberty engines of twelve cylinders and 8,000 of eight cylinders. In the single month of August 1918, the combined output of Liberty engines was 3,850.

As for the other Mercedes Grand Prix winner caught in France by hostilities, Ulmann writes, it was crated up and shipped to the Mercedes company's British concessionaires in London. The Royal Flying Corps, later the Royal Air Force, badly needed a good aviation engine and appealed to the automobile industry to

Robert Bosch, who introduced the magneto ignition system in European cars, as "Mephistopheles" in his company's advertisement, 1911. Bosch was also the first to install a horn inside an automobile, in 1921.

Benz advertisement for automobile and aircraft engines, circa 1915.

After Carl Benz moved to Ladenburg, in 1905, he established Benz Söhne, a company for his sons, Eugen (far right) and Richard. They produced two hundred fifty cars between 1906 and 1926. Circa 1908. (Printed from the glass plate).

Catalogue advertisement for a Benz double Phaeton, Ceylon, 1911.

supply one. The Rolls-Royce management, over the objections of the firm's founder that it wouldn't be cricket, sent its engineers prowling for the German car that had won the last Grand Prix, vaguely remembering that there was something they might learn from it. They found the car at the warehouse of British Mercedes.

The British Government gave permission to Rolls Royce to remove the engine but, as upright Englishmen, to keep their eyes closed to anything else they might see.

While the Allies learned from the German Grand Prix machines how to build better aircraft engines, enabling them to turn out an airplane like the Sopwith Camel by way of answer to Baron von Richthofen's Fokker, Mercedes engineers were busily preparing something else for them to worry about. This was the supercharger, which fed the engine compressed air, making up for the loss of oxygen in the thin air of the higher altitudes and thereby boosting power without increasing the size of the engine.

Daimler had supercharged airplane engines ready for action in 1915, only the second year of the war, Benz following with the same a year later. Daimler engines of five hundred and six hundred horsepower were in limited production at the signing of the armistice.

With the return of peace, the company set about adapting the supercharger, or *Kompressor*, to automobiles, chief engineer Paul Daimler himself leading the way. Working with the Roots blower, a crude supercharger from England, they redesigned it so that it could be cut in and out, using the clutch pedal. This had not been possible with the original. Many say the automobile supercharger was Paul Daimler's most important engineering achievement.

In an automobile, as in airplanes, the supercharger made a telling difference in the engine's performance. First tried in a Mercedes in 1919, it was installed in two production cars by mid-1920. In one car, as the driver engaged the blower, the horsepower leaped from twenty-five to forty, and in the other from forty to sixty-five, the car in each case shooting forward as if kicked by a rocket.

The day of the supercharger had begun. The man who would exploit it to the full was Ferdinand Porsche.

Advertisement, circa 1913.

Benz advertisement, 1917.

Advertisement, circa 1910.

Vintage brass plate from Maja cars sold in the United States.

# CHAPTER SEVEN

# The Folies Bergère and Carburetors

Ferdinand Porsche was a difficult man. "My predecessors more or less finished up in the lunatic asylum," said Ghislaine Kaes, Porsche's nephew, who served as his uncle's secretary. "They couldn't cope with the work they were supposed to do."

Porsche was a genius who belonged to that tiny company of hardheaded loners—the Daimlers and the Benzes—who were the true bellwethers of automobile development, daring to try the new while others only followed. Porsche was already well known when he took over as chief engineer at Daimler's Austrian branch at Wiener Neustadt in 1906, after Paul Daimler moved into Wilhelm Maybach's place at Untertürkheim.

Born in Bohemia, the son of a tinsmith, Porsche was briefly exposed to a technical education and at twenty-two went to work for Ludwig Lohner, coach builder for Austro-Hungarian royalty. Lohner,

having heard about the engines being built by Gottlieb Daimler in Germany, felt that horses might be on the way out and wanted to build vehicles that ran without them. Daimler, however, was unable to supply him with engines, because of his commitments to the French.

Young Porsche thereupon built Lohner an electric car. This was shown at the Paris Exposition Universelle in 1900, and Porsche overnight found himself famous. He followed this machine with an electric racer, which he drove to a record at the Semmering course that stood for years. For a customer in England, he designed an electric car with four-wheel drive and four-wheel brakes, delivering the machine himself.

But this car was inordinately heavy, the batteries alone weighing nearly two tons, and word got around that it was man's work to handle the machine. Porsche re-

Mechanics prepare Jellinek's Maja at the Villa Mercedes, in Baden-Baden, 1907.

sponded by designing a small car, or *"voiturette,"* especially for the ladies.

But Porsche could see no future in battery power; the weight was too much and the range too short. On the other hand, gasoline cars had a severe fault as well: the gears were hard to shift. Porsche got around this problem by combining the two kinds of power. The engine drove a generator that charged the batteries that ran the car. No gearbox was needed. Beginning in 1901 and continuing until he left Lohner for Austro-Daimler, in 1906, Porsche built "MIXT cars," as they were called, getting his engines from Daimler at Untertürkheim, where they were now available.

At Austro-Daimler, Porsche was first assigned the task of designing a gasoline engine of the company's own, saving the need to pay license fees to the Germans. Porsche replied with a car that was named the Maja, after Odette Maja Andrée, a half sister of Mercedes, born in 1906 of Jellinek's second marriage. This detail has escaped some historians, because, as explained by Guy Jellinek, Maja's brother, she was known as Andrée. "The other given names figured only on her birth certificate," Jellinek writes from his home in Nice.

In 1910, Porsche produced a racing version of the Maja that developed nearly 40 percent more power than the 60-horsepower Mercedes of 1903 James Gordon Bennett fame, while having only half the piston displacement. Driving one himself, Porsche entered three of the racing Majas in the Prince Henry of Prussia Reliability Trials of 1910, and the trio came home at the head of the field, in one, two, three order.

The Prince Henry Trials were promoted by Kaiser Wilhelm's brother, who is said to have invented the windshield wiper—and who always drove a Benz while his imperial brother became a strong Mercedes partisan. The Prince Henry runs succeeded the more leisurely Herkomer reliability tours of the Bavarian Automobile

The Kaiser and Princess Viktoria Luise in a Mercedes produced in 1907–9, Cologne, 1913.

Ferdinand Porsche admires the first car he built for Austrian coach builder Ludwig Lohner, using a Daimler engine, in Canstatt. Vienna, 1901.

A Mercedes Type 400, 15/70/100 (long-wheelbase version) transports Von Hindenburg in 1924.

Hans Nibel, center, poses at the Benz factory in honor of a guest, Prince Heinrich, who sits in his Mannheim-model Benz, 1926. Prince Heinrich patented the first windshield wiper, in 1908.

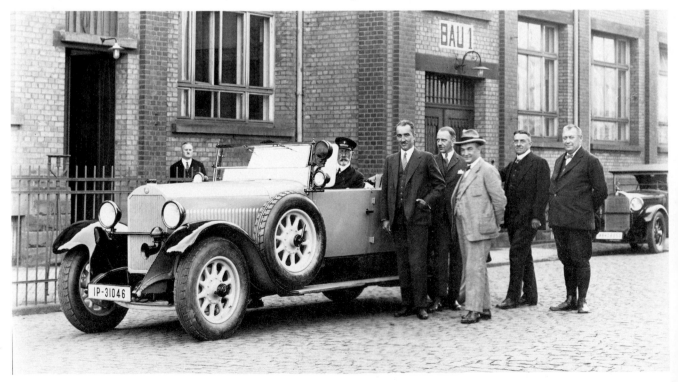

Club, between Frankfort and Innsbruck, founded by Sir Hubert von Herkomer, Bavarian-born painter knighted by King Edward VII of England.

It was a chassis design of Porsche's, shown at the Brussels auto show in 1922, that brought him to Stuttgart. A director of the Daimler company, admiring the design, invited Porsche to join the firm. Paul Daimler, like his father, had little patience with those who disagreed with him, and was leaving.

In Stuttgart, made director in charge of design, Porsche immediately was taken by Paul Daimler's supercharger and was delighted to have as his first project the completion of a new car with a "blower," at the same time getting off on the wrong foot by calling himself "doctor." He was directed by letter to refrain. Porsche perversely fought back, not because he cared about the title, his nephew Ghislaine Kaes said, but because an issue had been made of it.

After his supercharged car won both the Targa Florio and the Coppa Floria, in Italy, the following year, the company happily allowed Porsche to call himself doctor—in Germany as well as Austria. Before the year was out, they were pleased to let him call himself anything he wanted to. Of the 269 races won by Daimler and Benz cars in 1924, 93 were scored by machines with superchargers.

Next from Porsche were a pair of cars described as "The Stradivarius of the Road." While this description was applied by the company itself, retroactively, no dissenting voice was heard. The two Stradivari were but the forerunners of more to come. In the first, in 1926, Porsche shortened the wheelbase, inaugurating the K type—K for *kurz*, or short. All over the world, rich men who thought they had everything, realized how barren their lives were without a supercharged Mercedes in the garage.

The chassis of the K alone cost up to eight thousand dollars. If you wanted better than an apple box to sit on as you drove, you came up with half as much more, minimum, for a body, or "coachwork." In the United States, jazz singer Al Jolson rode around New York in a twenty-eight thousand dollar Mercedes K town car with gold fittings.

While Porsche bent over his drawing board, important corporate news was in the making. There were eighty-six automobile manufacturers in Germany, competing in a market shriveled by postwar depression, inflation, luxury taxes, and low import duties on foreign cars. A single company, using modern production methods, could have filled all there was of a German market.

Under the circumstances, Daimler-Motoren-Gesellschaft and Benz et Cie., in 1924 found it advantageous to enter into "an association of common interest," so that they might uphold the standards both were known for, rather than compromise on design and materials, as others were doing. They agreed to stop the duplication of products and to cooperate instead of competing with each other.

After two years of this informal association, they made it official, merging as Daimler-Benz Aktiengesellschaft, on June 28 and 29, 1926. Daimler's three-pointed star, standing for the threefold nature of transportation—on land, on sea, and in the air—was encircled by Benz's laurel branches, along with the names of the two firms, forming the trademark of the new company.

Although the two corporate bodies were now one, their human counterparts remained steadfastly aloof from each other, no Daimler yet meeting a Benz. Stories that Gottlieb Daimler and Carl Benz once came near to meeting on a street—in Paris or Berlin, depending on the source—are just that: "nice little fairy tales," said grandson Paul Gottlieb Daimler, an engineer for the city of Hamburg. Why did they never meet? He would say only that it was not nice to publish it.

It has been suggested that neither Benz nor Daimler knew the other existed, though they toiled in pursuit of the same goals, virtually in each other's backyard. "This is not plausible," declared Dr. Grube-Bannasch, the quiet-spoken, comely woman who used to head the Daimler-Benz archives in Untertürkheim. "They would have known of each other through the publication of their work."

Whatever the feeling between the two families may have been, it had mellowed enough by 1942 that grandson Carl Benz and his wife, Gertrud, named their newborn daughter Mercedes-Jutta Toni Marie— Mercedes Benz. Her father, who, like her great-grandfather, operates a machine shop in Mannheim, insisted that it was all just coincidence that, until only a few days before, no Daimler and Benz of the three generations had ever crossed paths; nobody was mad at anybody.

In 1927, Porsche produced the first of a legendary line of sports cars which one day, as they were fought over by collectors, would gain a value that would make them a sort of Fort Knox on wheels. They were much lower than any of their forerunners, and the engine and supercharger more powerful. If Porsche's first machines for Daimler were Stradivari, the S cars turned the Stradivari into country fiddles by comparison. Engine tolerances were so fine that the only gasket was the head gasket, between the cylinder head and the cylinder block. The Mercedes S honored its credentials by sweeping the inaugural event at the Nürburgring, a course encircling Nürburg castle, in the style of its forebears at the 1914 French Grand Prix: one, two, three. In 1928, the Mercedes S won fifty-three times and broke seventeen world records.

When 166 had been built, Porsche introduced the next step in his ascent toward an ever more perfect world in automobiles. This was the SS—Super Sport, of 1928. Again there was more horse-

Count Giulio Masetti, of Florence, drives his Mercedes through Sicily in the Targa Florio, April 2, 1922. Masetti took all honors, receiving the Polizzi and Termini trophies and a gold medal from the King of Italy.

Le Mans start, in which the drivers are clocked as they sprint to their cars, at the English Tourist Trophy, August 17, 1929. Caracciola won first prize. He drove the 414 miles in five hours, thirty-five minutes, forty seconds, set the lap record, and had the best round and the best time. The Le Mans start was named after the first twenty-four-hour Le Mans race, in 1923.

power, jumping to 225 as the super-charger took hold.

"They come from as far away as California to try to buy this car," said a Philadelphia matron whose husband is the proud owner today of an SS. "It is my husband's favorite toy—his favorite subject of conversation. It's the only picture he carries in his wallet. People don't understand," she went on to the stranger on the phone. "This car is not for sale—*at any price.*" After a thoughtful pause, she added, "And that, sir, is more than I can say for myself."

At the same time as the SS, whose count ended with 141, came the SSK—Super Sport Kurz. The SSK was marked by a shorter wheelbase—116 inches instead of 134—placing the driver and his lone passenger just in front of the rear wheels, where they looked out over a panorama of hood thrusting nearly six feet into the future, with the road sliding under the car at up to 126 miles an hour. Not shortened was the price: $13,550 for the bare-bones chassis. The body builders responded with coachwork to match, turning out some of their handsomest creations. Between the chassis and the body, and the fact that only forty-two were built, the Mercedes SSK is one of the rarest and most coveted of automobiles.

In their 1920s heyday, the Mercedes S cars ruled the raceways of Europe. An im-

At twenty-two, Rudolf Caracciola prepares to drive his first race in a supercharged 4-cylinder, 1.5-liter Targa Florio Mercedes, 1922.

portant factor in their success was Daimler-Benz race manager Alfred Neubauer, a portly ex-artillery officer, who ran his racing teams as if he were still in the army and being pressed by the enemy. It is said that when Neubauer in his later years entered the Daimler-Benz museum, opened in 1961, his voice was heard at the farthest corner of the building, many walls away.

Neubauer had been race manager for Porsche at Austro-Daimler, and when Porsche moved to Stuttgart, he brought Neubauer with him, as part of the arrangement. The two had met during the war, in which Porsche's skills were employed to design carriages for eighty-ton howitzers and the like. Neubauer served as liaison officer between the War Ministry and Porsche's company.

At Austro-Daimler, Neubauer had first tried his hand as a driver. "There were better ones," Ghislaine Kaes said, "but, being an officer, he was used to organizing things."

As boss of the race crews during the golden era of the S cars, Neubauer went at each event as he would a well-planned military operation. He and his troops visited the track well ahead of race day, studying the course until no detail of its surface, curves, and turns remained unknown. They rehearsed refueling and tire changing, reaching a proficiency no others were able to match.

Apart from the Mercedes cars, with their screaming superchargers, which added nothing to rival drivers' peace of mind, certain of the German drivers themselves became box-office draws. Rudolf Caracciola, who was victor more than one hundred times, is remembered for many things but in particular for the way he won the Irish Trophy Race of 1929, when he drove a Mercedes SS against a field of sixty-one. It began raining. The rain became a downpour. The cars slowed. Some drivers dropped out. Caracciola drove on, increasing his speed and

94

lengthening the lead he had taken after the first lap.

It was an awesome performance, for Caracciola drove without goggles. Alfred Neubauer, in his autobiography, wrote that Caracciola had abnormal eyesight. His eyes were insensitive, Neubauer maintained, giving him no problem of pain as he drove against the raindrops at 150 to 160 miles an hour, and his eyes admitted an unusual amount of light, so that he saw the rain-swept road ahead as others might see it at high noon.

But Caracciola had other things going for him as well, not counting his matinee-idol good looks. "His real asset as a racing driver was his absolute lack of nerves," said Allen Zane, an American friend. "Nothing disturbed him. You couldn't get him excited. On one occasion he almost missed a race because he was asleep. His wife woke him at the last minute. A taxi rushed him to the starting line and he made it just in time."

Adolf Hitler, something of a racing fan, wanted to meet the great Caracciola, who enjoyed similar popularity in Germany as Babe Ruth or Jack Dempsey in the United States, Zane said. Hitler mentioned his wishes to a functionary who was close to the automobile industry and who, in turn, conveyed the message to Caracciola. "Der Fuhrer wishes to meet you."

Caracciola reflected a moment, then replied quietly, "It can be arranged."

One time, as Caracciola drove Hitler through the streets of Munich, the nervousness was all on Hitler's side, as Caracciola told the story to Zane. "Not too fast!" Hitler cried. "Not too fast!"

Ghislaine Kaes fondly remembered when, at seventeen, he served as water boy for Caracciola, during school vacation. "I thought of myself in those days as being a person of some importance," Kaes said with dry humor. His job was to hand Caracciola a bottle of mineral water to drink during pit stops for fuel and tires. Caracciola would drink, and then let the dregs pour over his face. "A very pleasant gentleman," Kaes mused, "modest, friendly, all smiles—and the very best of drivers."

Ferdinand Porsche himself saw little of his Daimler-Benz creations in action. He left the company in 1928—when his

Rudolf Caracciola stands in front of a Mercedes SSKL, illustrated by Walter Gotschke.

five-year contract expired and the firm showed no interest in renewing it—possibly out of longing for a more tranquil life. There had been incompatibility between Porsche and Hans Nibel, Benz's young chief engineer, who had stayed on after Benz merged with Daimler.

"They didn't get along too well," Kaes said. "Porsche, being a genius, wouldn't stand to have another man next to him—a man with different ideas. Nibel was a German; Porsche was not a German. Nibel was a well-educated man, with perfect manners. Porsche didn't bother about manners. He would spend hours in the workshop lying under the automobiles trying to find out what was wrong, a thing Nibel for sure would never do.

"And besides," Kaes added, "Porsche was hot-tempered. He wouldn't stand for long talking. He was always asking for action."

In the summertime, Kaes remembered, Porsche went to the factory on Sunday, demanding that top management be there too. "He was, to put it mildly, not an easy man to get along with. He was never satisfied. The best you could ever hope for was that he not say anything at all."

At Austro-Daimler once, Kaes recalled, Porsche snatched the bowler from his head and dashed it to the floor. He stomped on the hat like a man putting out a fire, and threw it into an oil tank. The foreman, the current object of his wrath, retrieved the hat, restored it as best he could, and respectfully handed it back to Porsche, only to be scolded for his trouble and to see the hat hurled back to the floor for a fresh assault.

Kaes survived as his uncle's secretary, he believes, because of his youth. The time came, though, during a visit to New York, when he nearly broke. The work day ended at around eight, but before they went to dinner, Porsche wanted to go to a movie, preferably an American Western, where he promptly fell asleep. When the show was over, he hauled the starving Kaes off to a second film, resuming his slumbers.

Dinner finally came at midnight—after Porsche first had his whiskey. "He always enjoyed whiskey in the United States and England, but he never drank it in Europe—something having to do with the water," Kaes said. "In Europe, he drank beer and champagne."

Up in their rooms, Porsche said goodnight and went to bed, leaving Kaes to deal with a pile of paper work bearing on the activities of the day just ended and plans for the new one. Kaes got to bed about three, being careful to open the door to his uncle's room for ready communications when Porsche's phone began ringing and he needed Kaes to speak English for him. Kaes was brought up in England, where his father—Porsche's brother-in-law—represented Porsche's interests. The calls often began at five.

At seven, they went downstairs for breakfast. While they waited for the food to arrive, Porsche thought of things for Kaes to do. He sent him back upstairs to fetch extra money from a pocket, to the lobby to send telegrams. By the time Kaes was through with his errands, breakfast had long since been served and Porsche was finished.

"I'm sorry," he would say, getting to his feet. "We can't waste any time. I'm sure you can go without breakfast, and we'll have a good lunch."

But when noon came, Porsche used the time while others were eating to travel to the next factory. So there was no lunch either. And come evening—before dinner—there were the movies again.

"Not every day was like this," Kaes said, "but there were too many when I had my first meal at midnight."

The S driven by Christian Werner at the Nürburgring, July 1927. Werner, who joined DMG in 1911 as a mechanic and chauffeur, placed second, averaging sixty-six miles an hour.

The Benz Tropfen (Teardrop) racer at the Solitude Race, May 18, 1924. Designed by Hans Nibel, this machine was significant mainly for its advanced aerodynamic lines and rear mounting of its 80-horsepower, 6-cylinder engine, among other innovations. It was a poor match for the supercharged Mercedes creations of Dr. Porsche.

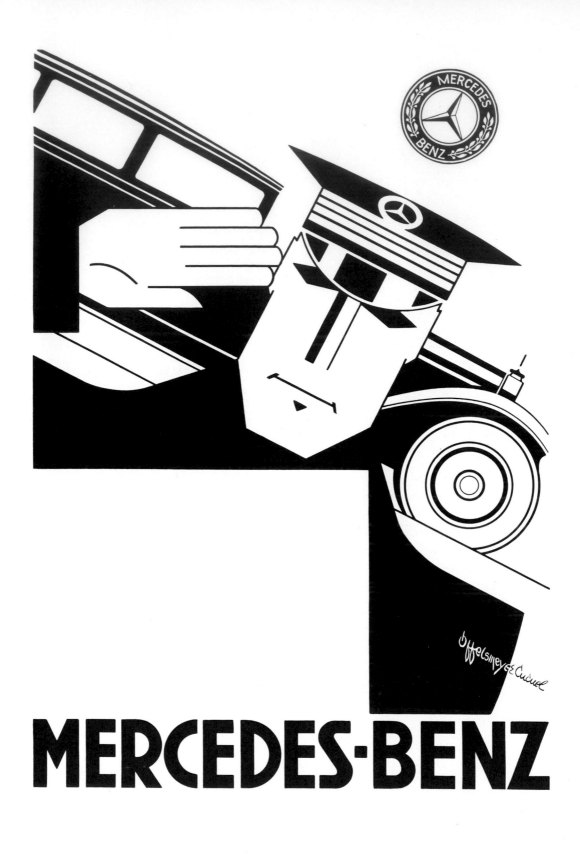

# MERCEDES-BENZ

The advertisements illustrated on these pages promoted the merger of Daimler-Motoren-Gesellschaft and Benz et Cie in 1926.

Der Stern
ihrer Sehnsucht

MERCEDES-BENZ

While Porsche was less somnolent at the Folies Bergère, it often appeared that he wasn't getting as much out of the show as he might. "While I was watching all the legs going up and down," Kaes remembered, "he all of a sudden would turn to me and say I should remind him of some technical matter after the show. Once, it was about a carburetor."

The momentum Porsche left behind at Daimler-Benz led to the SSKL, which was simply the SSK with a number of holes bored in the frame to lighten the car, the L standing for *leicht*, or light. Fitted with an "elephant blower," which pushed the horsepower up to three hundred, the SSKL grandly climaxed the company's sports-car dynasty of the twenties era. Caracciola easily drove it to victory in the 1931 Mille Miglia, of Italy, finishing the one thousand miles nearly nine minutes faster than the record of the year before,

despite stops to fix a puncture and to secure a silencer that had come loose.

Caracciola went on setting records in the same machine: in the Prague hill-climb, the Eiffel race on the Nürburgring, the German Grand Prix, and the Avus at Berlin, ending the year as the hill-climb champion of Europe. Next year, given a streamlined body, the SSKL carried Manfred von Brauchitsch through the Avus race at nearly 121 miles an hour, six mph faster than Caracciola's time. The SSKL probably won more races than any other sports car in history.

Not as many were built, by the way, as is suggested by the count of those cars in the hands of people who think they own an SSKL. The same can be said, in fact, of any of the Mercedes S cars. There are a number of them around that were not made by the factory in Stuttgart. This is not to say that these extraordinary ma-

1926 Mercedes-Benz 32/70-horsepower, 4-cylinder double-decker bus seating sixty passengers.

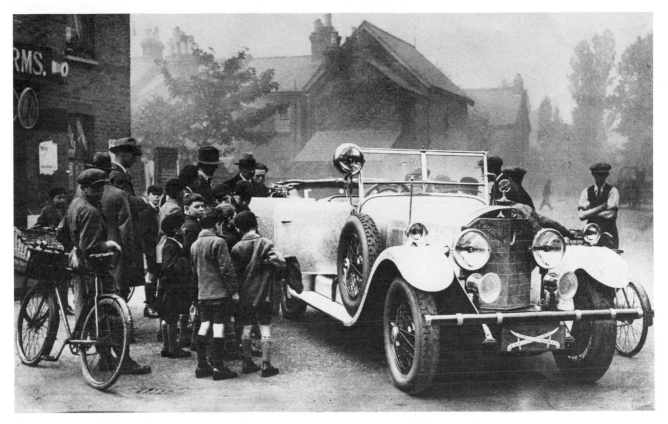

A Mercedes-Benz Type 600 Model K being delivered to Arabian sovereign Abdul Aziz Saud, London, circa 1927.

chines possessed biological capabilities, being able to reproduce themselves. The extra ones are fakes.

The most notorious of the forgers, appropriately operating underground in a vast, richly equipped space underneath his home, is known to have created at least six "SSKLs." This operator's work has fooled top experts. Some have bought his product knowing it was phony (or claiming they knew) on the theory, presumably, that a well-executed fake Rembrandt is better than no Rembrandt at all.

To an extent, his reproductions are authentic, many parts coming from cars innocently brought to him for work by owners who didn't know any better or couldn't believe that he was capable of the villainies ascribed to him. Uninhibited by the scruples of other men, he would fall on the car like a school of pir-

anha, stripping and gutting until there was little left. From a car that once belonged to Rudolf Caracciola, he took the engine and gearbox, defiling a classic of special distinction. Nor was the victim likely to know the difference when he got his car back. One man was two years discovering that the newly "restored" fenders of his SSK were fiber glass.

This master counterfeiter of automobiles is now living in France. He acquired a taste for residence abroad after going into the "restoration" of airplanes, the story goes, and someone was killed. He lives at Menton, on the Mediterranean coast, with Monte Carlo handy on one side and the Italian border a convenient two miles away on the other.

From the size of his spread—if appearances may be trusted—he was doing well . . . whatever it was he was doing.

101

1938 advertisement illustrating the diverse uses of Mercedes Benz engines.

# CHAPTER EIGHT

# A Bad Day at Pau

While Daimler-Benz may have found the days more restful in the wake of Porsche's leaving, the condition was transitory for events ordained that Porsche return to their lives as a competitor, bringing forth new flower in both them and him.

Porsche was working in Austria when "Black Friday" on New York's Wall Street, in October 1929, threw the world into the Great Depression. Like millions elsewhere, Porsche lost his livelihood, and he decided to strike out for himself. He returned to Stuttgart and looked up Adolf Rosenberger, a wealthy jewelry merchant and amateur race driver. They formed Porsche & Rosenberger, to design and build racing engines.

As Porsche worked at the drawing board and Rosenberger wrangled with bankers for additional capital, Adolf Hitler came to power as Chancellor of Germany, January 30, 1933. On February 11,

opening a motor show in Berlin, Hitler pledged to help the automobile industry, badly hit by the depression. Hearing of this, Porsche went to see Hitler, handing him his drawings of a V-16 engine. "You said you were going to help the automobile industry," Porsche reminded him, as told by Ghislaine Kaes. "This would be one way."

"I'm afraid you are a fortnight too late," Hitler replied. "Two weeks ago I gave 500,000 marks to the Mercedes-Benz Company, and they are going to design and manufacture a new racing car to compete with the rest of the world."

"Wouldn't it be wise to have two German cars competing?" Porsche countered. He mentioned the Alfa Romeo, Bugatti, and other machines they would be up against. "It would be a good idea to be on the safe side."

"But you haven't got a company to

Caracciola sets a record for the highest speed on a city road (198.9 miles an hour) in a special W 25 coupe. Gyon, October 28, 1934.

The Auto Union rivals Mercedes-Benz at the Avus race, Berlin, May 30, 1937.

manufacture a racing car," Hitler said. "Who would build your car?"

"The Auto Union," Porsche answered. This was a consortium of car builders—Audi, DKW, Wanderer, and Horch—recently formed to present a united front against the common enemy, lean times. Porsche had already designed two cars for them.

"They have never manufactured a racing car," Hitler pointed out.

"They haven't, but I have," Porsche retorted.

According to Kaes, the answer, direct and confident, impressed Hitler. He gave Auto Union the same stake as Daimler-Benz, and the new group went to work. In less than nine months, in January 1934, they had a car on the road powered by Porsche's rear-mounted V-16 engine and were breaking records. The immediate idea was to make the name Auto Union as widely known as possible in the briefest time.

To Daimler-Benz, commissioned by Hitler to develop a Grand Prix car to carry the colors of Germany at international events, the goings-on at Auto Union, with Ferdinand Porsche in the middle of the action, were disquieting. They looked on racing supremacy as their private fief. The company took steps to clear up any confusion in the matter. It set up a racing department, which was to function without regard to the rest of the establishment. Max Sailer was placed in charge, with three hundred specialists under him. Hans Nibel got the job of designing the car. Alfred Neubauer, back in a familiar role, was made boss of the racing team.

Max Sailer's answer to Auto Union's racer was the W 25, propelled by a supercharged straight-8 engine of 354 horsepower. The car was painted a gleaming white, with the paint laid on extra thick to ensure maximum smoothness. At the weigh-in for its first race, the Eiffel event at the Nürburgring on June 3, 1934, the car proved to be overweight by one kilogram (a little more than two pounds) in excess of the 750 kilograms allowed. The problem was remedied by scraping off the paint down to the aluminum. Mercedes racers thereafter were left unpainted, becoming known as "Silver Arrows."

Sans paint, the W 25 won the Eiffel race, along with four more during its first season. It finished the program for 1934 by setting a world record at the Gyon course, near Budapest, averaging 117.19 miles an hour and covering a mile at 199.36 miles an hour from a standing start.

In 1935, the Mercedes W 25 won nine out of its ten races, including six Grand Prix events—all but the German, which went to Auto Union when the Mercedes blew a tire in the last lap. The year 1936 passed rather quietly, Mercedes winning two Grand Prix, Auto Union and Alfa Romeo one each, but in 1937 Mercedes introduced a car that has been called the most remarkable automobile of any era. The W 125, chiefly the work of designer Rudolf Uhlenhaut, weighed the same as its predecessor, the W 25, but the power was nearly doubled, reaching 646 horsepower.

Just starting to move as another car went by at 100 miles an hour, the W 125 could overtake and pass the other *within one mile*. At 150 miles an hour, it spun its wheels on dry cement at the sudden depressing of the accelerator.

In 1937, the W 125 won the first four places in the Grand Prix of Switzerland, the first three in the Grand Prix of Monaco, the first two places in the Grand Prix of Germany and of Czechoslovakia, and first in those of Tripoli and Italy. In a special, streamlined version of the same machine, with twelve slightly smaller cyl-

Caracciola drives the W 25 at the Barcelona Grand Prix, June 30, 1935.

inders in place of eight, Rudolf Caracciola set an international record of 271.5 miles an hour for one kilometer on the autobahn between Frankfurt and Darmstadt, on January 28, 1938. This was the highest mark ever reached on an ordinary highway and still stands as of this writing.

Between the Mercedes cars and those of Porsche's Auto Union, racing in the thirties was essentially a closed issue to others. If anyone else won, it was usually because the two big fellows pushed each other so hard that their engines blew up. But Mercedes nearly always won. Between 1934 and 1939, they came in first thirty-four times, Auto Union eleven times.

For Mercedes in the thirties, as with the S cars in the twenties, much of the winning was done before the race and in the pits during the race. Weeks in advance, Neubauer and his forces visited the course, traveling by large Diesel trucks

loaded with spare engines, tons of equipment, and a portable machine shop, along with the racers. First the drivers reconnoitered the track, riding in their own sedans. Then they went around in practice cars, fixing such details as rises, bends, and turns in their minds. The cars were then returned to Stuttgart, where the gearing best suited to the track, selected from more than seventy combinations, was installed in them.

Each driver's seat was formed and adjusted to his body, to assure his comfort. The pedals were tailor-made to his needs and transferred each time he changed cars. Before final adjustments were made, the driver made a few tryout laps to see how the car felt, as one might try a new pair of shoes. One by one, the Mercedes drivers then took an all-out practice lap to decide the starting order for the team.

While the Mercedes drivers sometimes lost, this could not be said of the pit

106

Hermann Lang at the wheel of a
Mercedes-Benz at the Italian Grand Prix,
Monza, September 11, 1938.

Von Brauchitsch's Mercedes-Benz catches fire during refueling at the German Grand Prix of 1938.

crews. They were expected to change all four tires, put in seventy-five gallons of fuel, check the oil, clean the windshield, and hand the driver a new pair of goggles and a drink—all in thirty-two seconds. In drill they sometimes made it in twenty-eight. The performance of the German pit crews was the despair of the British, whose best time was fifty seconds for the fuel and oil alone.

Moreover, the Mercedes men were seemingly unflappable. At the 1938 German Grand Prix at the Nürburgring, driver Von Brauchitsch's car burst into flames as it was being refueled. Von Brauchitsch snatched the steering wheel from its post and stepped out of the machine while the crew efficiently went about smothering the blaze. Meanwhile, Richard Seaman, the English member of the Mercedes team, came in for fuel. As a mechanic bent over to restart Seaman's engine, presenting his backside to Von Brauchitsch's flames, his pants caught fire. The mechanic went on cranking, in unswerving commitment to the rule of first things first.

Von Brauchitsch, incidentally, could as well have stayed in the pits. In a rare slipup, he failed to lock the steering wheel when he got back into the car to resume the race, which he was leading. Not far down the road, as he hit a bump at 130 miles an hour, the wheel lifted off. He somehow got the machine off the track and brought it to a stop without untoward developments, presenting an unusual spectacle as he walked back to the pits carrying the wheel.

Inevitably, there came the day when all the dexterous expertise and self-control of the Mercedes men availed them nothing. This was in the Grand Prix at Pau in 1938. The company entered a new car in the race, the W 154. The new car had a lower center of gravity than the W 125, and pis-

ton displacement was cut nearly in half by the new formula, balanced by a higher rpm.

Driver Hermann Lang, with vapor-lock problems in practice, either didn't start at all in the race—accounts differ—or he went out early after sailing backward into some bales of hay. In any case, Lang's misfortune left the honors to Caracciola, who indicated his disdain for the proceedings by wearing an ordinary peaked cap in place of the usual cloth helmet.

The race soon settled down to a classic David and Goliath contest between Caracciola with his brawling, 483-horsepower Grand Prix machine (with two superchargers, nine oil pumps, and all five gears set especially for Pau), and René Dreyfus in a car with just over half as much muscle: a 250-horsepower Delahaye sports machine with a production-line engine, helped by no supercharger at all. Stripped, the Delahaye could do 150 miles an hour. Caracciola in his Mercedes had 195 at his command.

Dreyfus was considered to be done for even before the race began. Until the Germans came in, he had been expected at least to hold his own, even though he was competing with a couple of Alfa Romeos, a Bugatti, and a Maserati, all full-fledged Grand Prix machines. And all were in the hands of top drivers, including Tazio Nuvolari, the last man to beat the Mercedes team, in the German Grand Prix of 1935—but René Dreyfus was champion of France.

The last-minute entry of the team from Stuttgart, after long tests of their new car at Monza, drastically changed the outlook. Dreyfus would finish so far behind Lang and Caracciola, loftily wrote the sports oracles of the newspapers, that he wouldn't be able to see them.

''The outcome of this race is now such a complete certainty that no bookmaker

Frame of the Type 80, designed for Daimler-Benz by Ferdinand Porsche to break the world speed record. The car had six wheels and was powered by a 3000-horsepower aircraft engine. War ended the experiment before the machine could be tested for speed (calculated by slide rule at 404 miles an hour).

The Type 80 in its completed form. The body consisted of a welded-steel-tube frame covered with a light sheet of aluminum alloy. Two stub wings attached at a negative angle of attack were intended to keep the car from crosswind drifting at high speed.

would take any money on the Germans, even at heavy odds-on prices. . . . The Germans don't make the kind of mistakes peculiar to the average mortal, and with Caracciola and Lang driving, what is there to add?"

What could have been added was something about the course they would be traveling and how its character might affect the fortunes of the drivers. The course at Pau was a tight little ring less than a mile and three quarters around. It rose and fell a hundred feet and had thirteen bends and corners. Depending on his car, the driver shifted gears fifteen to twenty times on each circuit, which was lined with houses, walls, trees, and fences. The longest straightaway, on a downhill stretch, allowed a brief burst of 110 miles an hour for the fastest cars. Driving at Pau separated the men from the boys.

As the late Ken Purdy described the start, "[Caracciola] ran the W 154's big engine up to 3,000 revolutions a minute, let in the clutch, lighted up his back tires and was off, well ahead of the second car, Dreyfus's Delahaye."

Dreyfus bided his time, staying close behind for a few laps. "I wanted to see if Rudy and Herr Neubauer had been saving some little surprise," he said. "It was not the case. I could hold him without trouble." He dropped back in deference to the exhaust fumes from the Mercedes.

He moved up again. He dogged Caracciola through a number of hairpin turns; then, on a wide bend, squeezed past him, to show he could do it. Dreyfus was encouraged by his wife, Chouchou, posted at Station Hairpin to give him signals. She was smiling each time he came by, while Caracciola's wife, Baby, standing a little farther on, looked glum.

After twenty-five laps, Caracciola led by only eight seconds, not enough to allow a stop for fuel without losing the lead. His car begrudged him barely more than two miles to the gallon, while Dreyfus, with his smaller engine, got seven and a half. When Caracciola finally had to make the sacrificial stop, Dreyfus shot past him and won the race, by nearly a full lap.

It was a great day for France—and for everyone else. Only Germans were sup-

Caracciola breaks the world land speed record at 271.5 mph on the Frankfurt-Darmstadt autobahn, January 28, 1938. Known as the W 125 R, with twelve cylinders, this car was a streamlined version of the W 125. The speed record still stands as the highest speed ever recorded on a public road.

110

Porsche, center, works on a model-V3 chassis in his backyard. On Porsche's right is his nephew, Herbert Kaes, who served as a test driver and mechanic for his uncle. August 18, 1936.

posed to win races, if not Mercedes then Auto Union. "One cannot congratulate Delahaye enough for having beaten a rival as redoubtable as Mercedes-Benz," wrote Charles Faroux in *La Vie Automobile*.

On a rainy autumn day thirty-nine years later, René Dreyfus, the giant-killer of Pau in 1938, greeted luncheon guests at Le Chanteclair Restaurant, on Manhattan's East 49th Street, which he owns in partnership with his brother, Maurice, his racing-days manager. Slight and straight, carrying his arms flat against his sides, Dreyfus reminded one of the late acting star Edward Everett Horton. He hardly suited the image of a man who had once

been the terror of the racetracks, who had driven one hundred thousand racing miles on three continents in more than two hundred events, winning 106 prizes including thirty-six checkered flags—whatever the image of such a man might be.

Dreyfus was pleased to recall the golden moments at Pau, the high point of his career. Paradoxically, the strength of the Germans proved to be their weakness, he explained. "The Mercedes had too much power for the track. They kept spinning their wheels at the turns as they tried to get going again."

The losers took defeat with gallantry. "We have learned more with this race at

Pau than in twenty days of trials at Monza,'' Max Sailer said.

One of the things learned from Dreyfus apparently was how to drive at Pau with the German powerhouses. The following year, the invincibles from Stuttgart swept the race into their win basket along with every other Grand Prix on the board but the Yugoslavian, where they had to settle for second place.

It was the last time they would be driving for a while. On September 1, 1939, Adolf Hitler gave the order that set off World War II. As the panzers and the Stuka air fleets struck Poland, the ghosts of the winning Grand Prix cars of Lyon 1914 were preparing for the second time to haunt Germany at war.

Already in production in the United States was an engine based on the famous Liberty motor of World War I, which had its genesis in the engines of the Mercedes winners in the final Grand Prix before the First World War started. The engine was the Allison. It shortly became the primary engine of U.S. Air Force fighters, the American counterpart of the 1,200-horsepower, liquid-cooled DB-601, which powered, among others, the deadly Messerschmitt-109. Daimler-Benz built more than one hundred thousand of these engines in 1939 and 1940.

The Allison was named for Jim Allison, who, with Carl Fisher, founded the Indianapolis Motor Speedway, to test the racing engines built at Allison's shop. The engine grew out of what Allison and his superintendent, Norman Gilman, learned about the Liberty motor from overhauling it and from studying the liquid-cooled Maybach engines of the German-built airship *Los Angeles,* trophy of the First World War.

The Liberty had been a little late for battle, but the Allison was in the air before Pearl Harbor, beginning with the P-40s of the American Eagle Squadron, the group of Yankee volunteers who flew with the hard-pressed British in the melancholy days of 1940.

While the company's work of long before, ironically, was back for the second time to make trouble in the air, Daimler-Benz not only made the engines to counter the ghost but turned out the mechanized ground armor that characterized the new conflict. The Panther tank was rated by those in the most authoritative position to know as the best of the war.

The tanks, together with their engines, were designed by Ferdinand Porsche, who had shown in the First World War that he was able to design big things as well as small things. As the military situation worsened, it was Porsche who was called upon to design the weapon calculated to save the day.

The Maus was 33 feet long, with treads just short of 13 feet wide. It weighed 188 tons. It was shielded fore and aft by armor plate of special steel nearly three feet thick. The bore of the gun sticking out of the turret measured close to six inches, or about the same as those of a naval light cruiser. The Maus was built to cross rivers underwater, since few bridges could hold it. ''If I could have a hundred of these, I could stop the Russians,'' Hitler is supposed to have said.

Alas, what difference the Maus might have made will never be known, for it came too late, only three being completed before the war ended.

Besides the Maus, Porsche had a hand in creating a less formidable vehicle, the fabled Volkswagen, or people's car, which began as a peacetime item but turned into a military car along the way.

The forerunners of the Volkswagen appeared in 1932, when two motorcycle manufacturers, hard hit by the times, decided to try their luck building automo-

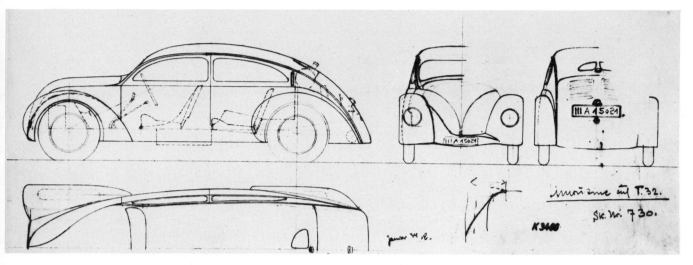

Porsche's drawings for a Type 32, one of two small cars he designed for the NSU, of Neckarsulm, a motorcycle manufacturer, Nürnberg, 1934.

biles. They asked Porsche to break trail by making them a small car. With his *voiturette*, of 1900, in the back of his mind, Porsche obliged with two cars for his clients, designating them Type 12 and Type 32. He later referred to both in designing Type 60, the VW.

Porsche had his two machines on the road being tested when there occurred an incident involving Adolf Hitler that is a key part of Volkswagen lore. As told by an inspired story in a Munich newspaper, Hitler was on his way to Munich on a raw, wet night in 1933 accompanied by Jakob Werlin, Daimler-Benz director and dealer in Munich, when his car overtook a couple on a motorcycle.

The sight of the pair riding along in the rain, drenched and cold, touched Hitler, not best remembered as a humanitarian.

The Porsche Type 32, with rear-mounted, 4-cylinder, air-cooled engine—forerunner of the Volkswagen.

Berlin Auto Show, February 16–25, 1939. Porsche (right) describes the Volkswagen chassis construction to Hitler. Dr. Robert Ley (fourth from left) and Dr. Bodo Lafferentz stand directly behind Hitler.

Hitler's sketches for the Volkswagen, 1932.

114

The first thirty of sixty Type V60 Volkswagen cars produced according to Porsche's design at Daimler-Benz in 1936 and 1937 by Hitler's order. The state built its own VW factory in 1938.

"It ought to be possible to design a small car to protect people from the weather for the same price as a motorcycle," Hitler remarked to Werlin, who planted the story in the paper. "The car shouldn't cost more than a thousand marks."

The account included two crude sketches of a car resembling the future Volkswagen, the caption saying the drawings had been made by Hitler in 1932, the same year Porsche designed his two small machines for the motorcycle builders.

Less apocryphal than the story accompanying the sketches is that Hitler got together with Porsche on the subject of designing a small car. On January 17, 1934, Porsche wrote down the specifics of his ideas for the vehicle, giving the measurements and sketching the beetle shape.

"He worked from what the needed space should be, starting with the husband, wife, and two or three children,

instead of building the car first and then squeezing people into it," Ghislaine Kaes said.

From time to time as Porsche worked on the project, Hitler phoned for a meeting to check on his progress and make suggestions. Hitler spoke more or less on equal terms to Porsche, who, besides being a fellow Austrian, was older and famous. "I have arranged for sausages and beer for you," Hitler would say. "Is this all right with you?"

In April 1934, the military for the first time joined in making the final design of the Volkswagen. In place of mother, father, and youngsters, the car now held three soldiers and one machine gun with ammunition.

Being without a workshop of his own, Porsche built the first two VWs by hand in his garage. He followed these with three improved models a year later, like-

115

**ein wirklich volkstümlicher Wagen!**

# MERCEDES-BENZ Typ 130

Der MERCEDES-BENZ-Heckmotorwagen „Typ 130" bereitet seinem Besitzer täglich neue Freude. Die Anerkennung, welche dieser wirtschaftliche, leistungsfähige und sehr bequeme Kleinwagen mit Vollschwingachsen gefunden hat, beruht auf seiner fortschrittlichen Konstruktion. Seine Fahreigenschaften sind überraschend. Auch durch seine traditionelle Hochwertigkeit in Material und Arbeit ist er ein echter MERCEDES-BENZ.

**Dieser Typ bleibt ein wertvoller Faktor unseres Fabrikationsprogramms**

| | |
|---|---|
| Limousine | RM 3 425.— |
| Cabriolimousine | RM 3 625.— |
| Offener Tourenwagen | RM 3 900.— |

Zu Auskünften jeder Art, sowie zu Probefahrten steht unsere gesamte Verkaufs-Organisation stets gern zur Verfügung.

**DAIMLER-BENZ AG STUTTGART-UNTERTÜRKHEIM**

Vertretungen an allen größeren Plätzen Deutschlands und des Auslandes

Company advertisement for Daimler-Benz's 130 H car, made between 1933 and 1936. It bears a striking visual similarity to Porsche's VW30 design.

Ferdinand Porsche (1875–1955).

wise turned out in his garage. Through Jakob Werlin, arrangements were made for Porsche workers to use the facilities of Daimler-Benz, which had been experimenting with a small car of similar measurements. This machine remains in the Daimler-Benz museum as a step in the development of the Volkswagen.

At Daimler-Benz, thirty Volkswagens were built in 1936 and a like number in 1937. These figures hardly encouraged hope for the million and a half cars a year Hitler wanted. When he pressured the automobile industry to get behind the car with their full resources, the auto men demanded a subsidy. They were unable, they said, to produce the Volkswagen profitably to sell at the one thousand-mark price Hitler had placed on the car. He decided the government would be money ahead to manufacture the car itself.

Hitler ordered Porsche to lay out a factory and put it up. Porsche visited the United States to learn how one goes about building 1.5 million automobiles a year. The information he gathered included the discovery that one did not need an office. This came to him as he was arranging to meet with Henry Ford, about as good a man as one could find to fill him in on car making in volume. Porsche suggested that they meet in Ford's office.

"Mr. Ford doesn't have an office," the secretary answered. "He feels that since he owns the company, he can sit anywhere."

Back in Germany, a site for the plant was found and the cornerstone laid on May 28, 1938, with Chancellor Hitler stressing the deep social implications of the moment. The first five hundred Volkswagens were scheduled to come off the lines by October 15.

They went not to people but to war, which was by then six weeks old.

The following three illustrations show examples of the Grosser (extra-large) Mercedes. Known as the Type 770 or Type 770 K, its engine size is denoted by "770" (7.7 liters) and "K" for Kompressor, or supercharger. This one is a 1938 Type 770 K (W 150) open tourer. All of the 770 cars have seven seats and extra side windows in the rear.

The 1930 Grosser Mercedes Type 770 (W 07) cabriolet F. This early version had solid axles and was available with or without a supercharger. The driver and passenger sections are divided. Kaiser Wilhelm II's chauffeur Walter Lang is at the wheel. The Kaiser had replaced the three-pointed star with the Hohenzollern coat of arms.

The 1939 Grosser Mercedes Type 770 K (W 150) Limousine. The W 150 version improved upon the W 07 model with swinging axles and integrated supercharger. Passenger versions of the Grosser Mercedes weighed from 3.6 tons to 4.8 tons as armored vehicles.

Type 170 V, 1938.

Mercedes-Benz Type 200 V, G 5 (W 152) open cross-country vehicle, produced from 1937 to 1941.

A WWI Daimler utility vehicle, Type LG652, negotiating a 33-degree grade. The truck weighs five tons.

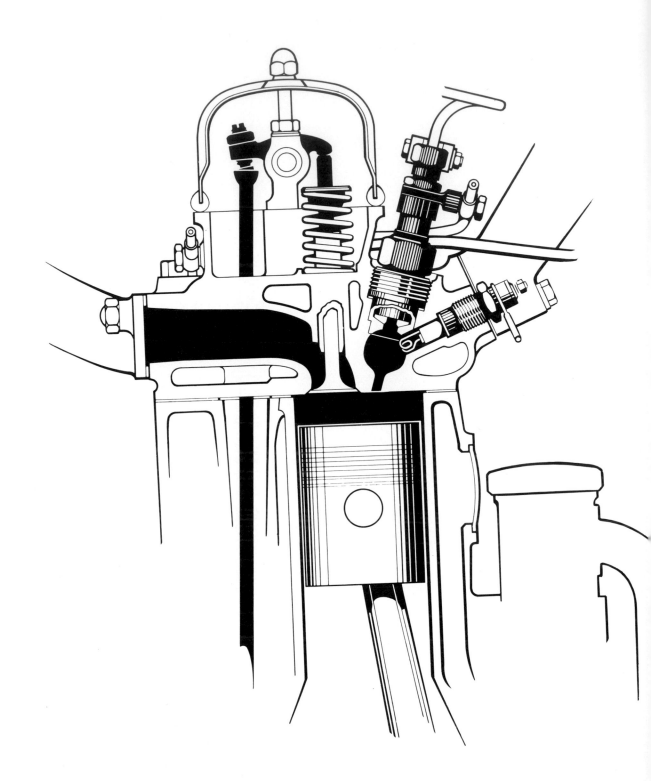

The first Diesel passenger-car engine.

# CHAPTER NINE

# Mr. Daimler, Meet Mr. Benz

"It began with clearing a path through the rubble."

The Second World War ended thirty-five years ago. In the Daimler-Benz organization, not many are left who know the story firsthand of the company's rise from the ashes. One of the few is Allen Zane, "an American who came to Germany to shoot and stayed to live," in the words of Günther Molter, director of DB's Public Relations Department.

For Lieutenant Zane, of the 10th Armored Division, United States Army, the war personally ended at Garmisch. It was a gloomy day of fog and rain, and Zane was as anxious as the next man to get home, in his case New York City. Next day, however, was clear and warm. To the south, the silver-topped Alps glistened in the sun. It was springtime. The scent of lilacs was in the air, and the storybook Bavarian countryside lay fresh and green everywhere.

"It looked good—all very different from New York," Zane remembered. He decided to stick around a while.

With a master's degree in industrial engineering from Lehigh University, Zane joined the Military Government, which took over the country's administration at the close of hostilities. Thus he came to have a direct hand in reviving Daimler-Benz, in line with the American occupation policy of getting Germany back on her feet as quickly as possible. Later, in 1950, Zane devoted himself to these same goals as a member of the Daimler-Benz firm, working with Dr. Wilhelm Haspel, chairman of the board of management, who had taken a liking to the young American.

Zane reminisced about those early postwar days on a cool evening in June, sitting before a crackling fire in the patio fireplace of the home he had built in suburban Stuttgart—a house of stone

A 1952 Mercedes-Benz 170 V, model b (1952–53), which looks the same outside as the 170 D, model b. The b is characterized by three-part bumpers, a 15-percent-enlarged windshield, two horizontal gills on the hood (vs. the inclined 28 gills), and many technical refinements. The 170 "bread and butter" car, first produced in 1935, was discontinued with this model in 1953.

throughout, with interior walls a foot thick. A descendant of the pioneer family that founded Zanesville, Ohio, Zane was a lanky, genial man with blue eyes and thinning blond hair. He spoke with deliberation.

"One of the first things that the civilian population started to do right after the war was to clean up the rubble," he said. "It went surprisingly fast. The bricks and stones were moved off the streets and paths and neatly piled along the side. At Daimler-Benz, the first thing was to clear passages among the various buildings and offices that were still left, so people and trucks could move."

To Zane, these spirited clean-up activities spoke of more than practical concerns. "There was something psychological involved, as I look back. It was the idea of making a new start."

For the Daimler-Benz industrial com-

plex, there was a long way to go. As the chief source of engines to drive the German war machine, it had gotten special attention from the bombers. By the company's own figures, the home plant at Untertürkheim was 70 percent destroyed, Sindelfingen 85 percent, Gaggenau 80 percent, and Mannheim 20 percent. What remained at Marienfelde was pulled down entirely, not worth saving. Branches also were hard hit.

For all that, though, the destruction apparently was overestimated, Zane said. "Dr. Haspel told me that the bombing raids had not done as much physical damage as one might have expected. Roofs were blown off the buildings, but in many cases the walls stood up. The debris fell inside, and it was possible to clear this away, put a tarpaulin over the top to keep the rain out, and still keep producing."

Dr. Haspel, Zane explained, headed a committee of manufacturers who made aircraft engines, some their own but most under license to Daimler-Benz, with Haspel answering directly to production minister Albert Speer. Because of his responsibility for aircraft-engine production throughout Germany, Haspel kept a close watch on the statistics of production and the effects of air raids.

"Dr. Haspel said the most devastating aspect of the raids, as far as production was concerned, was the wearing down of the workers," Zane went on. "When the raids came, several times during the night, they got out of bed and into the air-raid shelters. They would hardly be back in bed when the next raid came along. There were absenteeism and illness, and the morale and physical strength of the workmen disappeared. This wearing down of the workers was a larger factor even than the physical damage."

Sometime after Zane began his work

A 1955 300 S. Painting (original in color) by Hans Liska.

with the Military Government in Stutt-gart, assigned to the Economics Section, he received a visit from one of the unit's German advisers, a carefully chosen group of knowledgeable men and women with business and professional back-grounds who spoke English. The caller asked Zane if he would care to join him in a visit to Dr. Haspel.

"I said, 'Who is Dr. Haspel?'

"He said, 'Dr. Haspel is the head man of Daimler-Benz.' He pointed out that Haspel was the leading industrial figure in the area and said he would like to take a few of us out to his home so that we could meet him and he could meet us."

In the course of the evening, Zane and Haspel discovered that they shared a fondness for hunting, Zane said. "So Dr. Haspel and I started doing a lot of hunt-ing. He wasn't permitted to own guns, but he had the shooting grounds and I had the guns. The two of us got along fine. He had no children. I was a young-ster of twenty-five, so I suppose he and his wife did not take too unkindly to hav-ing a young fellow always coming to the house for dinner and spending time with them. We became very good friends. He was a man from whom I could learn a lot."

Meanwhile, the work of rehabilitating German industry in general and Daimler-Benz in particular, Zane's immediate area of interest, proceeded apace, with the two erstwhile enemies going at it shoulder to shoulder like American pioneers at a barn raising.

A 1957 Mercedes-Benz 300Sc (W 188 II), with 3-liter, 6-cylinder, fuel-injected 175hp engine. A total of two hundred of these cars were built between 1955 and 1958. Daimler-Benz ended separate chassis and body construction with the type 300 model. Restored by Willard Powell, Los Angeles, California, 1977.

"There was a tremendous scarcity of materials," Zane said. "But it was interesting that everyone seemed to be pulling in the same direction, beginning with the Americans. We did everything we could. It was our highest priority to get German industry back on its feet—to get production going and to get exports going. The Marshall Plan, which came along at this time, was also a very significant factor. The Marshall Plan was, for the conditions at the time, perfect." He mentioned the famous airlift of 1948 by which the U.S. Air Force kept Berlin alive by flying in supplies after the Russians barricaded access to the city.

"Then, on the other hand, you had the will of the Germans to start up again," Zane said. "It began with clearing a path through the rubble. And here it must not be overlooked that the German workers, also as represented by their unions, took a very constructive attitude. There was no

question of how much they were going to be paid. It was a question just of working. Everybody knew there wasn't going to be much pay. As long as one could be fed, that was the first thing.

"Of course, in line with all this, the money reform in 1948 was a key step. The Reichsmark was eliminated and everybody started off with 40 D-marks [deutschemarks], but the D-marks had a lot of purchasing power. It was more than the old Reichsmark of the same amount. You had a currency in which people had confidence."

The rate was 4.20 marks to the dollar (compared to less than two to the dollar as this is being written). "The mark was purposely made very cheap in relation to the dollar, because the United States had all the marbles," Zane continued. "If we were going to get the German economy back on its feet, we had to make it possible for them to export, and who were they

Mercedes-Benz Diesel dining car, circa 1938.

Princess Grace and Prince Rainier of Monaco with a Mercedes-Benz Type 180a. This was the first Daimler-Benz car designed with platform construction and safety body. Both gasoline and Diesel versions were produced from 1953 to 1962. The 180a (W 120 II) illustrated was produced from 1957 to 1959.

going to export to? They had to export to us. It was like a healthy man giving a sick man a blood transfusion. This blood transfusion was made more possible through an exchange rate which favored German exporters."

(The Daimler-Benz company itself had a word on this subject in its *History*, published in recent years: "The effect of the currency reform of June 21st, 1948, was startling; conditions began to improve rapidly; the beneficial effects of the end of financial paralysis, together with the adoption of a sound government policy, spread to every branch of the economy, including, of course, the Daimler-Benz company. . . . Again, the Mercedes-Benz star appeared on world markets.")

By 1949, Daimler-Benz had risen to its knees, if not yet to its feet. The company introduced its first new-model car since the war—a pair of them: the 170 S and the 170 D, the last a diesel. Up to then, the company had put together some prewar models, the first as early as 1946, from leftover stocks. The new models flung the company all the way back upright. It built 137,431 of the new cars the first year.

Now that there was something to export, Zane acted on a standing invitation from Dr. Haspel and joined the Daimler-Benz company, taking a post in the export division. Dr. Haspel first sent him to India, where he laid the groundwork with the great industrial conglomerate Tata Enterprises for the assembly and partial manufacture of a Mercedes-Benz truck suited to India. "They finally were producing the entire truck under our license and distributing it," Zane said.

The arrangement worked well for both sides. "We had opened up a completely new form of help for developing countries, because here was Germany, herself just getting back on her feet, contributing to India's progress through helping them

Engineering and design directors at the Italian Grand Prix, September 9, 1954. Center, left to right: Rudolf Uhlenhaut, Hans Scherenberg, and Fritz Nallinger.

411/950 Harold James Cleworth

England's most successful Mercedes Benz race car driver, Stirling Moss.

manufacture trucks. We were bringing their technicians and apprentices here for training, and our experts were going there. It was also for us a very profitable association."

After India, in 1954, Zane was sent to the United States "to try and help get things started there," as much as possible seeking to combine Mercedes-Benz sales with Volkswagen dealerships, in New York, Los Angeles, San Francisco, and San Antonio. "The naysayers were plentiful," Zane said. "What I find interesting in retrospect was that all the dealers of that time failed to see the big boom coming in Volkswagen."

While Zane and his colleagues of the Daimler-Benz Export Division looked for customers abroad, the company's engineers and designers were hard at work on a project aimed at restoring the name Mercedes before the world. What they were building was heralded with excited rumors much like those which preceded the first Mercedes, back in 1901. The machine was a new, 215-horsepower sports car with fuel injection for each cylinder— the 300 SL (Sports Light).

At a New Year's celebration, January 1, 1952, Dr. Haspel announced that the three-pointed star was going to be seen again at international racing events, as carried by the 300 SL. After doing no better than second and fourth in its first effort, at the Mille Miglia, the new car pretty much picked up where Mercedes racers left off when the war intruded, in 1939.

The 300 SL won the Swiss Grand Prix at Bern, sweeping the first three places. It came in first and second in the twenty-four-hour Le Mans endurance grind, both cars beating the record by three miles, with an average of better than ninety-six miles an hour. The two winners were then driven the 525 miles back to the factory, where it was found that the big turbo brakes were good for still another thousand miles.

At the fifteenth running of the German Grand Prix, August 3, 1952, on the Nürburgring, the 300 SL made it a quadruple victory before a half million spectators. The Jaguars, Allards, Healeys, and Ferraris, which had been expected to give the Germans a battle, never came close. It was old times again.

The 300 SL climaxed the year's triumphs by taking first and second places in the third Carrera Panamericana México, an ordeal of 1,934 miles nearly spanning the length of Mexico, leading through jungle and desert heat and over mountains two miles high. At one point, Alfred Neubauer, directing his drivers from a DC-3 flying overhead, was unable to keep up. The leader had dropped out and Neubauer couldn't tell his own driver to slow down.

There were those who thought the race would go to the Ferraris, which had more power and speed and whose drivers enjoyed the advantage of having been over the course the year before, winning the race. These did not include Günther Molter, automobile journalist hired to publicize the event. Within an hour after the race was over, Molter airmailed victory posters in eleven languages to Mercedes dealers around the globe.

The 300 SL led to the 300 SLR (Sports Light Racer), which was to the 300 SL much as the SSKL had been to the SSK in another time. Neubauer's immediate purpose with the 300 SLR was to win the 1955 Mille Miglia and to do it in the heroic style in which Rudolf Caracciola had captured the event in an SSKL in 1931. With but one exception, the Mille Miglia had belonged to the Italians ever since.

Chief engineer Rudolf Uhlenhaut, who had the unusual ability of being able to drive a race car as well as design it, per-

The Eiffel race at the Nürburgring, 1955. Fangio placed first, averaging eighty-one miles per hour. He was the world champion driver for the third consecutive year. Moss came in second.

sonally took a hand in testing the new flag carrier. On one occasion, in practice at the Nürburgring, he trimmed five seconds off the lap time of world champion Juan Fangio.

With his customary thoroughness, Neubauer, who believed that 99 percent of winning a race lay in getting ready for it, took his men back and forth over the one thousand-mile course until it seemed they must know it as a country mail carrier knows his route. Still, the odds favored the Italians, who knew the road as natives.

To help improve the odds for British ace Stirling Moss, a new member of the

Mercedes team, Moss's co-driver, Denis Jenkinson, former motorcycle sidecar champion, hit on a novel idea. He and Moss had made copious notes about the route to be traveled, but there were obvious problems in leafing through a notebook in an open car at three miles a minute. Jenkinson transcribed the notes to a seventeen-foot roll of paper contained in a box with a window to read them through as he unreeled the notes by crank, relaying the information to Moss by hand signals. Thus informed of what lay ahead, Moss could sail up hills and around blind curves at full speed. He topped one hill at 175 miles an hour and

Alfred Neubauer and Juan-Manuel Fangio, 1955.

Stirling Moss with his goggles off
after a race.

Neubauer clocks Fangio at the Argentine Grand Prix, 1955. Fangio won at 75.1 miles per hour. He was the world champion driver for the third consecutive year.

The 1955 Italian Grand Prix, Monza. The winners: Fangio (Mercedes), 128.5 miles per hour; Taruffi (Mercedes); and Castellotti (Ferrari). The circuit combined a road course with a new, banked track.

at one point Jenkinson noticed they were passing an airplane.

Things went well until, on a flat stretch inviting full-out going, they hit a low place in the road not programmed on Jenkinson's scroll. The car took off like a sandpiper downwind. After some two hundred feet of air travel, the car returned smoothly to earth and unwaveringly continued the passage to Rome, demonstrating that even in flight the 300 SLR showed the well-known Mercedes-Benz road-holding qualities. The question of whether Moss might have been disqualified on the grounds that he flew part of the way, sportingly was never raised.

Moss won the race, covering the one thousand miles from Brescia to Rome and back—without relief—in 10 hours, 7 minutes, 48 seconds, averaging 97.9 miles an hour, an all-time record. Moss also broke the tradition that "he who leads at Rome never leads at Brescia"—that the first man into Rome never wins. Thirty-two minutes after Moss crossed the finish line, Fangio roared in, making it another one-two win for Mercedes-Benz.

It was a feat of endurance not only for the drivers but for the 300 SLR as well. The machines held up without complaint all the way, requiring no stops except for fuel and a set of tires in the rear. Back at

The 220 SE sedan driven 2,874 miles by Walter Schock and copilot Schiek to victory at the Argentine Grand Prix, 1961. Schock was European Rallye champion of 1960. The Hermann-Günzler team finished second, also in a Mercedes.

the factory in Stuttgart, tests showed Moss's car to have the same power curve as before the race.

Next for the 300 SLR: Le Mans—and catastrophe, with much the same shock effect as the Paris-Madrid debacle of 1903. The race was some two hours old when Pierre Levegh, driving one of the three Mercedes cars in the race, swerved to avoid an Austin Healey coming into the pits. Levegh's machine was deflected from its course and sent hurtling over the safety embankment into the crowd. Eighty-three died, among them Levegh.

Sunday morning, after an emergency meeting of the board of directors in Stuttgart, Alfred Neubauer stood at the pits with a black flag and brought in his two remaining cars in the race—one leading by two laps, the other crowding a Jaguar for second place.

Daimler-Benz finished out its committed schedule for the year, then retired from racing. But the goal of restoring the name Mercedes-Benz to its prewar eminence had been richly served by the 300 series. Except for Le Mans that year, where it had been winning again when Neubauer called the cars in, the 300 SLR had won every race it entered.

After more than forty-four hundred victories since it all began with the Paris-Rouen Reliability Run, in 1894, it was time to leave racing anyway. "In Germany you make a basic distinction between the reason and the trigger," Allen Zane explained. "Le Mans was the trigger. The basic reasons go a bit deeper. Automobile racing does not have the same significance as before the war. The ownership of automobiles had become broader. People had their own cars and were more interested in getting away on weekends and driving around themselves than in going to an automobile race.

"Also, we here at Daimler-Benz were not competing against our commercial competitors. We were competing against specialist firms like Ferrari, Maserati, and so forth, who were not competitors in the normal market. We also were faced with the fact that our cars were becoming extremely popular around the world. We had to put considerable effort into design, and to bring out new models, to improve what we had. Greater demands were being placed on our technical people—our design staff, our testing staff, the research people. We were overworking key people to keep up the racing effort when we really needed them for something else.

"Also, the old argument about testing being necessary to prove a product is becoming obsolete, because with modern electronic devices it's possible to get the same results which in the old days you only got from practice. So a lot of the old classical reasons for racing were gone with the passage of time." Zane had in mind the C111, which, for the past several years, has served as a rolling test bed. In April 1978, powered by an improved five-cylinder diesel engine supercharged by the Airesearch Company, of Los Angeles, California, the third-generation C111/111 established nine absolute world speed records for land vehicles, previously held by gasoline cars.

On a twelve-hour endurance run, the car averaged 194.967 miles an hour. It covered one thousand miles at 197.836 miles an hour. The top speed reached with the diesel engine, pioneered for passenger cars by Daimler over forty years ago after Carl Benz had led the way on tractors and trucks, was 201.5 miles an hour.

This performance ought to appease the spirit of Rudolf Diesel, the Paris-born German of Swabian ancestry who invented the engine bearing his name, in which the heat of compression is the sole means of igniting the fuel. Diesel died a

Willy Mairesse wins the Liège-Rome-Liège Rallye in a 300SL, 1956.

Mercedes-Benz taxis are common in Western Europe, and are equipped by the factory with taximeters. Production of this model began in 1976.

tormented man, before he saw its potentials fully exploited. He drowned in the English Channel after falling (or jumping) overboard from a steamer in 1913. It was the mid-twenties when Robert Bosch, the ignition wizard, produced the pump that satisfactorily got the fuel into the cylinders at the instant of peak compression, when the pressure was many times that of the atmosphere and the temperature about 1000 degrees Fahrenheit. Bosch's fuel-injection pump vastly improved the diesel engine, which is twice as efficient as the gasoline engine, and cleared the way for its use in automobiles.

In October 1977, Daimler-Benz rolled out Mercedes-Benz Number 5 million since clearing away the wartime ruins and starting up again in 1946. The three-pointed star was seen in ever more places, with the car being sold in 171 countries. It had become the most wanted and most imitated automobile made. The time had come to celebrate.

The occasion chosen was the anniversary of the Deutsches Museum in Munich, sprawling over an island in the middle of the Isar River. The museum was founded over seventy-five years ago by electrical engineer Oskar von Miller to house "the masterpieces of science and technology." One of the museum's most distinguished

tenants is Carl Benz's original *Patent Motorwagen,* history's first gasoline-driven automobile. To honor this common ancestor in a four-day celebration, Daimler-Benz trucked all her vintage machines from the company's Stuttgart museum to Munich, to join the scores of other antiques being brought there by their owners from all quarters of the wind.

"Internationale Sternfahrt Zum Auto Nummer 1," proclaimed the banner unfurled above the stage of the banquet hall at the Sheraton Hotel the night before—literally translated, "International Star Trip to First Car." High on a wall, accenting the universal flavor of the occasion,

A 1950s advertisement.

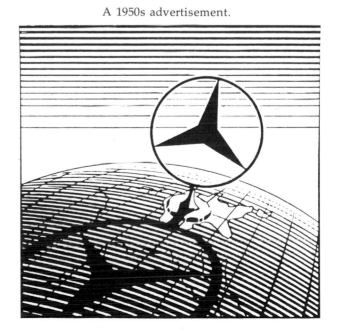

hung the flags of a dozen nations, among them in identical size as the national banners, in white on a blue field, the three-pointed star of Daimler-Benz.

"I think this one is more permanent than any of the others," wryly muttered Bodo E. Schütt, a lawyer from Heidelberg, referring to the Daimler-Benz colors.

Next morning, under the aegis of the Snauferl Club, the old cars were off early on a rally around the Starnberger Zee, southwest of the city. One by one they struggled gaseously up the ramp from the garage under the Penta Hotel. Traffic waited more or less patiently at the upraised hand of Dr. Huegel, outgoing director of the Daimler-Benz museum in Stuttgart, as the ancient machines turned into the street and scrambled off in a great to-do of shivering, wheezing, and coughing, trailing exotic fumes.

Each driver intently followed a printed itinerary in his hand, which instructed: Turn right into Hochstrasse for one kilometer, then right into Franziskanerstrasse, etc. Between nursing his engine and consulting the directions, the driver had his hands full. In the narrow, tortuous streets of medieval Munich, a miscue could quickly put him out of the game.

A 1911 Opel Torpedo with an Oregon license led the way out of town. Others appeared in front as the fortunes of the drive kept shifting. Cars were stalled by the side of the road, their drivers industriously turning the crank to bring them back to life. Fred Lustig, inveterate rally-goer from California, trundled along in grim concentration aboard his Benz Ideal, his faithful wife, Anita, at his side, wearing a look of patient amusement.

At nine-thirty, the gasping cavalcade began to reach Tutzing, halfway down the east shore of the Starnberger Zee, the first checkpoint. The machines labored up the drive and into the grounds of the laundry and dry-cleaning emporium of August Wurth, who was on hand to greet the travelers. They steered between two umbrella-covered stands, receiving a cloth rose from the lady on the one side, a miniature beer stein from the other. There was a handshake for the adventurer at the wheel, and off they went again.

In halting English, not helped by the cigar stub in his mouth, Herr Wurth told of having owned the first truck ever registered in Munich, a chain-drive Benz. He proudly showed a picture of the truck, AUGUST WURTH lettered on the side, in an advertisement in the rally program. The tires were of solid rubber and the engine did 980 revolutions a minute, the description read. Wurth apparently started a trend with his truck, for it was followed by three more in the city within the year.

A car with a single-cylinder engine arrived. The one-lunger trembled with the violence of an alcoholic in the throes of delirium tremens as it staggered between the two memento stands. He was followed by a Benz touring car with the top down as a pair of NATO fighters slashed past low over the water. There were a Bouton from London and a sedate Benz sedan, driven by Heidelberg lawyer Schütt.

The first Mercedes appeared. A Lorelei and a Didion came chugging daintily up the drive, overwhelmed a moment later by one of Ferdinand Porsche's legendary SS cars, bellowing with authority. The driver received his souvenirs, then went blasting out the gate and up the road like a retreating thunderstorm, making up time.

"It's an interesting hobby," observed a white-haired matron in a red jacket, looking off in the direction of the retiring SS. "But *very* expensive."

The Oregon Opel arrived late in the morning, preceded by a car under tow. The old fellows kept coming, each adding

Cars on the test track
at Untertürkheim,
circa 1968.

Close-up of a Mercedes hood at the test track.

a fresh load of fumes to the miasmic cloud that hung heavily over the scene. Herr Wurth scribbled the final total—between 90 and 100—for the outsider's convenience. With a break for lunch at the lakeside Strandhotel, memorable for the insolence of its waiters, the rally finished up back at the Penta Hotel in Munich by early evening.

Next afternoon, a group gathered on the Oskar von Miller Ring, a small street on the grounds of the Deutsches Museum, for the dedication of a memorial tablet to Carl Benz, the man who built the car that begat all the visiting progeny. As Helmut Paul Hahn, president of the Snauferl Club, made the officiating remarks, two men drifted up from separate directions and stood on the perimeter of the gathering, listening to the proceedings.

Hahn recognized the pair, having invited them to attend the museum celebration, though without telling either that he had invited the other. Concluding his words, Hahn hurried forward and caught the two as they moved close to each other. He introduced them.

"Mr. Daimler, meet Mr. Benz. Mr. Benz, meet Mr. Daimler."

After three generations, for the first time—though their grandfathers and their fathers lived and worked 60 miles apart, each engrossed with the development of a machine which would change the world perhaps as no other—after all this, a Daimler and a Benz had finally met. The grandsons looked at each other and warmly shook hands. Daimler presented his wife, Ira, a handsome woman who smiled brightly. Mrs. Benz was at home in Mannheim, Benz apologetically explained. "I invite you to come there next week so you can meet her."

Soon afterward, far down in the bowels of the museum, a crowd clustered around an old machine in an alcove at the foot of the escalator. Raised on an 18-inch platform, the machine was being explained by museum director Strassl. "Das Auto No. 1," read the sign over the car—Carl Benz's three-wheel *Patent Motorwagen*. On a matching platform toward the back of the alcove, stood Gottlieb Daimler's Steel-Wheeler, the first four-wheel automobile.

Down the corridor strolled the pair of new friends, Carl Benz and Paul Gottlieb Daimler. They readily agreed to sit at the tillers of their grandfathers' machines, Benz on the Motorwagen and Daimler on the Steel-Wheeler, making an historic photograph.

On the fourth day, after an address in the museum auditorium by President Walther Scheele of West Germany, followed with music by the Munich Symphony Orchestra, the Deutsches Museum celebration ended. Daimler-Benz loaded their venerable machines back aboard vans and returned them to Stuttgart, to get on with the work of building more new ones.

With upward of a million unfilled orders waiting, and each new day putting them yet farther behind, management had decided it was no stricture on the rule of keeping "all four feet on the ground" to add some more plant capacity. Bremen had just started to build station wagons, hoping to turn out 30,000 in 1979. "This could be called the start of expansion," said Sindelfingen personnel director Waldemar Bubeck, adding that the company planned to keep expanding for the next five years, investing a billion deutschemarks in new facilities.

And what would Max Kaspar Rose, Carl Benz's disapproving partner, think of all this? "My God, my God!" Rose had cried despairingly 90-odd years ago, "where is all this going to end?"

Herr Rose, nobody knows.

The Mercedes-Benz C111, an experimental sports car built in a small series beginning in 1968 under the direction of Rudolf Uhlenhaut. This car was used as a rolling test-bed for the Wankel rotary engine. The C111 has an aerodynamically designed resin body reinforced with glass fiber and equipped with a steel-frame floor unit. The engine is in front of the rear axle.

In the fourth step of its development, the C111/IV broke five of its previous records, powered by a V-8 gasoline engine. Turbocharged, developing 500 horsepower, it reaches well over 250 miles an hour.

Bud Cohn's car collection serves as background for a 1977 450 SEL. From left to right:
1964 Type 600 Limousine, 1933 Type 540 K Cabriolet B, 1936 Type 500 K roadster, 1929
Model SS 27/180/250 hp sport roadster, and 1955 300 SL Gullwing coupe, California 1976.

Paul Gottlieb Daimler (left) and Carl Benz pose on their grandfathers' first automobile at the Deutsches Museum, photographed by Wendy Grad, 1978. The two had been introduced only minutes before—the first time any members of the two families had met in three generations.

# CHAPTER TEN

# Yesterday and Today

## It Goes Like a Scared Rabbit

It was common knowledge in the brotherhood of classic-car people that Mahlon E. Patton owned an antique Mercedes that was as fine a specimen as one could find. IIe had driven it in shows and won prizes with it, one was told. "The car is in beautiful shape," all agreed.

Reached on the telephone at his home in Elizabethtown, Patton was cagy. "Is this a commercial enterprise?"

We told him we hoped so, briefly explaining, "If people buy our book, we stand to make a little. If they don't, we don't,"

"I hate to see these old cars exploited."

"We hear you've got a very interesting one."

"It's probably the outstanding car in the country."

The rolling Pennsylvania countryside,

with its red barns and herds of fat Holsteins grazing in the pastures, looked prosperous as we rode Amtrak out from Philadelphia a few days later. Patton arrived five minutes after we called from the phone booth outside the station—a point of mild interest since he had said he lived "way out in the country" and wondered how we planned to get to his house. He whistled us up from the other end of the tunnel under the tracks through which we had wandered while we waited.

Looking us over with chill blue eyes, he wheeled around a couple of corners and there we were—in the presence of the prize. Indeed, it was something to see! Painted white with brown trim and resplendent with polished brass and copper, it was a model of the car that thrilled autodom back in 1902 as the second-generation Mercedes—the forty-horsepower racing machine that swept all events at

Nice Week, whisked Baron de Caters through the flying mile at seventy-five miles an hour, and wound up the year stealing the show at Paris's Grand Palais in December.

"When I bought it, somebody said it was an oh-two," Patton said, referring to the date, speaking with a crisp, no-nonsense manner. "I said it was about a six. So I compromised and called it a five, but it is actually a four."

Records from Daimler-Benz showed that the car had been ordered by Emil Jellinek on June 6, 1903, for his customer Baron de Caters of Brussels, and was delivered October 29, 1904—the same unhappy year in which Camille Jenatzy, hero of the 1903 James Gordon Bennett race in Ireland, lost the Bennett trophy back to France. For starting and taking third place in the 1904 event, driving a ninety-horsepower Mercedes, the baron was presented with the forty-horsepower car by Jellinek and the Daimler company as a gift.

"This has the greatest history of any car in the country," Patton declared.

The venerable machine surfaced in Iowa in the early sixties as one of about four hundred old-timers offered for auction. The finder, George Norton, of Reading, Pennsylvania, on the prowl as head of the Antique Automobile Club of America, got word of his discovery to Patton, himself once head of the AACA. "I made a down payment on it before I ever saw it, then I went out and picked it up," Patton said tersely, not one to waste time with minutiae.

Patton, who used to make roller skates, did most of the work of restoring the bedraggled relic personally, as he had done with other oldsters in his collection of eight or ten cars. "Having been in the manufacturing business, I can make a lot of the parts," he said.

The job he did on the 1904 Mercedes won it the laurel of "best restored European car" from the AACA—gratifying but hardly surprising to Patton, who looked on at least one aspect of his work as being superior to the original.

"Daimler painted them a dead white," he said critically. "I've been in this thing long enough to know what colors go well and what colors don't go well. A dead white to me is not good on an automobile, so I made it with a little bit of brown in it. Then I followed through with brown for the upholstery, flooring, and striping. I think my selection of colors couldn't have been better with all that brass on there."

The conversation had a tendency to stall —like the early cars. "Where can you get tires like that nowadays?" we asked.

"You don't."

"You don't?"

"No."

We timidly inquired if he might lift the hood, held in place by clamps of solid brass. He silently obliged. We exclaimed admiringly at what we saw: the glittering brass, the copper. "You don't find that any more, do you? They don't even know what it is in an automobile factory."

No reply.

"This is one of Maybach's jobs, isn't it?"

"Yes."

We bent over to study a name plate. "How do you say that?"

"I wouldn't."

We spelled out the name—C-A-R-R-O-S-S-E-R-I-E. "Is that the body builder?"

"That's the body builder."

The next question brought improved ignition: Did he drive the car?

"Oh, yes! If they won't run, I don't want 'em," he replied emphatically. But he drove the car, he made clear, on his own terms always—never to impress anybody. "If they want to hand me a trophy,

I'll take it," he said. "I'm not going to kill myself to get trophies."

How did the car run?

"It goes like a scared rabbit. At this time Cadillac was one-cylinder. Ford was two-cylinder. Reo was one-cylinder. They'd do about fifteen miles an hour. This damn' thing would do seventy." Patton had more respect for his 1904 Mercedes than for some of the modern cars. "That damn' Chevrolet I just bought stops on me every time I go downtown," he said of the car he had driven to the station.

"What kind of mileage does this old car give you?"

This dumb question nearly used up what was left of Mr. Patton's patience. "That's one thing you don't concern yourself with!" he snapped. "If you have to worry about the mileage, you shouldn't have the car. If you can't stand the heat, get out of the kitchen."

He had entered his Mercedes in the coming London-to-Brighton run, but a dock strike on the East Coast had kept him from getting the car shipped to England. "I went to see about flying it over, but that's out of the question," he said. "Hell, it costs forty-six hundred bucks just to send it one way."

But missing out on the next London–Brighton scarcely laid him low with melancholy. "I've been in it five times," he said. "One time I rode with Lord Montagu in his oh-three Mercedes. Another time I drove a four Peugeot. Another time I drove an 1898 Daimler. Another time an oh-four Humber. Another time I drove a three-wheel motorcycle. So it isn't anything new to me."

"Five times in the London–Brighton!" we exclaimed. "That must be a record."

"Probably is."

With no London–Brighton to bother with, Patton was putting his machine away for the winter. "Then it'll be all wrapped up—the brass all covered—everything protected." He seemed relieved.

In the spring, the car would start to be seen once again on the streets of Elizabethtown, Patton at the wheel. Unlike most antique-automobile drivers, who generally rate second fiddle to their machines, Patton had gained an identity above his car. As he piloted his splendid old Mercedes around town, he said with uncustomary animation, "People cry out, 'Here comes old man Patton again!'"

## This House Was Designed around the Mercedes

The 1836 Blacksmith's Forge, at Gladstone, New Jersey, is a one-time smithy. Built of native stone on the shaded banks of Peapack Brook, the old shop, along with the 1820 frame house adjoining, was restored and is now the residence of a vintage Mercedes touring car, which shares the premises with Mr. and Mrs. Roland P. Beattie II. The machine has its own room, enclosed with stone from a fence matching the stone of the Blacksmith's Forge. The room also serves as the foyer, so that the first thing callers see from the front door is the car.

"Young people become transfixed," Lynn Beattie said. "They ask to see it. It is something brand-new and strange to them—something where every part has its number and tells the pride of workmanship that went into it. They have never known a time before the phrase 'built-in obsolescence.'"

She showed snapshots of the car as it looked when it arrived at the Beattie home back in 1953, a battered, grimy tramp. "We built the house for that?" she exclaimed in disbelief.

"A hideous-looking affair," Beattie remarked. He had been privileged to buy the car from Henry Austin Clark, the well-known museum and archives keeper on Long Island, in exchange for having bird-dogged another relic for Clark. For a couple of years, while the architect got used to the idea of featuring an automobile in the house as a piece of sculpture, the Beatties stored the car in the barn at the back. When at last the house was ready, the machine was pulled from the barn to its place in the front hall by cable winch operated from a truck stationed in the street in front, with the cable running through the house.

"The tow-truck operator was so excited that he decided to do the job for nothing," Beattie said. "He had never pulled a car into a house before. It was always the other way around."

As he slowly took the machine apart to begin the long task of making it new again, Beattie came across a clue to the old car's background. "In the bottom of the oil pan, buried in all the goo, was a hand-made, open-ended flat wrench," he said. "Stamped very neatly across the front were the words 'Otto Hammer.' I showed the wrench to Charlie Stich"—about whom more later— " and he said, 'Roland, would you like to meet Otto Hammer?'"

It was arranged to call on the man with the name on the wrench at the Hudson View Hotel, in Cold Spring, New York. "Charlie and I walked in about six in the evening, and here was this slight little gentleman, ramrod straight, with snow-white hair and a waxed mustache, sitting at a table for two, with a shrimp cocktail and a martini, straight up, in front of him. He was maybe seventy-five years old."

Otto Hammer, long ago, had been chauffeur for a family that owned an estate near Cold Spring. Beattie's old Mercedes was the car Hammer had driven for the family, acquiring it as his own when he retired. He knew the car from the body, which was a hybrid. He had put it on himself, because his wife hadn't felt right about sitting in the back, comfortably enclosed from the weather, while her husband rode out in the open.

Beattie's affinity for Mercedes cars had begun when, as an undergraduate at Princeton in the 1940s, he hung around Charlie Stich's Manhattan garage on weekends. "Charlie had all kinds of fancy cars there," Beattie said, "but I was most impressed with the antique Mercedes, of which he had three or four in various stages of rehabilitation. I felt that it was the finest-built motor car you could buy— in design, quality, and workmanship. You've got to see Charlie Stich. He enjoyed a fabulous reputation without advertising—all on performance and word of mouth." Stich's old sign, CHARLIE STICH, INC. AUTOMOBILE MACHINIST, was now mounted over the door of Beattie's barn.

Beattie took steps to own his own Mercedes. He began with a Stanley Steamer, paying $30 for it. He sold the Stanley to James Melton, the singer, for $200 and with this bought a Stutz Bearcat with an ailing rear end from a man whose fiancé wanted him to get rid of it. Beattie corrected the car's affliction and sold it for $2,700. With $450 of the Bearcat money, he completed his ascent to what he was after, buying a Mercedes S.

"I got this from a fellow I met at Charlie Stich's who also had one of those peculiar girls that didn't want him to have the car," Beattie said. "I completely rebuilt the car and had all kinds of exciting experiences with it. I used to frighten all others off the road because of the supercharger. Horses bolted. People ran out of their houses to look."

Then Beattie received what some might

Workers in the basement of the Daimler-Benz Museum, Untertürkheim, refurbish cars from the collection. On the left is Daimler's motorcycle of 1885, and to the right is Benz's *Patent Motorwagen* of 1886. Both are replicas.

call his comeuppance. "At that time I found myself alone in life and I was spending too much time in the evening living loosely and dangerously," he said. "One night I was driving home. The road was a little wet and I lost it. This was my second experience of terror. I scared myself so badly that I put an ad in the New York *Times* offering the car for sale. I got responses from all over the United States."

A doctor from Oklahoma City eagerly paid $14,000 for the car. This was over thirty-one times the $450 Beattie had paid

for it, a profit of 3,000 percent. "I thought this was a fantastic capital gain," Beattie said. "I had a great sense of relief that I made out fine."

Not long afterward, Beattie learned that the new owner of his Mercedes S had turned down an offer of $100,000 for the car. Beattie laughed hysterically. "You win a few, you lose a few—right?" He paused reflectively. "It never occurred to me that people would pay that kind of money for something like this."

Meanwhile, the restoration of the old hulk in the foyer was coming along. "We started really with just a chassis," said Beattie, a manufacturer of photographic equipment for the printing trade. "Everything that was worn we replaced with new pieces—of course, I had my own shop." Some parts he found at Hershey, the great annual massing of the world's old-car faithful featuring a flea market covering many acres just outside the chocolate town. If you can't find it at Hershey, you probably can't find it at all.

Beattie's biggest problem was what to do about a body for his 1904 Mercedes, to take the place of the mutation Otto Hammer had put on it. He remembered a couple of brothers in Morristown who ran a store in what had once been a carriage shop, and who shared his interest in vintage autos. "On the third-floor loft was a magnificent wooden automobile body but no automobile to go with it"—a body that had once belonged to a Clement-Bayard owned by a pair of elderly sisters, Beattie found out later. "I was able to procure this body for a very modest sum and it fitted perfectly."

The main thing needed was to fill in the space at the back that had been occupied by the rise in the Clement-Bayard's chassis—the Mercedes chassis being flat. There were a pair of rear fenders to provide, either by renovating those of the Mercedes or making new ones, and that was it.

"All it really took was time," Beattie said. One detail alone, the making of some brass castings, consumed a whole winter. What with the intrusion of such subsidiary concerns as running the family industry and bringing up three daughters, more than twenty years had passed since Austin Clark delivered the old Mercedes to the Beattie door.

Only once had there been a slight hitch. After Beattie finished painting the chassis and running gear "a very choice shade of tan," Lynn made him do the job over to match the burnt orange of the drapes at the door behind, where the car had been winched in from the barn.

"But that was a small price to pay," he said gallantly. "As a matter of fact, I think it's a real nice color. After all, this whole house complex was designed around the Mercedes."

The hope was to have the car ready for the 1978 London–Brighton run. "As that date approaches, we are commencing to worry a little," Beattie confided. "I've had this car since 1953. When I received it, one piston was seized. The car wasn't running. Now we've gone through the restoration. I've never heard it run up to now." He mused that he would have the winter to finish the assembly of the car, and then all spring and summer to make good any problems that showed up.

*Postscript:* November 5, 1978. Call from collaborator Grad in London, who had just ridden in the London-to-Brighton run, traveling with the photographer of the National Motor Museum at Beaulieu: "The Beatties made it!"

## Nobody Does It That Way Any More

There was no way to miss Charlie Stich as we stepped from the Trailways bus at Grand Gorge, a tidy old town with bracing fresh air, in the James Fenimore Cooper country of the Catskills. Charlie would be the lean, spare-built man in a blue beret with the three-pointed star in front, his eyes holding ours and grinning in mutual recognition as we approached. He seemed a long way from eighty-five years old.

As we slid into a booth at the nearby diner for a lunchtime hamburger, he was eager to tell of something that had happened to him the day before. He had found a one-time girl friend whom he hadn't seen in more than fifty years. He used to visit her—or try to—on selected occasions such as his own birthday and then on hers, a month later, but each time he set out for her home driving his 1909 Mercedes, something went wrong. It was the only time the car ever failed him. And if it wasn't the car that thwarted his plans, it was something else. "I always had bad luck," he said. "Once, I was hit at a crossroads. One year I tried the train: halfway there we hit a bridge washout."

Charlie gave up. He couldn't phone her, because she refused to give him her number—just as Charlie stubbornly refused to give her his own. That was in 1924. Yesterday, fifty-three years later, he somehow had gotten the number and called. "Her voice was as clear as a bell— just as strong as always," Charlie said, though she was now eighty-one. "I said, 'Is that you, Judith?' She knew me right away. 'I know you, Charlie.'"

He abruptly changed the subject. "Let's get started," he said, getting up. "We got a lot to see before it gets dark."

The dates 1565 and 1846 appeared on a pair of houses as Charlie left the street and headed for the country. "I'm going to take you to the woods," he said. His home, several miles out, was a trim little house with white-painted aluminum sides overlooking a broad valley with a backdrop of wooded mountains flecked by the first colors of autumn.

Charlie turned into the driveway, which was flanked by stone walls with "C. Stich" painted on either side. "Do you see anything?" he asked, switching off the engine. At the center of the garage door was a large three-pointed star. There were other decorative effects. By the foot of the steps leading up to the porch and front door, a small crankshaft stood endwise on a pedestal with four legs made of pipe interspersed with metal filigree.

"That's from a Fiat 500," Charlie said.

The railing of the steps, continuing around the porch at the top, was all his own handiwork, Charlie explained as we went up. The graceful curves and wheel-like forms of the ornamental ironwork, he had wrought with a vise and a monkey wrench. Where these tools weren't enough, he had gotten the curves by bending the metal around lengths of pipe of assorted diameters.

He pointed out that the ironwork was fastened in place with copper rivets— eighteen hundred of them—every one annealed (made soft) "so you could hammer it" and fitted in a hole drilled three times —this rather than welding. "This is the way things used to be done," Charlie said sadly. "Nobody does it that way any more. There isn't time and nobody cares."

Grease cups from an old-time automobile provided lubrication for the hinges of the little gate to the porch, the floor of which was flagstone. Connecting rods from an automobile engine clamped to the railing gave sturdy support to the framework of the porch awning. "I make use of everything," Charlie said.

On the front door again appeared the three-pointed star of Mercedes-Benz. Inside, he led the way down the interior stairs to his workshop, in the basement. As we descended, he told of having had to repair a gap in the railing of the staircase, using the casing from the exhaust pipe of a Mercedes. Reaching bottom, he went to a corner of the room and pulled aside a cover, revealing his 1909 Mercedes, painted a fire-engine red.

"She'll go to Los Angeles if somebody will buy the gas," he said proudly. "This was a town car when I got it. You know what a town car is? The chauffeur was in front, and in the back the passengers were enclosed in a carriage. In those days— 1908, 1909—the Mercedes was king of the road. It was the only car that would take you anywhere—go, and come back."

This dependability was helped out by one of the conditions of purchase, Charlie explained. "When a man wanted to buy a Mercedes, he would go to Europe. He went to the factory, which kept a roll call of mechanics who wanted to go to different parts of the world. The customer wouldn't buy the car unless he had a mechanic-chauffeur, so in case anything went wrong with the car, the mechanic was there to fix it. Nobody here could do it. The chauffeur was part of the deal."

The owners of automobiles were "oh, God, the richest men you could think of—the Vanderbilts—people like that," mostly living on great estates on Long Island, Charlie remembered. "They had the best roads there, because they were rich people and could afford the roads, and the cars. Most of them had Mercedes,

and they used the Mercedes for long-distance driving." For local trips, they used their lesser cars.

Each Croesus owned enough automobiles that he was not inconvenienced if one or two were laid up for repairs. If the problem became too much for his chauffeur-mechanic, he took the car to a public garage for help. "That's the way I learned my apprenticeship," Charlie said. "I worked in a public garage." It was one of the first jobs he found after his mother brought him to the United States in 1906 from his native France, where he was born on a farm.

A Mercedes was the first automobile he ever rode in. "I thumbed a ride from Columbus Circle to the Mercedes repair shop, about a half mile," he said. "I fell in love with the maneuvering—the driver, what he was doing—all the gadgets that he was working on."

John F. Kennedy rides in a Mercedes-Benz 300D (fuel-injected) Cabriolet D (produced 1958–62) in Mexico City, June 29, 1962.

150

But it would be a dozen years before Charlie owned one of these bedazzling machines himself. The opportunity came after he opened his own repair shop, in 1918, at 89th Street and First Avenue, Manhattan. A family at 80th Street and Fifth Avenue, with four cars, chose to get rid of the Mercedes, a 1909 model, to make room for madame's Lancia. The Lancia needed work, and if Charlie would take care of that, the chauffeur proposed, he could have the Mercedes for four hundred dollars.

Since the Mercedes was a town car, a little overboard for Charlie's needs, he replaced the body with one from a Renault, cutting it in half and lengthening it to fit. He put on leather fenders—car fenders were the same as on carriages—found in a junkyard. He installed four-wheel, hydraulic brakes—practically unknown at the time.

"I became swamped with orders," he said. "Everybody wanted four-wheel brakes. I put things on my car for the fun of it, and the customers would want the same innovation: leather on the steering wheel, a cluster of brass horns that played a tune. My car was a showpiece wherever I went."

Clearly, in Charlie's mind it still was. He moved about the old machine, pointing out its features. On the front seat rested a three-pointed-star radiator ornament. "We used to put those things on the hoods, on the front of the radiator, any part of the car it would show up best. I devised the idea of making a ring around the star and a stand to carry it on the radiator cap. I wanted to make the star more eye-catching. Your eye sees the large ring first." He formed a circle with his hands. "Up to that time all they had was the star."

Evidently, as Charlie told it, among the eyes caught by the ring around the star were those of the New York Mercedes dealer. "I used to park at the Mercedes showrooms at 56th and Broadway. In about 1927, Mercedes cars from the factory began to carry the emblem on the radiator cap."

The secret of making a car last a long time, Charlie stressed, was to take care of it. His machine of sixty years had carried him a half million miles, he estimated, and was still going. "It outlasted me. I've replaced the spark plugs and so forth but, what the hell, the fundamental parts are good as new." He raised the hood. The engine's identification shown clean and bright: "Mercedes-Simplex Daimler Motoren Gesellschaft No. 10364."

Charlie Stich's reputation after fifty-two years as mechanic for New York's "400" pursued him after he quietly closed up shop in 1970 and disappeared into the Catskills. Although he told no one of his plans, his old customers somehow found him. Hence, the presence of the towering black hulk in another corner of his garage.

Partly dismantled, this behemoth supposedly had belonged to Joseph Goebbels, Adolf Hitler's Minister of Propaganda. "Don't use Hitler's name any more than you have to," Charlie said. The car was one of six Mercedes machines specially built for the Hitler Cabinet, Charlie had been told. (Daimler-Benz built no cars for individual members of the Hitler government but filled orders for a number of cars that were used interchangeably by the officials, according to the company.)

The car in Stich's hands had been sent to him by a client who had tracked Charlie down in his pastoral solitude from England. Charlie had once restored a purported Hitler car for the same customer. Like the first machine, the second weighed about four tons. It stood eight feet high and cleared the floor by only an inch or so—"a monster," Charlie called it.

After it was deposited by a huge van at the foot of Charlie's driveway, it had taken a farmer with his tractor to push it into his garage.

The car was giving Charlie headaches. Many parts were not to be had, so that it was necessary to have them made, along with special tools to work with. "This is a tool to pull the axles out," he explained, indicating a hefty implement on the floor. "That cost me fourteen hundred dollars." Another device, with a long handle for extra leverage, fitted over the hubcaps like a collar, permitting their removal without hammering on the ears and rounding them. Stich had made this one himself.

The machine had been badly abused. Charlie picked up a gasket that fitted between the exhaust pipe and the engine—it was made of tin. "Mercedes would never have used that kind of thing," he said disgustedly. "These are used only on cheap cars." His replacements for the tin gaskets were massive bronze affairs a quarter inch thick, made to his order. The brake drums were "works of art," but they were so severely scored and out of round that Charlie had to take them to New York to have them reground, at a cost of $140 for the pair.

"So far, so good," he mused. But after having been three years on the project, he longed for something else in life. "I wish it was tomorrow I could start it and get it out of here," he said impatiently. "Morning, noon, and night I think of Mercedes. How shall I meet the problems that keep coming up?"

And there was still the engine to worry about. He had found the cylinders in good condition but the manifold cracked. What might that portend? "When I start it, what the hell do I know what else I may find?"

Was it a good car?

"It will be," Charlie said, looking us hard in the eye, "when I'm finished with it."

## You Don't See Girls Driving 540 Ks

A thunderstorm enlivened the night as Bill Adamson, at his home in Princeton, New Jersey, talked about his Mercedes 540 K. He was an articulate, handsome man, with a John Barrymore profile and thinning white hair, combed back.

The 540 K was a snazzy sports car of mid-thirties vintage, which succeeded the 500 K. Weighing nearly three tons, the 540 K had an eight-cylinder engine of 115 horsepower, boosted to 180 by the supercharger. Polished exhaust pipes curled from the left side of the hood in the style of its ancestors, Dr. Porsche's fabled Mercedes S series, of the late twenties. The 540 was priced at twelve thousand dollars, a lot of money in those Depression times.

(Even so, the car was a good investment. On Sunday, February 25, 1979, at the Los Angeles Convention Center, a 500 K, a slightly less powerful machine, sold for four hundred thousand dollars—plus forty thousand dollars for Christie's, the auctioneers, for its five-minute toil of selling the car. It was the all-time-champion high price ever paid for an automobile. The occasion was the sale of the estate belonging to M. L. "Bud" Cohn, internationally known among classic-car folk as the man they could count on to supply the part not to be found elsewhere. Eighty-two years old, the beloved Cohn died of a heart attack in London while he was preparing with his friend Bill Post for the 1977 London–Brighton run.)

Bill Adamson's 540 K was unusual in that it combined one of the last of the 500 K cabriolet bodies with one of the first 540 chassis. "So it really is the best of two worlds," Adamson said. "This particular body is distinctive because the spare tires are in the rear instead of being mounted in the fenders. My 540 K is the only one of its kind that I know of."

A special joy for Adamson was the supercharger. "When you kick it in, it sounds like thirty Banshee airplanes diving on you. I have actually raised the ears of a Basset hound horizontal," he said. But the supercharger also had a more practical use: It got him away from gawking motorists closing in on him in traffic. "When you get that pincers effect at fifty miles an hour, it's very harrowing." There was a puff of smoke at the tailpipe, and he was gone. "People can't believe that a car that age could move that fast."

There were yet other rewards from the machine. "The 540 K exemplifies, for me, one of the last bastions of male supremacy on the highway," Adamson said. "You don't see girls driving 540 Ks. It takes a lot of beef, and unless they are Russian weight lifters . . . there is something about this car which you just feel is a male animal."

But driving the 540 K called for alertness as well as muscle. "You really have to think or you are in serious trouble," he said. "They don't stop in five feet. You have to keep in mind what gear you're in and so forth. When you have to think as you drive, it keeps you awake."

One of his more exhilarating moments with the car occurred one evening after he picked it up at the paint shop and was crossing a viaduct on the Pennsylvania Turnpike. "Suddenly, in the rearview mirror I see my right rear wheel bouncing down the road," he said. His first thought was that the axle would rake the guardrail, throwing the car off the highway and into the swamp. "I leaned to the opposite side as far as I could. I looked in my mirror and saw the radiator of a Diamond-T truck right on top of me. The driver nearly jacknifed the rig getting it stopped."

Adamson brought the car to a stop at the edge of the road, with the machine precariously balanced on three wheels but without so much as a scratch to his new paint—and with Adamson never more awake in his life.

Next day, using a small boat, he looked for the errant wheel but without success. "There were no bubbles and it wasn't floating," he said. "The wheel weighed one hundred and fifty pounds." It was finally located by the members of a Philadelphia social organization—"a group of gentlemen," Adamson explained, "who like to drink while riding horseback." They were practicing in the vicinity for an exercise with the National Guard. Looking for the wheel from the 540 K gave them a chance to try out their new mine detector—and, presumably, was good for a few more drinks.

The wheel had wound itself off because the paint-shop employees had inadvertently reversed the axles.

Adamson traced the origin of his interest in automobiles to his grandmother. "When I was eight years old, she gave me a pair of scissors every Sunday because she didn't know what else to do with me and told me to cut out the advertisements in *Town and Country*, *Vogue*, *The Saturday Evening Post*—the beautiful colored ads for these cars."

As he grew older, remembering the pictures of those that appealed to him most, he began looking around for his dream car. "When you're collecting automobiles," he said, "I consider it a twelve-year project—four years to determine what you want, four years to try and spirit it away from whoever owns it, and four years to restore it. Then, if you are unhappy with it, four years to sell it. It could be a sixteen-year project for each car."

Adamson at length found a 540 K with the style of body that he wanted in Paris,

A 1933 Mercedes-Benz Type 380 (W 22) 15/90/120 hp Cabriolet B before restoration. It was found in a small village near Prague, Czechoslovakia, in 1972.

The same car restored, Stuttgart, Germany, 1976. Parts were located by owner, Hans Polack, from all over the world. The headlights, side lamps, taillights, gas caps, and spare wheels came from Switzerland, the upholstery from Argentina, fog light and central lubrication system from Czechoslovakia, generator from Luxembourg, trunk with trim and rear bumpers from East Germany, tires from Great Britain, and the water pump from the United States.

but the owner refused to sell. "All cars have stories attached to them," Adamson says. "Here's the story that was given to me about this one: The man who originally bought the car was a French aviator. When the war broke out, he drove it down to his family's farm at Lyon and hid it in a silo, with thirty feet of hay on top of it. Then he went into the Air Corps. He was shot down, and the car passed into the hands of his best friend—the man in Paris who now owned it—by the terms of a letter which the flyer left behind with his family."

Adamson lost track of the 540 K when the late flyer's friend came to the United States in the early fifties. Picking up the trail again, Adamson found the machine in Beverly Hills, California, owned by a man who headed a foreign-car dealership there—and at long last the car was Adamson's. He had it shipped to Chicago and from there drove it home to New Jersey, battling snowstorms most of the way.

He soon discovered that he was lucky for other reasons than the weather to have made it to Princeton with the car. "I took the wheels off to look at the brakes, and I found I had no brakes. I was stopping on the brake shoes. Then I realized that the mechanical condition of the car was zero. I took it apart and put it into twenty-one boxes, and I started my restoration from scratch. I was a bachelor then. When you are a bachelor, you can work much harder on these things than when you are married."

The steepest part of the Mount Everest before him, as all soon learn who set out to restore an old car, was to find parts. "The Daimler-Benz people repeatedly referred in their letters to our success with the Norden bombsight on Stuttgart during the war. They said if it hadn't been for that, they could be more helpful."

Adamson's best friend in the matter was Bud Cohn, in Los Angeles, the cornucopia of pieces for the old ones. "He has done more things for me than anyone else."

Adamson, a chemical engineer, learned about engines in the Navy and so was able to do the work himself, saving on costs. "I think I came out quite well. Ten or eleven thousand dollars is my total investment. The car is probably worth seventy-five thousand dollars today." (This was before Bud Cohn's 500 K sold for four hundred thousand dollars.)

But with the hobby being taken over by hustlers, Adamson had a word of advice for those thinking of investing in an old machine. "My suggestion is to buy a car already restored," he said. "The cost of restoration today can go as high as fifty thousand dollars."

For those who already have one of the old ones, he emphasized the importance of knowing something of what went on under the hood. "Many never know what to do when they get into difficulty. They pull over to the side of the road, and if they leave it there it will be stripped in twenty minutes. The owner should know as much as he possibly can about his car, and keep it in good running order."

As for himself, Adamson went somewhat further in being prepared for road emergencies. On his forays to Boston or Washington, his favorite loops with his stable of relics, he hauled a trailer along behind, "for purposes of what I call a hospital ship. If a car gets sick, I never tow it. I put it on my trailer and take it to where I can get it fixed. I think I have found the best mechanics for each of the cars I own. There are a few honest, dedicated ones left who really love working on old engines. They are older men—like Charlie Stich."

When he was married, Adamson took steps to avoid the problems of friends who had trouble mixing marriage and automobiles. "They get carried away with the hobby," he explained. "They lose all contact with the family and everything else. I made an arrangement with my wife not to have more than six mistresses, as I call my cars—one for each work day of the week, with the day of rest for the real one." As further insurance, he added, "I keep an unheated garage, so I can't stay there very long."

## I Felt Like Moses at the Red Sea

At meetings of the Classic Car Club of America, the best-selling postcard is Austin Clark's picture of a canary-yellow Mercedes-Benz Sport touring car with a black stripe around it, standing in the snow in a pine forest. The car belongs to John Riegel, squire of a 25-acre estate of forest and fields near Montchanin, Delaware, not far from where General Howe routed George Washington at the Battle of Brandywine, clearing the way for the capture of Philadelphia.

Distantly related to the DuPont Family, "like nearly everybody around here," Riegel estimated he is the twelfth owner of the machine. The first owner is believed to have been "Little Willie" Hohenzöllern, who had been in line to follow his father, Kaiser Wilhelm II, as emperor of Germany when World War I brought a change of plans.

"We can't make sure it was Hohenzöllern because purchases for the family were made through agents and the records are lost," said Riegel as he leafed through the binder holding papers having to do with the car. The entries were kept in script by Riegel's brother-in-law, a lettering hobbyist. "We do know that in May 1928 the car was delivered to a Louis Zeller, a Mercedes-Benz dealer in Dresden."

In 1938, the car turned up in England, where it passed through a number of ownerships, seemingly declining in value as it went. In 1953, one British owner offered the Mercedes S for sale at $1300, compared to an original price of $10,000. Brought to the United States, the car came into the hands of Ed Jurist, owner of the Vintage Car Store, at Nyack, New York.

It was at Jurist's place that Riegel's brother, Jerry, spotted the car. Jerry telephoned John, who was in the navy at the time, serving aboard a ship at San Francisco. "He told me the price," Riegel recalled. "It sounded reasonable. He said the car was pretty racy looking. I said all right, I'll buy it."

Jurist, a man of humor, confirmed the sale with a letter to Jerry in San Francisco. "Dear Jerry: Sieg Heil! You iss now der owner of a 1928 Mercedes."

"I didn't get home for two and a half years to see the car," Riegel went on. "When I got home I was amazed at what I had bought. It was all-white then, with red leather interior and red wheels. Almost every Mercedes you run into is either white or silver, the German racing colors. I didn't want just another white Mercedes. Paint it yellow and the judges walk by and say, 'Good heavens!'"

Unlike most, Riegel did none of the work personally of restoring the car. He left that to George Waterman of East Greenwich, Rhode Island, one of the first to collect and restore the classics of the road. Bud Cohn, as for other cars Riegel has owned, was a great help in supplying parts. "He almost always has what I need," Riegel said. "He will say, 'I either have it right now or I'll find one for you. Give me a few weeks.' So a little time goes by and all of a sudden a UPS package arrives from California and here are the parts."

Riegel alone of the family drives the

Bud Cohn observes the judging of the restoration of his 1936 Mercedes-Benz Type 500 K roadster at the Ambassador Hotel, Los Angeles, 1977. The car sold at auction in 1979 for $400,000.

veteran car, he being the only one willing and able. His brother refuses on general principles, and the house mechanic has a bad back and leg, serious deficiencies in a man operating a Mercedes S clutch. "At slow speeds it's a bit of a truck," Riegel said. "It's hard to steer. It's hard to get around corners—it's just plain hard to drive."

But on the turnpike at 50 or 60 miles an hour, it's a different story. "It's the most beautiful handling car you've ever driven —very light steering, very responsive." There was only one problem. "It takes forever to stop, because of the mechanical brakes." He recalled Bugatti's famous retort to the criticism that his cars were hard to stop, "I make them to go, not to stop!" —finding a seeming parallel in the view of the German car builders. As someone had written in a magazine, "The chassis is always faster than the brakes."

"I can put both feet on the pedal, pushing with all my might, and still not get the wheels locked up," Riegel said. There have been a couple of close calls. "I was able to drive up a driveway, or get into a different lane—or do something." But then came the time when no such options were open to him. He reached an intersection just as the light changed.

"I came steaming down an incline at about 40 miles an hour and there was no way in the world I could get stopped. I just leaned on the horn good and hard and went through. I felt like Moses at the Red Sea the way traffic stopped on both sides. They could see this huge grill and these headlights that are 12 inches across coming at them. It threw the fear of God into them."

To limit adventures of this kind, Riegel continually adjusts the brakes, the drums of which are of castiron with copper plat-

157

An SSK engine fitted with an eighteen-fin "elephant" blower (supercharged), used on special racing cars. Ordinary SSK engines were equipped with fifteen-fin blowers, as were all K, S, and SS cars.

1) Supercharger.
2) Carburetors.
3) Air inlet when engine runs normally expirated.
4) Heavily finned air-pressure tube supplying carburetors with air when supercharger is in operation.
5) Inlet tube heated by exhaust gases.
6) Isolated tube guiding exhaust gases.
7) Six spark plugs out of twelve in dual ignition system (others on right side of engine).
8) Intermediary fuel tank by which the carburetors are supplied with fuel flowing under gravity.
9) Air pump driven by the camshaft to force fuel from the main tank toward the intermediary tank. (There was also available a vacuum fuel-feed system on S and SS engines, but it was never used on SSK engines.)
10) Steering-gear housing. This racing engine has as extras: eighteen-fin blower with blower clutch carrying a higher amount of drive disks and no brake disks, high-compression pistons, cylinder linings of special material, oil pump with two chambers, of which one limits the oil in the sump to a certain level, and generator creating 200 watts at 1300 rpm.

ing on the outside, theoretically for better heat dissipation. Each time he drives to Hershey for the annual old car jamboree and flea market, he adjusts the brakes first thing when he gets there. "It's very simple. Just you get a little dirty. You have to get under the car and turn four great big knobs about one click. This tightens the whole system and you're in good shape until you use up the next one-thousandths of an inch of brake lining."

As we rose from our chairs to go and look at the car, Riegel called attention to some items of decor in the room. On the wall, framed in chrome and yellow to match the car, was a pen and ink drawing of the machine done in vertical lines only. A wooden pedestal held a three-pointed star radiator ornament incorporating a temperature gauge. "It reminds me of my car," Riegel said, adding that it was a spare, matching one on the machine.

There was a cartoon showing two elderly ladies indignantly exclaiming at the sight of the Blitzen-Benz: "200 horsepower—all for one selfish brute who never took his wife anywhere!"

The yellow Mercedes S was housed in the 11-car garage of his mother's home nearby. Riegel removed the cover, commenting that the car had not been driven since June, three months before. "We go away during July and August, when it's too hot to drive the car—have to work too hard and sweat."

With the help of the garage crew, we pushed the machine toward the door, bringing it close enough to the car we arrived in to attach a cable to the battery for extra juice to swing the engine of the Mercedes. Riegel pumped up the fuel pressure and tried the starter. The engine turned over heavily—grindingly. It coughed, and was silent. Riegel tried again. "We're out of gas, Parky," he said to one of the men. He poured fuel from a small can into the vacuum tank. "Once I

get this full there are some 30 gallons back in the main tank," he said.

The vacuum tank filled, Riegel turned the engine once more. It chortled to life, quickly running up to a deep, cackling roar. Riegel backed the car out into the open and motioned us to get in. "We'll go for a quick ride," he called over the racket. "You'll have to pick up on that door a little as you close it—that's it." The gears thrashed and we were off.

"They break their necks looking at you," Riegel said of other motorists as we reached the road, sounding a little like a running gun battle. "It's carburetion causing that backfiring," he explained, expertly wrangling the car around the bends. "When she gets warmed up she'll run a little better. We're doing about 36 now. We're still in third gear. I doubt if I'll ever get it in fourth."

At the first hill he lost ground, shifting down to second. "Something wrong with the carburetor," he repeated. "No power. We should be flying up this hill in fourth." We reached the top and started down. "Maybe we can get the supercharger going," Riegel said.

A rising howl began somewhere under the floorboards, and the car gained momentum as the supercharger took hold. Riegel's face relaxed into a smile. "She handles beautifully at speed," he said happily. Moreover, the speed wasn't costing much. "At 60 miles an hour in fourth gear, I'm only turning about 1200 rpm. A modern car would be turning twice that."

Back at the garage the exhaust covers were blue with heat. "There are judges at meets who would find fault with that," Riegel observed. "They believe the car ought to look like it did when it came out of the showroom. I believe that if you show a little bit of grease here, a little bit of dirt there, a little bit of oil dripping— the car's been run."

Unlike Mahlon Patton in his Baron de

Caters 1904 Mercedes, Riegel passed unrecognized in his machine while everyone seemed to know the car. At shows, people said, "Oh, you're the guy that owns that big yellow car! I've seen it around for 10 years." Riegel keeps even by then asking the other what kind of car he has. "I own that green Duesenberg (or whatever it is)." "Oh, you're the guy!" Riegel replies. "I've seen that car everywhere up and down the east coast."

At auctions Riegel used to have a standard flip answer to all who asked the price of his Mercedes: "$200,000. I thought that was such an utterly ridiculous answer that they would think I didn't want to sell it. The last time I gave that answer, the man said, 'Let's go outside and talk about.' I said, 'Wrong again. The price is three hundred thousand dollars.' He said, 'Oh, you don't want to sell it?' I said, 'That's the general idea—I don't want to sell it.'"

Riegel doesn't quote a price anymore. He's afraid somebody will snap him up on it.


## It Could Cost Fifty Thousand Dollars

Ralph Buckley's automobile restoration shop lies in the woods outside Pleasantville, New Jersey, a few miles inland from Atlantic City. The address is unpublished, for Buckley does no advertising—never has during his thirty years in the business. He makes not even the concession of a sign at the turnoff from the highway to tell of the shop's presence.

"Those who want my services know where to find me," Buckley said with dignity.

And find him they do—from all parts of the United States. Buckley's clients include Briggs Cunningham, the former race driver whose museum at Costa Mesa, California, shelters one of the more distinguished assemblages of historic automobiles in the Southwest; Cameron Peck, prominent collector of the Chicago area; and Austin Clark, the Long Island museum curator and archivist. Buckley's customers have found him from Connecticut, Vermont, Pennsylvania, Texas.

Not that there are no other restorers to go to. There were at least twenty within a hundred miles, Buckley said. This compared with two when he started—the other besides himself being Charlie Stich. "It wasn't the in thing then," said Buckley, who converted his hobby into a business after the failure of the boatyard where he worked. "We were just the nut with the old car. You could buy one for three hundred dollars that now sells for two hundred thousand dollars." The difference, he said, had been brought about by the razzle-dazzle of advertising and promotion.

Buckley advised the owner of an antique car who planned to restore it, to be prepared for a lot of pitfalls and expense. He could know nothing of what lay ahead from what he saw on the outside of the machine. "When you tear it down, that's when you find out what you're into," he said. He gave the estimates for a Mercedes-Benz. "If the crankshaft is bad, that means getting a new one made." In one case, this alone had cost him twenty-five hundred dollars. "Maybe all your cylinder blocks are cracked. That runs into all sorts of money. Pistons may run one hundred dollars each. Wrist pins are about thirty-six dollars. It could cost fifty thousand dollars, all told."

Few are as fortunate as Austin Clark, whose Mercedes Simplex, a type of passenger car built by Daimler in 1902–6, had been dragged from a pile of ashes—"the worst thing you ever saw," Buckley remembered. "We tore the motor down and all it needed was a set of piston rings. The motor looked like it had just been rebuilt. Austin was lucky."

But the engine is not necessarily the critical expense, Buckley cautioned. "The woodwork alone can cost fifteen hundred or two thousand dollars. In the old days, cars were all framed in wood—mostly ash, but many bodies were made of poplar." A restoration, to be authentic, must use the same materials as the original.

There is the question of which restorer to use. Not all remember their Sunday-school lessons too well, or know what they are doing. "Check with collectors," Buckley advised. "They usually know who is good and who isn't."

Some of the best restoration jobs, he conceded, were done by the owners themselves—when the owner was qualified. "Many just get into trouble, then leave you to straighten them out. Sometimes that takes twice as long. Or they lose interest after taking the car apart, making a basket case out of it. They'll leave it maybe twenty years, then bring the whole mess to you and tell you to put it together. Meanwhile, pieces have been lost and nobody remembers how anything was."

Buckley also recommended that no one buy a car sight unseen, as he had done in the case of a Mercedes 540 K from England that had belonged to Peter Ustinov. "He's a fine actor, but you should have seen his car," Buckley said. "They said it was nearly immaculate, with white rubber floor mats and so forth. The car arrived in Philadelphia. I would have pushed it into the Delaware River if I could. The white rubber floor mats were in it, all right; only, Peter's heel had worn through the rubber, through the insulation, and was almost through the floorboards."

But the painful part was that after Buckley restored the Ustinov 540 K, he sold it for thirty-five hundred dollars. How could any sane man have known that one day such a car would fetch one hundred times that amount?

## They Don't Know What They're Doing

Fred Hoch, operator of a restoration shop at Magnolia, across the state from Buckley's place, said the craze to bring back the old cars began in the 1950s. "Up to then, if you had an old automobile, you were looked on as some kind of eccentric. Then the picture started to change. One guy would paint his car and get it running. Then the next guy would paint one a little bit better."

Competition developed among the owners of the old machines, all trying to outdo one another in making them look new again. It became stylish to own a renovated antique. "Then along came the entrepreneurs," Hoch said. "They started to say these cars are selling for money. Let's promote them—catalogs, auctions, promotion of all kinds.

"Now everybody who has a two-car garage is restoring cars—everybody," Hoch went on. "Most of them are just painting them up and calling them restored. There are all degrees of restoration. You can paint a car and call it restored. You can take it apart from the frame to the ground, check every rivet, check it for square, clean all the paint off and sandblast it—all the rust bits—rebuild every part, fit every part—build the car up to the same or better condition it was in when it left the factory, and call that restored. You can clean it down, put in new upholstery, and paint it, and call that restored."

Overall, Hoch had another word for what was going on: destruction. "There is more destruction in the name of restoration than anything else," he said feelingly. "They take real good cars and they destroy them. They throw the upholstery away. They throw the paint away. They make them look shiny and pretty, and they've destroyed an authentic, real piece of history. They don't know what they're doing."

Hoch gave the same low marks to contemporary methods of repair as to restoration. "The name of the game is to get it done real fast. It's expensive and it takes too long to fix it right."

A badly battered Mercedes 280 SL in the shop offered a case in point. The car had been in a number of accidents, and after the ministrations of successive repair shops, had come to resemble the final loser in a destruction derby. "They did it cheap," Hoch said. He showed where holes had been drilled in the body to admit a slide hammer to pull back the dents. What had been left of wrinkles and pockets after the slide-hammer treatment was filled in with plastic, now beginning to separate from the metal.

"Here's a place they never touched," said John Schaefer, Hoch's partner, running his hand over a fender. "See the rust—all the holes? They went right over it. Years ago, whenever we had damage like this, we repaired it to the extent we could, then we used lead," explained Schaefer, who had been doing this kind of work all his adult life. "Lead stayed in place because it reacted to temperature changes the same as the metal of the car. Plastic doesn't do that."

It would take two months to put the Mercedes back in shape, Hoch estimated, compared to a week or ten days for one of the slapdash-and-plastic operators, and the cost to the owner would be about forty-five hundred dollars. "It will be a new car," Hoch said.

It might even turn out to be the job

Hoch said he hoped one day to be satisfied with.

## There Have Been Great Frauds

Ed Jurist, owner of the Vintage Car Store, at Nyack, New York, was a man to see for what he knows and what he thinks; he was rated strong on both counts. Vigorous and forthright, with a full mustache and dark hair flecked with gray, Jurist delivered his mind of a number of things as he sat in his wood-paneled office just off the showroom floor. Among the paintings of race cars on the walls was a frame document showing he had been shot down as a Flying Fortress pilot in World War II, bailing out over Germany on March 6, 1944.

As a collector, feeling deeply about the old automobile masterpieces, Jurist was outraged by what had been done to the legendary Mercedes sports cars designed by Ferdinand Porsche—"the cars that made Mercedes racing history. There have been great frauds perpetrated on the public in the name of Mercedes-Benz," he declared.

At the end of the war there had been only one specimen of the SSKL left in the world, he said. "It was in the Dresden Museum, and it disappeared. Then, all of a sudden, here in the United States, a spate of SSKLs suddenly comes into existence, done by one of the master counterfeiters of the automotive years—a man by the name of Ray Jones. Underneath his home, which was surrounded by verdant lawns and shrubs, was an actual underground factory where he fabricated—counterfeited—SSKs, converting them from S types, from SS types, and K types, destroying great cars in the process of shortening them."

Jones was satanically thorough, Jurist

said, "He acquired the numbers of every car that was produced and where it was produced. He forged new manufacturer's plates, fabricating new numbers for those plates, and giving the car a new birth certificate. As a result, about five or six SSKLs suddenly came into being. It is now very, very difficult to determine the real McCoy from these frauds."

One of Ray Jones's home-made SSKLs apparently was bought by restorer Alex Dearborn, who visited Jurist and offered it for sale. "This SSKL was a total, obvious fraud," Jurist said, his voice rising. "I took issue with him. I take issue with all sorts of criminal behavior, and I consider this to be criminal behavior. Fraud and counterfeiting are criminal arts. I told him if you were to sell me an SSKL, giving me a document saying you had sold Jurist a 1929 Mercedes-Benz SSKL, serial number so-and-so, and I paid for it, I would immediately sue you for criminal fraud. You know damn well there are no SSKLs in existence!"

Jurist had had his own experience with Jones. It began one day after he received a phone call from a lawyer settling the estate of an elderly woman on Long Island. The lawyer wanted to know if Jurist might be interested in a dozen or so ancient automobiles that the brother of the deceased had collected on the premises.

"Needless to say, I went roaring out to Southampton," Jurist said. "It was an extraordinary experience. The brother had great taste in cars: Three or four of them were Mercedes S types, and he had used these great old Mercedes to pull tree stumps. When he ran out of space, he put them all in line like elephants, tail to nose, and then built a shed over them. The shed ran into an old barn in which more cars were stacked. Between the greenhouse and the barn was a huge Mercedes chassis of about 1928 vintage with engine, gearbox—everything but the body, with a tree about eight inches in diameter growing through the car. It took a two-man saw to cut the tree, and the car was hoisted over the stump with a block and tackle."

Jurist bought the entire lot of old ma-

Ray Jones driving an original SSK. Photographed by Martin Schroeder at the Nürburgring Veteran Rally, Germany, 1975.

chines. "We gave some of them away—nonsense cars like the Jupiter—and brought the rest here," he said. "One turned out to be William K. Vanderbilt's S Mercedes—not a racing car, but a beautiful touring car. This fellow Jones came here and bought the Mercedes cars—these great, historic cars. They should have been left in a room as one would a Rembrandt or a Botticelli. The canvas may be torn and the paint blurred. What you do is restore them. You don't mutilate them. This man proceeded to mutilate these cars!"

Unfortunately, ordinary men were slow to believe what they heard about Ray Jones. Jurist told of a collector friend of his, Ed Malley, of Greenwich, Connecticut, who came to him seeking advice on an offer from Jones to make a new set of fenders for one of his cars, a Mercedes that had belonged to Rudolf Caracciola. "Don't do it," Jurist said. "Because if you

do, you're not going to see your car again."

"Impossible," Malley responded. "He couldn't do a thing like that. Nobody could."

"Mr. Malley, I'm warning you," Jurist pleaded. "Don't do it. Your car is super. It's beautiful. It's original. It's historic. Don't do it!"

Malley was not persuaded. He sent his car to Jones for the fender job. "You know what he got back?" Jurist asked. "The shell of the Caracciola car. Jones had stolen the engine, stolen the gearbox, fiber-glassed the fenders, fabricated new plates. Jones has the original, basic components of the Caracciola car. Poor Malley has the remains."

When the collecting fraternity finally realized that Jones was real, many of his victims tried to sue him but found they couldn't, Jurist said. "He was judgment-proof. His assets were in the names of

A 1931 Mercedes-Benz SSKL rebuilt by Ray Jones with its owner, General Motors design consultant William L. Mitchell, at its side. Photographed by Jim Israel, Detroit, 1968. Authentic SSKL cars were modified from SSK cars of the twenties by drilling holes into the longitudinal and cross members of the chassis frame. The modern Ray Jones SSKL modifications were copied from a Daimler-Benz press photo of car number 18. The number 18 car existed, but was never entered in any race. Correct SSKL pictures from Daimler-Benz are identification photos, without fenders, numbers or drivers. Pictures of the cars with drivers, race numbers and victory laurels were faked. An historical racing picture of a genuine SSKL is not available.

Pablo Picasso, his wife Françoise Gilot, and David Douglas Duncan in photographer Duncan's 300 SL Gullwing. Photographed by Gerald Cramer at Duncan's villa, La Californie, Cannes, France, 1956.

other people. He ultimately wound up fleeing the country. He became involved in restoring airplanes, with no license to do so. He sold one to a chap. The guy got up in the air and killed himself."

Jurist was all the more sensitive to the defilement of the few remaining specimens of the car that inscribed the name Mercedes in the pantheon of motordom, because of the cars that were produced to take its place, appeasing the demand for a sports car after production of the others stopped. These were the 500 K and the 540 K—"a monstrosity," Jurist said, "as incomparable to the S type as the moon is to the sun. And yet it would be easier to sell—and at higher prices as well—a 540 K or a 500 K than it would be to sell a real thoroughbred like an S, an SS, or an SSK. Only the collectors of thoroughbreds realize what a lousy car the 540 K is. It is a disaster."

Another thing galling Jurist was auctions. "Auctions, in my opinion, are dishonest, manipulated, notoriously fraudulent—attributing values and virtues to cars that are devoid of these values and virtues, so that a 1932 Chevvy gets on the block for thirty-five thousand dollars. It's

really worth about seven thousand dollars, because it was a piece of tin when it was built and it's a piece of tin now. Auctions involve interstate fraud. The whole collecting hobby is so confused that people can no longer tell the difference between a thoroughbred and a dray. We, here, are involved with a thoroughbred."

Jurist led the way downstairs and pointed to an SSK. It was a machine that he and George Waterman, owner, among other classics, of Christian Lautenschlager's standby car at Dieppe in 1908, had brought out of Argentina and restored. "This was a racing car," Jurist said. "It is a racing car. It is documented. It could be driven right now. It would probably just loaf at 110."

### It Was All Done By Hand

We were a little late. Except for one or two that had refused to start, the old cars were already sputtering on their way down Wilshire Boulevard on a run from Santa Monica's Miramar Hotel to the Ambassador, in Los Angeles. Hurrying to catch up, we overtook a high-riding little machine with bicycle wheels whose driver presented the image of a man happy in his work.

On the lawn of the Ambassador a little later, we made the acquaintance of Anita and Fred Lustig and their 1898 Benz Velo. The car had given them no problems on the drive from Santa Monica, except for a broken brake link. Lustig had borrowed a pair of pliers from a passing bicyclist, fashioned a new link from a length of rod that he carried for just such emergencies, and after applying a little rosin to the drive belt while he was at it, he and Anita were off again.

The Velo finished the trip of ten miles without further ado, as befitted its status as a London–Brighton veteran, having conquered the British passage the year before. After seventy-nine years, the Benz Velo still met or exceeded all performance specifications of its builder, including speed, said Lustig, a friendly, informal man. It was supposed to do fourteen miles an hour. Actually, it would do nineteen.

This was not the only Benz Lustig owned. He had twenty-five more, making his collection of Benz cars likely the largest in the world. Some months later, then, at his invitation, we drove up for a longer visit with him and his wife at their home in Saratoga, California. Present with us in the den as we had lunch was the Velo we had seen in Los Angeles. It sat on a carpet centered by the Benz laurel branches, in the place where the pool table would have been if there had been a pool table.

"This old bus has been a very fond part of our lives," Lustig said. "We rather treat it as a piece of furniture. It's a conversation piece."

Attentions to the car that went beyond conversation were forbidden. "We make it quite clear that the car is not to be sat on, and we don't mind telling people that those are the ground rules," Lustig said. We were careful to keep our hands at our back as we briefly inspected the machine close up. We had learned by now that one did not touch a finger to one of these old treasures, much less apply his seat to it. We had read of a man being shot for laying his profane hands on a car. On social occasions, such as the annual party for the Mercedes-Benz Club, the Lustigs prudently push the Velo into a corner at the end of the fireplace, behind a barrier of potted plants.

Now and then, with no small bother, they manhandle the car outside and run the engine. "We take the furniture away from the side of the room and roll the car out through the sliding glass to the swimming-pool area, in the backyard," Lustig explained. "We remove one of the stationary plate-glass windows in the wall of the living room to the left, push the car into the living room, then down past the dining room, through the hallway, and out the front steps to the side yard."

Fuel for the Velo is lacquer thinner, not easy to find in the grade needed. "Standard sells it, but in fifty-five-gallon barrels," Lustig said. "A barrel would last us forever. I think our burn rate is probably a gallon an hour. So, through the Special Products Division of Standard Oil, I've found a radiator shop in San Jose that lets me have five or ten gallons of this stuff at a time."

The Lustigs bought the Velo, once owned by Winthrop Rockefeller, when the late William Harrah, of Reno, disposed of his Rockefeller collection. "The car came in a covered truck and we were so delighted with it that we decided to give it a baby-arrival party," Lustig said. There were about sixty-five guests.

"Even got presents," Anita put in.

They keep their other Benz machines at scattered locations, fourteen of them in a heated, air-conditioned warehouse a dozen miles away. They began collecting them in the late sixties, more or less in-

Mrs. Anita and
Dr. Fred Lustig
on their 1898
Benz Velo, Sara-
toga, California,
1978.

advertently. "All of a sudden we had two
Mercedes and then three, and I thought,
you know, maybe this is a pretty doggone
good idea," Lustig said. "We sought
models that I was interested in and Anita
was interested in, and this is how the
collection got started. We're specializing
at the present time in Benz. For some
reason there are more old Benz cars that
have come our way than Mercedes."

Lustig has done more than gather a
substantial portion of the world's surviv-
ing Benz cars under his wing. He has set
up the Benz Registry to find out where
the rest of them are, so that more can be
learned of when and how the various
Benz models were built. While the Daimler historical records are intact, those of
Benz are not. They were destroyed in
World War II.

"The Benz records had been hidden in
a cave, as the story comes to me from
individuals in Stuttgart," Lustig said. "I
have no reason to doubt it, because it's
plausible. The cave was overrun by the

French, and when they learned this was
German property, they fired the cave."

Joined with Lustig in the effort to hunt
down what are left of the Benz automobiles are Benz's grandson Carl; Max J. B.
Rauck, of the Deutsches Museum, in
Munich; Max-Gerrit von Pein, director of
the Daimler-Benz Museum, in Untertürkheim; and Bernard W. Garrett, of England. As the Benz cars are found, most of
the sleuthing being done by mail, they
are registered as to performance specifications, engine number, and individual
characteristics. By the spring of 1978, a
line had been gotten on 164 machines.

"There is no one in the world today
who has the knowledge to reconstruct
what vehicles were built when," Lustig
said. "They have a pretty good idea, but
we're not satisfied that it is totally based
on fact."

Besides having no documents to go by,
they were up against another obstacle.
"We have to fight an entirely irresponsi-
ble system known as the Benz numbering

167

system," Lustig said. "It was not consecutive. We have instances where four-digit numbers were used on an engine series before three-digit numbers were used. It was if Carl had these number plates engraved, put them into a drawer, and as the cars were finished, irrespective of the model, he reached into the drawer and put the number plate on it."

Old sales brochures were some help. "From these we've been able to get a reasonable cross section of what Benz was selling in what year," Lustig said. But the sales brochures were not accurate either, because of the requests for changes in the details of a car by the customers—"a little seat here, a wicker basket there, or this engine and that body"—making each car more or less custom-built. Many things happened along the way from order to delivery, which was how models evolved, Lustig explained.

But if Benz was a little relaxed with his numbering, this could not be said of his work in the shop. "Considering that there was a lot of blacksmithing in a car—it was all done by hand—I'm amazed at the accuracy of the gears," Lustig said admiringly. "Being a mechanical engineer myself, I went to the technical things first, to see how they were built."

A well of information was *Karl Benz und Sein Lebenswerk* (his lifework). "If you have one of these, believe it, it'll be a hen's egg," Lustig said as he brought out his own copy of the volume. "They're no longer available." He gently laid the book open and began explaining the sketches from Benz's work diary, translating from the German. These were the sketches Benz made as he worked out each problem of his *Patent Motorwagen:* the ignition, carburetor, cooling, steering, flywheel, followed by further drawings as he made improvements through the years.

How remarkable that he was right in so many fundamentals at the very outset! "He was a master mechanic. He was a master blacksmith. He was ingenious. Sometimes I wish," Lustig said nostalgically, "that I might have lived in Benz's time and seen the development going on.

"It really must have been a fascinating thing to see."


## There Was a Small Conflict

Closing time approached and traffic grew thicker. Paul Gottlieb Daimler glanced anxiously at his watch. Abruptly, he swung the car off the street and raced across the airport on a shortcut. He stopped to open gates to let the car through, then stopped again to close them, moving at a dogtrot.

"How does he get away with this?" we asked interpreter Hedy Murtihardjana, a native of Indonesia, having in mind that, in the States, driving on the runways of international airports is severely frowned on.

"He is a well-known man and he has privileges," she replied.

Our destination was Daimler-Benz's main showroom, repair, and parts center for the Hamburg area, northwest of the city, opened two years before but already being expanded. Karl Martin Schroth, the man in charge, was waiting for us at his desk. Tousel-haired and smoking a pipe, he heaped us with books and folders, humorously referring to "good public relations" as he provided a fancy bag with the company name and colors to carry them in.

Each day, twice as many orders for cars came in as could be filled, he said. "Models become obsolete while the customer waits"—although this hardly mattered, since there was so little change between

Stephen and Jocelyn Pitcairn with three of their Mercedes-Benzes: a 1928 Model SS, a 1955 300 SL Gullwing, and a 1968 280 SL. Bryn Athyn, Pennsylvania, 1968.

Gertrud (Trudel) and Carl Benz drive guests Ira and Paul Daimler through Stuttgart, celebrating the ninetieth anniversary of Bertha Benz's drive from Mannheim to Pforzheim. Stuttgart, 1978.

models. Last year, fifty-four thousand cars were sold out of Hamburg, but only eighteen thousand were delivered. It was all quite frustrating.

More fulfilling were other operations at the Hamburg center. Spare parts flowed in at the rate of fifty thousand items daily, ranging from *Pfennig*-size washers to multi-ton bus engines. It was a matter of pride that 92 percent of all parts requests were filled at once. The shop turned out four hundred repair jobs a day, including work on trucks, buses, and Unimogs, the mechanical version of the Missouri mule that does everything.

One repair job still on the floor showed how the Mercedes-Benz "safety cell" passenger compartment, patented by the company in the fifties, works out in practice. The car had been hit from behind with an impact that normally could be expected to pop the doors open and tele-

scope the back seat into the front, with likely fatal results to the passengers. Instead, protected by the steel framing enclosing it, the passenger compartment had come through the crash without damage. Even the rear window was still whole.

Daimler, the last of his clan, was a slightly built man with an anxious expression and a fringe of gray hair allowed to grow long, who might have stepped from the pages of *The Pickwick Papers*. Back at his home, a tastefully furnished walk-up apartment on a tree-lined street, his handsome wife, Ira, joined in as he talked about his father and his grandfather, whom he never knew directly, having been born in 1908, eight years after his grandfather's death.

"They were two of a kind," Daimler said. Both men were introverts and had few interests outside of technology. His father's only diversions were an occasional swim and a walk, sometimes with his wife but usually alone.

As with his father, Gottlieb, before him, he said nothing of his affairs to his wife—all very different from the relationship between Carl and Bertha Benz, Daimler noted. "Literature shows that Madame Benz had a very good technical contact with her husband," he commented, in English.

His father was iron-handed with the children, demanding instant obedience when it was time for play to end and study to begin. Failure to jump at the paternal order brought "a clap on the back"—for Paul up until he was fifteen.

"He could dominate the family but not his associates," Daimler said. This gave him a feeling of failure despite such acknowledged accomplishments as his contributions to the design of the first Mercedes. It also made him advise his son to seek some other calling than engineering. Technical questions from the boy, who precociously showed signs of interest in technology at the age of six, were curtly dismissed by his father with the reply that he was too young for such things and to mind his homework.

The reason his father left Daimler-Motoren-Gesellschaft in 1923, to be succeeded by Ferdinand Porsche as chief engineer, was "a small conflict" between him and the company over the supercharger, which his father had developed for aircraft engines during World War I and afterward adapted for use in automobiles. The supercharger, his employers felt, wasn't worth the extra expense. They argued that it would only add to the cost of the car while making little or no difference in sales.

"My father was thinking from the technical point of view and the salesmen from the sales point of view," Daimler said.

It can have done little to improve Paul Daimler's feelings afterward, as Porsche's supercharged sports cars held the world's motoring spotlight, that Porsche had been more persuasive with his erstwhile bosses than he himself had been. It rankled, too, that his successor was awarded an honorary degree for his work, while Daimler received no such honor.

Paul Daimler died when our host was thirty-six. He was fifty-seven before the company that began with his grandfather found a place for him. In ten years he was retired for age, and he returned to his former engineering post in Hamburg.

Now that we had come to see him, Daimler and his wife were concerned that we also visit their new friends the Benzes. "They are very nice people," Mrs. Daimler said.

## Medieval Is Recent

Like the Daimlers, Carl and Gertrud Benz live in a walk-up flat. Their home occupies the top floor of a sturdy three-story white-painted brick building on the Ilvesheimerstrasse overlooking the wide, placid Neckar River, in Ladenburg, on the edge of Mannheim. The second floor is the home of Carl Benz's sister, Anneliese Elbe, and her husband, Wolfgang.

On the ground, a side room contains family memorabilia: a bust of grandfather Carl Benz, a painting of him and two of his wife, Bertha. There are tables, chairs, clocks, cabinets, a safe, a black trophy cabinet with a luminous likeness of Ladenburg's ancient city gate on the front, given to Bertha Benz on her ninetieth birthday. There is a functional replica of Carl's *Patent Motorwagen* on a scale of 5:1, presented to Bertha on her ninety-fifth birth anniversary.

At the back of the building is the machine shop that provides the livelihood of both families, Benz handling the technical end of the work and his brother-in-law the business part. At the moment, the work included an order for truck axles from Daimler-Benz.

Thus, the building continues to serve as home and workshop for the Benz family as it has done since 1905, when Carl Benz put it up for Eugen and Richard to build gas engines, Wolfgang Elbe said as he showed the visitors around. In 1908, gas engines having been rendered obsolete by diesels and electric motors, as Elbe explained it, Eugen and Richard gave up gas engines and began building automobiles, with a look-in from time to time from their father.

The machine was the twenty-five-horsepower Benz Söhne (Benz Sons) touring car—which seems to have come and gone with all the fanfare of an owl in the night, not many today knowing about it. The brothers built two hundred and fifty of the machines, according to Elbe; then, in 1922, they surrendered to postwar inflation.

When Benz visited his sons' shop, he hadn't far to go. The three-story mansion where he lived from 1904 until his death, in 1929, is on Ladenburg's main street, a quarter mile or so away. Bought by the city in 1974, the house is now a football club and wholesale beer outlet. The grounds in the back are a public park, and "the world's oldest garage," built by Benz for his *Patent Motorwagen*, is a restaurant.

The Benz family car, a ten-horsepower, 1899 Tonneau, moldered untouched in the garage until only recently, when the members of the family finally agreed among themselves to part with the machine, selling it to Gerhard von Raffay, Hamburg Volkswagen distributor and widely known collector of some of the finest vintage cars. Raffay had to conduct a considerable timbering operation in order to get the old car out to the street, the grounds having grown up into a forest during the decades since it last was driven.

Sadly, not salvaged were Carl Benz's personal papers from his sanctum over the garage. In a family dispute arising from the Benz distaste for celebrity, the documents were burned.

This aversion for the limelight was still strong in Carl Benz's great-granddaughter, schoolteacher Jutta Mercedes Benz, who was staying in her parents' apartment while they were away on vacation in Switzerland. She hid her identity as a Benz by retaining the name of her divorced husband. To be a Benz meant to play a role and to keep up a front, she explained as she poured wine. Besides, the subject of automobiles bored her.

A stroll in the twilight, amid the antiquity of her town, was more inviting. "Anything here that is merely medieval is recent," she said. She pointed out the crumbling remnants of walls and foundations left by the Romans more than two thousand years ago, the pocks in the stone above the town gate made by cannon or catapult, the tower where witches were tortured to prove their guilt before being burned. And there were the streets—narrow, tortuous, and cobblestoned—built for carts and chariots. No wonder the fragile gadgetry of her great-grandfather's first machine kept shaking apart as he strove to complete his two circuits of the city.

Next morning, the home of Carl Benz was left to us as our hostess departed for school, apologetically explaining that because of examinations, she was unable to take the day off. We washed the breakfast coffee cups and were careful to leave the kitchen as tidy as we found it. On our way through Mannheim, we discovered

Anneliese and Walter Elbe (left) and Trudel and Carl Benz with a pair of family cars outside their home and machine shop: a 1914 three-seater Benz sports machine with a 4-cylinder, 20-horsepower engine, and a 1914 Benz Söhne with a 25-horsepower, 4-cylinder engine and custom body by Stadler and Jest, Ludwigshafen. Ladenburg, 1978.

that there were still pockets where the Benz renown hadn't penetrated.

"Where is the Benz memorial?" we asked the blonde behind the desk at the Park Hotel.

She looked blank. "Never heard of it."

The Benz Memorial turned out to be the tall, rectangular slab looming at the head of the parkway in the next block.

Jutta would have liked that.

## He Always Wore Shoes

Our Mercedes-Benz 240 Diesel hummed a contented tune as it sped southward through the Swiss wonderland at a steady 140 kilometers (87 miles) an hour. In early June, water still plunged down the verdant peaks in long streamers from the melting snows beyond the clouds. At Kandersteg, with snow in the passes, we drove the car aboard a train and rode through the mountain in Stygian darkness, coming out on the other side somewhere in the heavens high above the Rhone River Valley.

"I-e-e-e, yi-yi!" yelled Frohmund Wiedmann, ordinarily a cool fellow, as he stole a look over the side at the first hairpin turn on our way down.

At the hot-springs resort of Brigerbad, Mr. and Mrs. Carl Benz, tanned by the Alpine sun, appeared in the lounge moments after their names were called over the loudspeaker in the camping area. We were soon seated in camp chairs under the awning of the Benz trailer, the 450 SL that had hauled it here from Ladenburg parked nearby. As he brought beer from the icebox, Benz told of the kick he had gotten out of being addressed as "Doctor" in our letter from Stuttgart. He laughed at our joke that we had conferred an honorary degree on him. In fact, he and his wife both laughed a great deal, seeming to find many things in life to laugh about.

Benz was but a boy when his grand-father was alive, but he still had memories of him. One that stood out was that when his grandfather went over to the shop that he built for Benz's father, Eugen, and uncle, Richard, he always walked. The inventor of the automobile scorned its use for commuter uses.

Eugen moved to the shop from the family mansion as soon as he was married. Uncle Richard was a life-long bachelor. Grandfather Benz, in those waning days of his life, spent most of his time tinkering in the little workshop he kept in his home, going over to see his sons when they called for advice.

With much merriment, the Benzes recalled grandfather Benz's nose-blowing ceremony. He spread the palm of his great hand—he had remarkably large hands—and over this, with exaggerated attention to details, draped his handkerchief, which was printed with red squares. With all finally in readiness, he clapped the handkerchief to his nose and noisily blasted until it seemed the dust at his feet stirred.

There was amusement again when the subject of the Benz memorial in Mannheim, erected in 1933, came up. Grandmother Benz, seeing the slab for the first time, objected that the bas-relief of her husband, wearing a toga-like garment as he stood by his three-wheeler, showed him barefooted. "Well," she exclaimed indignantly, "he always wore shoes!" (Actually, a close look shows sandals on Benz's feet.)

"My grandmother was a very resolute person," Benz said. "She was very strong-minded." She was "boss of the family." Mrs. Benz vigorously agreed, "Ja, ja!" that was the word—"boss." The two laughed heartily.

"She always kept pushing," Benz went on. "If it hadn't been for her, nothing would have happened. She was the one that said what was what. All the others

The world's first garage, built by Carl Benz around 1900, and the inventor's personal car, which he drove until 1910. The machine is an 1899 Tonneau with a 2-cylinder *Kontra-Motor* (opposed twin engine) of ten horsepower and would do thirty-one miles an hour, photographed on the Benz family estate (which is now owned by the city of Cadenburg) by Robert Haüsser, 1969.

were children." It was fully in character that she took matters into her own hands and made the celebrated jaunt to Pforzheim with the *Patent Motorwagen* that day in 1888. "She wanted to prove to her parents that her dowry had not been wasted," Benz said.

As Carl and brother-in-law Wolfgang Elbe turned out parts for Daimler-Benz, was there any advantage in the name Benz? None whatever. "We have to scramble for orders the same as anybody else." Was he perhaps thinking of designing a self-propelled vehicle in his machine shop, bringing things full circle? Benz laughed.

Back in Fellbach, the long day came to a surprise ending. In the darkness of the driveway, we struck our forehead on the upraised lid of the car trunk, instantly bleeding like the French Revolution. We were shortly stretched on a table in the emergency room of the hospital in Cannstatt, undergoing repair with needle and thread.

It could have been worse. The edges of Mercedes-Benz trunk lids are nicely padded.

# A P P E N D I X

## *The Mercedes-Benz Production Program*

### A Reference Guide to All the Vehicles Manufactured

Compiled by Dr. Claus–Peter Schulze of the Daimler-Benz Museum.

Daimler motor bicycle, 1885
1 cylinder • bore/stroke: 58/100 mm • 0.26 lit.
0.5 HP at 600 rpm, 12 km/h

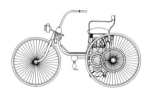

Daimler wire-wheel car, 1889
2 cylinders • bore/stroke: 70/126 mm • 0.97 lit.
1.65 HP at 920 rpm, 18 km/h

Daimler motor carriage, 1886
1 cylinder • bore/stroke: 70/120 mm • 0.46 lit.
1.1 HP at 600 rpm, 18 km/h

Benz Viktoria, 1893
1 cylinder • bore/stroke: 150/165 mm • 2.92 lit.
5 HP at 700 rpm, 25 km/h

Benz patent motor car, 1886
1 cylinder • bore/stroke: 91.4/150 mm • 0.99 lit.
0.89 HP at 400 rpm, 15 km/h

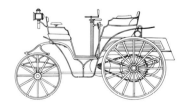

Benz Vis-à-Vis, 1893
1 cylinder • bore/stroke: 150/165 mm • 2.92 lit.
5 HP at 700 rpm, 25 km/h

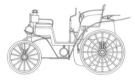

Daimler belt-driven car, Vis-à-Vis, 1894
2 cylinders · bore/stroke: 75/118 mm · 1.04 lit.
3.7 HP at 670 rpm, 18 km/h

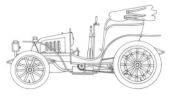

Paul Daimler Phaeton, 1901
2 cylinders · bore/stroke: 88/116 mm · 1.14 lit.
6.7 HP at 8000 rpm, 40 km/h

Benz Velo, 1894
1 cylinder · bore/stroke: 110/110 mm · 1.05 lit.
1.5 HP at 700 rpm, 21 km/h

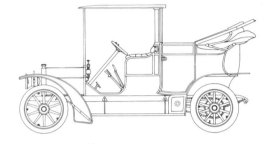

Mercedes Simplex, 1902
4 cylinders · bore/stroke: 90/120 mm · 3.05 lit.
22.6 HP at 1200 rpm, 70 km/h

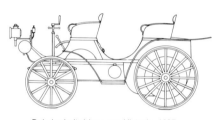

Daimler belt-driven car, Victoria, 1897
2 cylinders · bore/stroke: 100/140 mm · 2.20 lit.
7.91 HP at 720 rpm, 40 km/h

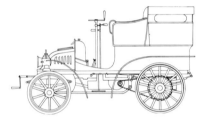

Benz Tonneau, 1902
2 cylinders · bore/stroke: 100/110 mm · 1.73 lit.
12 HP at 1280 rpm, 50 km/h

Benz Landaulette Coupé, 1899
2 cylinders · bore/stroke: 115/110 mm · 2.28 lit.
9 HP at 1000 rpm, 30 km/h

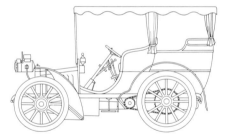

Mercedes Simplex Tonneau, 1903
4 cylinders · bore/stroke: 100/130 mm · 4.08 lit.
18 HP at 1200 rpm, 60 km/h

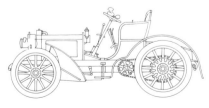

First Mercedes car, 1900
4 cylinders · bore/stroke: 116/140 mm · 5.93 lit.
35 HP at 1000 rpm, 72 km/h

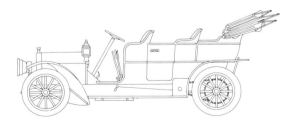

Mercedes Simplex Tourer, 1903
4 cylinders · bore/stroke: 120/150 mm · 6.78 lit.
40.3 HP at 1040 rpm, 70 km/h

Mercedes Simplex Phaeton, 1903
4 cylinders · bore/stroke: 140/150 mm · 9.23 lit.
60 HP at 1060 rpm, 90 km/h

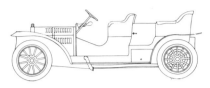

Benz 28/50 Tourer, 1907
4 cylinders · bore/stroke: 130/140 mm · 7.43 lit.
50 HP at 1350 rpm, 90 km/h

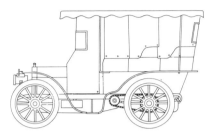

Mercedes Simplex Double Tonneau, 1904
4 cylinders · bore/stroke: 100/130 mm · 4.08 lit.
18 HP at 1200 rpm, 50 km/h

Benz limousine, 1907
4 cylinders · bore/stroke: 105/130 mm · 4.5 lit.
28 HP at 1300 rpm, 70 km/h

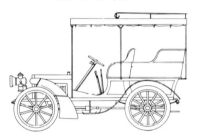

Benz Parsifal Tonneau, 1904
4 cylinders · bore/stroke: 90/110 mm · 2.80 lit.
18 HP at 1280 rpm, 50 km/h

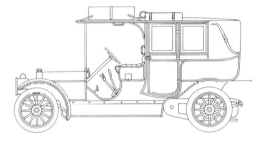

Mercedes Landaulette, 1908
6 cylinders · bore/stroke: 120/150 mm · 10.18 lit.
70 HP at 1280 rpm, 95 km/h

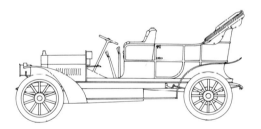

Benz Double Tonneau, 1905
4 cylinders · bore/stroke: 90/110 mm · 2.80 lit.
14 HP at 1200 rpm, 60 km/h

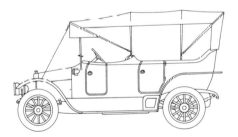

Mercedes 14/30 Tourer, 1910
4 cylinders · bore/stroke: 90/140 mm · 3.56 lit.
30 HP at 1600 rpm, 80 km/h

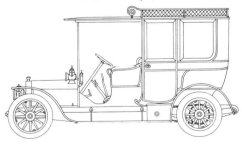

Mercedes Tourer, 1906
4 cylinders · bore/stroke: 120/150 mm · 6.78 lit.
45 HP at 1200 rpm, 85 km/h

Mercedes 28/60 Landaulette, 1910
4 cylinders · bore/stroke: 120/160 mm · 7.24 lit.
60 HP at 1250 rpm, 80 km/h

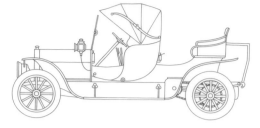

Mercedes 28/60 double Phaeton, 1910
4 cylinders · bore/stroke: 120/160 mm · 7.24 lit.
62.4 HP at 1250 rpm, 85 km/h

Mercedes 22/50 limousine, 1911
4 cylinders · bore/stroke: 110/150 mm · 5.7 lit.
54 HP at 1400 rpm, 89 km/h

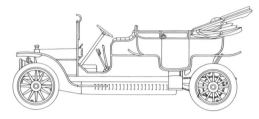
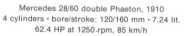

Mercedes 28/60 Landaulette, 1910
4 cylinders · bore/stroke: 120/160 mm · 7.24 lit.
62 HP at 1250 rpm, 85 km/h

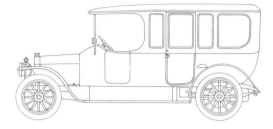

Mercedes 22/40 Tourer, 1912
4 cylinders · bore/stroke: 110/148 mm · 5.62 lit.
40 HP at 1250 rpm, 80 km/h

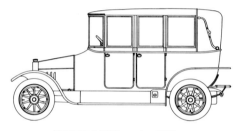

Mercedes 14/30 limousine, 1910
4 cylinders · bore/stroke: 90/140 mm · 4.08 lit.
35 HP at 1500 rpm, 80 km/h

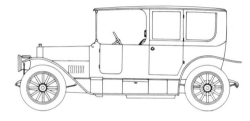

Benz 29/60 limousine, 1912
4 cylinders · bore/stroke: 125/150 mm · 6.76 lit.
60 HP at 1400 rpm, 95 km/h

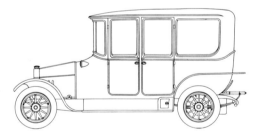

Mercedes 16/40 Knight, 1911
4 cylinders · bore/stroke: 100/130 mm · 4.08 lit.
43 HP at 1800 rpm, 80 km/h

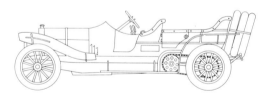

Mercedes 38/70 Sports Phaeton, 1912
4 cylinders · bore/stroke: 140/160 mm · 9.85 lit.
95.8 HP at 1200 rpm, 85 km/h

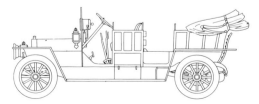

Mercedes 16/40 hunting car, 1911
4 cylinders · bore/stroke: 100/130 mm · 4.08 lit.
40 HP at 1800 rpm, 85 km/h

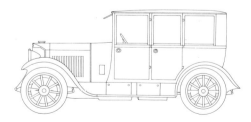

Benz 16/50 limousine, 1921
6 cylinders · bore/stroke: 80/138 mm · 4.16 lit.
52 HP at 1950 rpm, 95 km/h

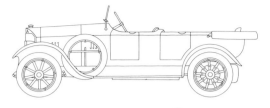

Mercedes 10/40/65 Tourer, 1922
4 cylinders · bore/stroke: 80/130 mm · 2.61 lit.
66 HP at 2800 rpm, with supercharger, 135 km/h

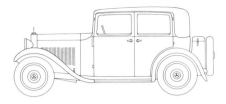

Mercedes-Benz limousine type 170, 1931
6 cylinders · bore/stroke: 65/85 mm · 1.69 lit.
32 HP at 3200 rpm, 90 km/h

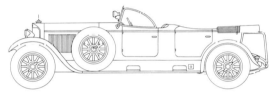

Mercedes type 15/70/100 limousine, 1924
6 cylinders · bore/stroke: 80/130 mm · 3.92 lit.
100 HP with 3100 rpm, with supercharger 104 km/h

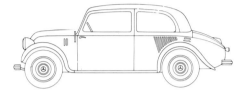

Mercedes-Benz limousine type 130 with rear engine, 1933
4 cylinders · bore/stroke: 70/85 mm · 1.3 lit.
26 HP at 330 rpm, 92 km/h

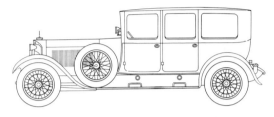

Mercedes type 24/100/140 Tourer, 1924
6 cylinders · bore/stroke: 94/150 mm · 6.25 lit.
145 HP at 3000 rpm, with supercharger 125 km/h

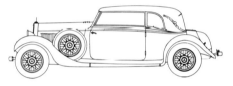

Mercedes-Benz convertible type 290, 1933
6 cylinders · bore/stroke: 78/100 mm · 2.85 lit.
68 HP at 3200 rpm, 108 km/h

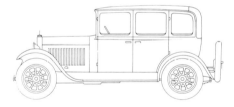

Mercedes-Benz type 200 Stuttgart, 1926
6 cylinders · bore/stroke: 65/100 mm · 1.98 lit.
38 HP at 3500 rpm, 80 km/h

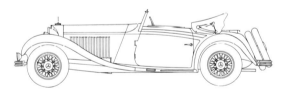

Mercedes-Benz convertible type 380, 1933
8 cylinders · bore/stroke: 78/100 mm · 3.8 lit.
140 HP at 3300 rpm, with supercharger 140 km/h

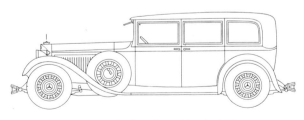

Mercedes-Benz *Grosser Mercedes*, 1930
8 cylinders · bore/stroke: 95/135 mm · 7.66 lit.
200 HP at 2800 rpm, with supercharger 160 km/h

Mercedes-Benz limousine type 170 H, 1935
4 cylinders · bore/stroke: 73.5/100 mm · 1.7 lit.
38 HP at 3200 rpm, 100 km/h

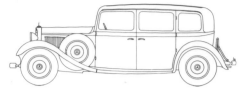

Mercedes-Benz limousine type 260 diesel, 1935
4 cylinders · bore/stroke: 90/100 mm · 2.55 lit.
45 HP at 3000 rpm, 95 km/h

1st diesel-powered production-line passenger car in the world

Mercedes-Benz limousine type 170 S, 1949
4 cylinders · bore/stroke: 75/100 mm · 1.8 lit.
52 HP at 4000 rpm, 120 km/h

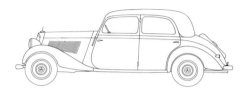

Mercedes-Benz limousine type 170 V, 1935
4 cylinders · bore/stroke: 73.5/100 mm · 1.7 lit.
38 HP at 3200 rpm, 110 km/h

Mercedes-Benz convertible type 220, 1951
6 cylinders · bore/stroke: 80/72.8 mm · 2.2 lit.
80 HP at 4600 rpm, 145 km/h

Mercedes-Benz convertible type 170 V, 1935
4 cylinders · bore/stroke: 73.5/100 mm · 1.7 lit.
38 HP at 32 rpm, 108 km/h

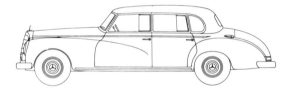

Mercedes-Benz limousine type 300, 1951
6 cylinders · bore/stroke: 85/88 mm · 3.0 lit.
125 HP at 4500 rpm, 162 km/h

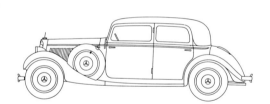

Mercedes-Benz limousine type 320, 1937
6 cylinders · bore/stroke: 82.5/100 mm · 3.21 lit.
78 HP at 4000 rpm, 126 km/h

Mercedes-Benz limousine type 180, 1953
4 cylinders · bore/stroke: 85/83.6 mm · 1.89 lit.
52 HP at 4000 rpm, 126 km/h

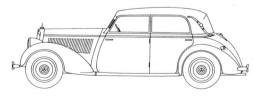

Mercedes-Benz convertible type 230, 1938
6 cylinders · bore/stroke: 72.5/90 mm · 2.23 lit.
55 HP at 3500 rpm, 116 km/h

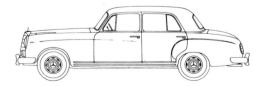

Mercedes-Benz limousine type 220a, 1954
6 cylinders · bore/stroke: 80/72.8 mm · 2.2 lit.
85 HP at 4800 rpm, 150 km/h

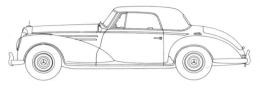

Mercedes-Benz coupé type 300 Sc., 1955
6 cylinders · bore/stroke: 95/99 mm · 3.0 lit.
175 HP at 5300 rpm, 180 km/h

Mercedes-Benz limousine type 300 D, 1951
6 cylinders · bore/stroke: 85/88 mm · 3.0 lit.
160 HP at 5300 rpm, 160 km/h

Mercedes-Benz limousine type 190, 1956
4 cylinders · bore/stroke: 85/83.6 mm · 1.9 lit.
75 HP at 4600 rpm, 139 km/h

Mercedes-Benz coupé 220 SE, 1959
6 cylinders · bore/stroke: 80/72.8 mm · 2.2 lit.
120 HP at 6000 rpm, 170 km/h

Mercedes-Benz limousine type 219, 1956
6 cylinders · bore/stroke: 80/72.8 mm · 2.2 lit.
85 HP at 4800 rpm, 148 km/h

Mercedes-Benz limousine type 220b, 1959
6 cylinders · bore/stroke: 80/72.8 mm · 2.2 lit.
95 HP at 4800 rpm, 155 km/h

Mercedes-Benz convertible type 220 S, 1956
6 cylinders · bore/stroke: 80/72.8 mm · 2.0 lit.
110 HP at 5000 rpm, 165 km/h

Mercedes-Benz limousine type 190c, 1961
4 cylinders · bore/stroke: 85/83.6 mm · 1.9 lit.
80 HP at 5000 rpm, 150 km/h

Mercedes-Benz limousine type 180a, 1957
4 cylinders · bore/stroke: 85/83.6 mm · 1.9 lit.
65 HP at 4500 rpm, 136 km/h

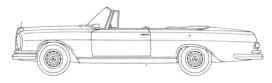

Mercedes-Benz convertible type 220 SE, 1961
6 cylinders · bore/stroke: 80/72.8 mm · 2.2 lit.
120 HP at 4800 rpm, 172 km/h

183

Mercedes-Benz limousine type 300 SE, 1961
6 cylinders · bore/stroke: 85/88 mm · 3.0 lit.
160 HP at 5300 rpm, 175 km/h

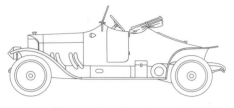

Mercedes 37/90 HP sports car, 1911
4 cylinders · bore/stroke: 130/180 mm · 9.55 lit.
90 HP at 1300 rpm, 114 km/h

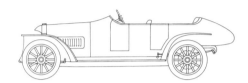

Benz sports car 28/80, 1909
4 cylinders · bore/stroke: 115/175 mm · 7.27 lit.
104 HP at 2050 rpm, 134 km/h

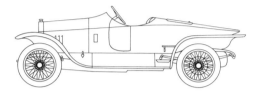

Mercedes 14/35 sports car, 1913
4 cylinders · bore/stroke: 90/140 mm · 3.56 lit.
35 HP at 1700 rpm, 90 km/h

Mercedes 14/30 sports car, 1910
4 cylinders · bore/stroke: 90/140 mm · 3.56 lit.
30 HP at 1600 rpm, 70 km/h

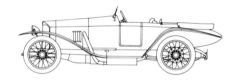

Benz 6/18 sports car, 1921
4 cylinders · bore/stroke: 68/108 mm · 1.57 lit.
18 HP at 3200 rpm, 120 km/h

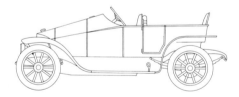

Mercedes 38/80 sports car, 1910
4 cylinders · bore/stroke: 140/160 mm · 9.85 lit.
75 HP at 1280 rpm, 90 km/h

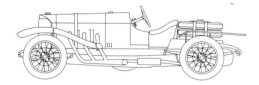

Mercedes 28/95 sports car, 1921
6 cylinders · bore/stroke: 105/140 mm · 7.27 lit.
95 HP at 1800 rpm, 110 km/h

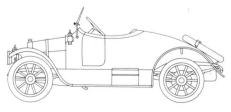

Mercedes 10/20 sports car, 1911
4 cylinders · bore/stroke: 80/130 mm · 2.61 lit.
20 HP at 1500 rpm, 65 km/h

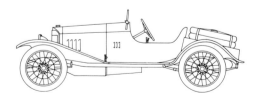

Mercedes 6/25/40 sports car, 1921
4 cylinders · bore/stroke: 68/108 mm · 1.57 lit.
43 HP at 2800 rpm, with supercharger 135 km/h

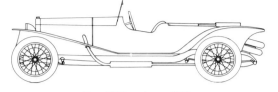

Benz 16/50 sports car, 1924
6 cylinders · bore/stroke: 80/138 mm · 4.16 lit.
50 HP at 1950 rpm, 90 km/h

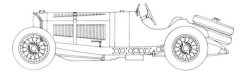

Mercedes-Benz type 720, model SSKL, racing sports car, 1931
6 cylinders · bore/stroke: 100/150 mm · 7.1 lit.
300 HP at 3400 rpm, always with supercharger 235 km/h

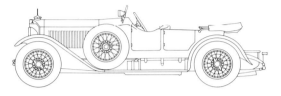

Mercedes-Benz type 630, 24/110/160, model K, 1927
6 cylinders · bore/stroke: 94/150 mm · 6.24 lit.
160 HP at 3000 rpm, with supercharger 145 km/h

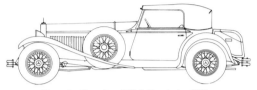

Mercedes-Benz type 370 S Mannheim, 1931
6 cylinders · bore/stroke: 82.5/115 mm · 3.66 lit.
78 HP at 3200 rpm, 110 km/h

Mercedes-Benz type 680, 26/120/180, model S, 1927
6 cylinders · bore/stroke: 98/150 mm · 6.79 lit.
180 HP at 3000 rpm, with supercharger 160 km/h

Mercedes-Benz roadster 500 K, 1934
8 cylinders · bore/stroke: 86/108 mm · 5.02 lit.
160 HP at 3400 rpm, with supercharger, 165 km/h

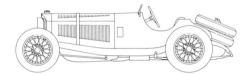

Mercedes-Benz type 710, 27/170/225, model SSK, 1928
6 cylinders · bore/stroke: 100/150 mm · 7.1 lit.
225 HP at 3200 rpm, with supercharger 175 km/h

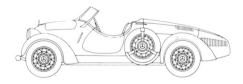

Mercedes-Benz type 150 with mid-engine, 1934
4 cylinders · bore/stroke: 72/92 mm · 1.49 lit.
55 HP at 4500 rpm, 125 km/h

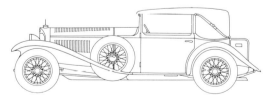

Mercedes-Benz type 700, 27/140/200, model SS, sports car, 1928
6 cylinders · bore/stroke: 100/150 mm · 7.02 lit.
225 HP at 3300 rpm, with supercharger 185 km/h

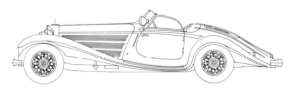

Mercedes-Benz roadster 540 K, 1936
8 cylinders · bore/stroke: 88/111 mm · 5.4 lit.
180 HP at 3600 rpm, with supercharger 170 km/h

Mercedes-Benz sports car 300 SL, 1954
6 cylinders · bore/stroke: 85/88 mm · 3.0 lit.
215 HP at 5800 rpm, 260 km/h

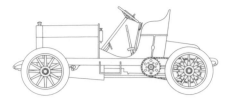

Mercedes racing car, 1903
4 cylinders · bore/stroke: 140/151 mm · 9.29 lit.
65 HP at 1100 rpm, 128 km/h

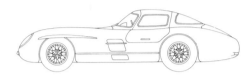

Mercedes-Benz racing sports car 300 SLR, 1955
8 cylinders · bore/stroke: 78/78 mm · 2.98 lit.
300 HP at 7500 rpm, 290 km/h

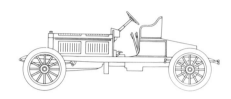

Benz Parsifal racing car, 1903
4 cylinders · bore/stroke: 160/140 mm · 11.26 lit.
60 HP at 1200 rpm, 120 km/h

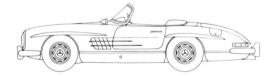

Mercedes-Benz sports car 190 SL, 1955
4 cylinders · bore/stroke: 85/83.6 mm · 1.9 lit.
105 HP at 5700 rpm, 175 km/h

Mercedes Grand Prix racing car, 1908
4 cylinders · bore/stroke: 155/170 mm · 12.8 lit.
120 HP at 1400 rpm, 155 km/h

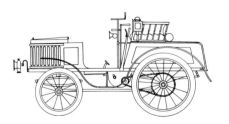

Mercedes-Benz 300 SL roadster, 1957
6 cylinders · bore/stroke: 85/88 mm · 3.0 lit.
215 HP at 5800 rpm, 260 km/h

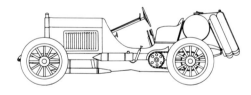

Benz Grand Prix racing car, 1908
4 cylinders · bore/stroke: 155/160 mm · 12.08 lit.
120 HP at 1550 rpm, 160 km/h

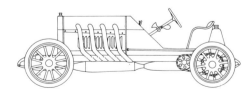

Benz racing car, 1900
2 cylinders · bore/stroke: 120/120 mm · 2.71 lit.
10 HP at 1000 rpm, 50 km/h

Benz racing car, 1909
4 cylinders · bore/stroke: 185/200 mm · 21.5 lit.
200 HP at 1500 rpm, 210 km/h

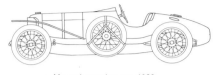

Benz racing car "Blitzen-Benz," 1911
4 cylinders · bore/stroke: 185/200 mm · 21.5 lit.
200 HP at 1500 rpm, 228 km/h

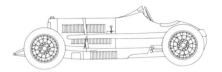

Mercedes racing car, 1923
4 cylinders · bore/stroke: 65/113 mm · 1.5 lit.
65 HP at 3600 rpm, with supercharger

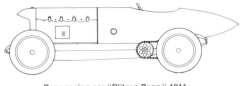

Mercedes Grand Prix racing car, 1914
4 cylinders · bore/stroke: 93/164 mm · 4.45 lit.
117 HP at 3180 rpm, 180 km/h

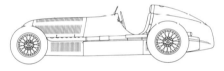

Mercedes racing car, 1924 Monza
8 cylinders · bore/stroke: 61.9/82.8 mm · 2.0 lit.
160 HP at 6000 rpm

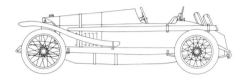

Benz 10/30 racing car, 1921
4 cylinders · bore/stroke: 80/130 mm · 2.61 lit.
30 HP at 3100 rpm, 130 km/h

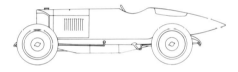

Mercedes-Benz W 25 racing car, 1935
8 cylinders · bore/stroke: 82/102 mm · 4.3 lit.
462 HP at 5800 rpm

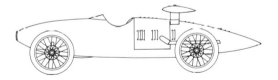

Benz drop-shaped racing car, 1922
6 cylinders · bore/stroke: 65/100 mm · 2.0 lit.
90 HP at 5000 rpm, 160 km/h

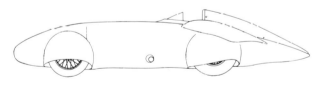

Mercedes-Benz W 25 record car, 1936
12 cylinders · bore/stroke: 77.5/88 mm · 4.98 lit.
540 HP at 5800 rpm, 372 km/h

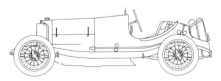

Mercedes racing car Targa Florio, 1923
4 cylinders · bore/stroke: 70/129 mm · 1.98 lit.
120 HP at 4500 rpm

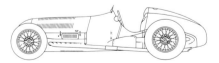

Mercedes-Benz W 125 racing car, 1937
8 cylinders · bore/stroke: 94/102 mm · 5.66 lit.
592 HP at 5800 rpm, 320 km/h

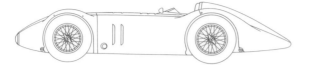

Mercedes-Benz W 125 racing car, 1937
8 cylinders · bore/stroke: 94/102 mm · 5.66 lit.
646 HP at 5800 rpm, 380 km/h

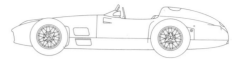

Mercedes-Benz W 196 racing car Monoposto, 1954
8 cylinders · bore/stroke: 76/68.8 mm · 2.5 lit.
280 HP at 8500 rpm, 265 km/h

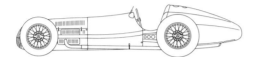

Mercedes-Benz W 154 racing car, 1938
12 cylinders · bore/stroke: 67/70 mm · 2.96 lit.
468 HP at 7800 rpm

Mercedes-Benz W 196, streamlined, 1954
8 cylinders · bore/stroke: 76/68.8 mm · 2.5 lit.
280 HP at 8500 rpm, 275 km/h

Mercedes-Benz W 125 record car, 1938
12 cylinders · bore/stroke: 82/88 mm · 5.57 lit.
736 HP at 5800 rpm, 433 km/h

Daimler truck, 1896
2 cylinders · bore/stroke: 90/120 mm · 1.53 lit.
5.27 HP at 720 rpm, 1.5 tons payload

1st motorized truck in the world.

Mercedes-Benz W 154 / M 163 racing car, 1939
12 cylinders · bore/stroke: 67/70 mm · 2.96 lit.
483 HP at 7800 rpm, 320 km/h

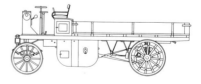

Benz delivery van, 1896
1 cylinder · bore/stroke: 150/165 mm · 2.92 lit.
5 HP at 700 rpm, 0.3 ton payload

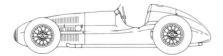

Mercedes-Benz W 165 racing car, 1939
8 cylinders · bore/stroke: 64/58 mm · 1.49 lit.
254 HP at 8000 rpm, 245 km/h

Daimler truck, 1896
2 cylinders · bore/stroke: 100/140 mm · 2.20 lit.
7.3 HP at 720 rpm, 2 tons payload

Daimler truck, 1897
2 cylinders · bore/stroke: 130/160 mm · 4.24 lit.
12.9 HP at 600 rpm, 5 tons payload

Benz 35 HP truck, 1913
4 cylinders · bore/stroke: 105/150 mm · 5.19 lit.
35 HP at 1100 rpm, 1.5 tons payload

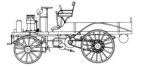

Daimler truck, 1898
2 cylinders · bore/stroke: 90/120 mm · 1.53 lit.
5.5 HP at 750 rpm, 1.7 tons payload

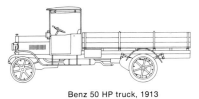

Benz 50 HP truck, 1913
4 cylinders · bore/stroke: 125/150 mm · 7.4 lit.
50 HP at 1300 rpm, 3.5 tons payload

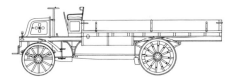

Daimler truck, 1899
2 cylinders · bore/stroke: 90/120 mm · 1.53 lit.
5.5 HP at 600 rpm, 2.2 tons payload

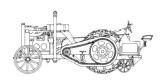

Benz-Sending S 7 motor plow, 1922
2 cylinders · bore/stroke: 135/200 mm · 2.86 lit.
30 HP at 800 rpm

1st diesel-powered rail-less vehicle in the world

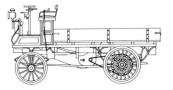

Benz truck, 1901
1 cylinder · bore/stroke: 115/110 mm · 1.15 lit.
7 HP at 980 rpm, 1.25 tons payload

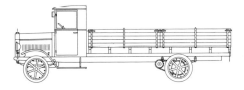

Benz truck 5 K 3, 1. diesel truck, 1923
4 cylinders · bore/stroke: 125/180 mm · 8.83 lit.
50 HP at 1000 rpm, 5.5 tons payload

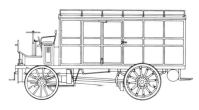

Daimler truck, 1902
2 cylinders · bore/stroke: 120/160 mm · 3.62 lit.
10.2 HP at 640 rpm, 2 tons payload

Mercedes-Benz L 1, 1926
4 cylinders · bore/stroke: 95/130 mm · 3.68 lit.
45 HP at 1800 rpm, 1.5 tons payload

Mercedes-Benz L 4000, 1931
6 cylinders · bore/stroke: 100/150 mm · 7.07 lit.
70 HP at 1500 rpm, 4 tons payload

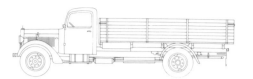

Mercedes-Benz L 2000, 1937
4 cylinders · bore/stroke: 100/120 mm · 3.77 lit.
55 HP at 2000 rpm, 2 tons payload

Mercedes-Benz L 2500, 1931
6 cylinders · bore/stroke: 80/130 mm · 3.92 lit.
50 HP at 2000 rpm, 2.5 tons payload

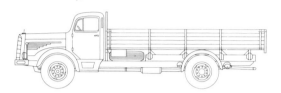

Mercedes-Benz L 5000, 1952
6 cylinders · bore/stroke: 105/140 mm · 7.27 lit.
120 HP at 2250 rpm, 5 tons payload

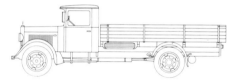

Mercedes-Benz LO 2000, 1932
4 cylinders · bore/stroke: 100/120 mm · 3.77 lit.
55 HP at 2000 rpm, 2 tons payload

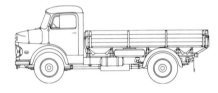

Mercedes-Benz L 322, 1958
6 cylinders · bore/stroke: 95/120 mm · 5.1 lit.
110 HP at 3000 rpm, 6 tons payload

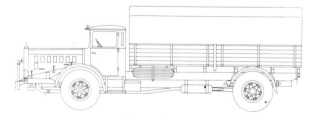

Mercedes-Benz L 6500, 1935
6 cylinders · bore/stroke: 125/170 mm · 12.52 lit.
150 HP at 1700 rpm, 6.5 tons payload

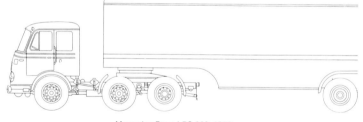

Mercedes-Benz LPS 333, 1958
6 cylinders · bore/stroke: 128/140 mm · 10.81 lit.
192 HP at 2200 rpm, 10 tons payload

Mercedes-Benz L 10000, 1936
6 cylinders · bore/stroke: 125/170 mm · 12.52 lit.
150 HP at 1700 rpm, 10 tons payload

Mercedes-Benz unimog, 1951
4 cylinders · bore/stroke: 75/100 mm · 1.8 lit.
24 HP at 2350 rpm, 1-ton payload

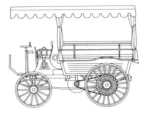

Benz Break, 1898
2 cylinders • bore/stroke: 130/160 mm • 4.25 lit.
15 HP at 910 rpm, 12 seats

SAF Gaggenau (Benz) Omnibus, 1910
4 cylinders • bore/stroke: 90/140 mm • 3.51 lit.
25 HP at 900 rpm, 12 seats

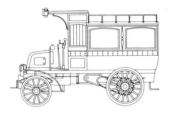

Daimler Omnibus, 1898
2 cylinders • bore/stroke: 120/160 mm • 3.62 lit.
10.2 HP at 640 rpm, 12 seats

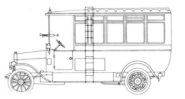

Daimler Omnibus, 1919
4 cylinders • bore/stroke: 110/150 mm • 5.7 lit.
35 HP at 1000 rpm, 18 seats

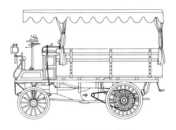

Benz Omnibus, 1902
2 cylinders • bore/stroke: 100/110 mm • 1.73 lit.
12.2 HP at 1280 rpm, 14 seats

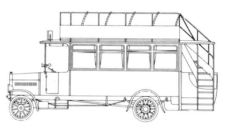

Daimler Omnibus, 1921
4 cylinders • bore/stroke: 80/130 mm • 2.61 lit.
35 HP at 1500 rpm, 36 seats

Daimler Post Bus, 1906
4 cylinders • bore/stroke: 100/130 mm • 4.08 lit.
28 HP at 1100 rpm, 17 seats

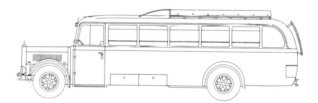

Mercedes-Benz O 4000, 1931
6 cylinders • bore/stroke: 105/150 mm • 7.79 lit.
110 HP at 2000 rpm, 42 seats

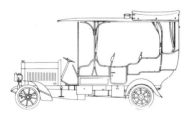

Daimler Post Bus, 1908
4 cylinders • bore/stroke: 110/140 mm • 5.3 lit.
35 HP at 1200 rpm, 15 seats

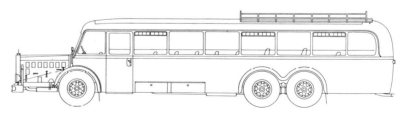

Mercedes-Benz O 10000, 1936
6 cylinders • bore/stroke: 125/170 mm • 12.5 lit.
150 HP at 1700 rpm, 80 seats

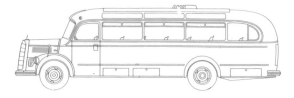

Mercedes-Benz O 3500, 1950
6 cylinders · bore/stroke: 90/120 mm · 4.57 lit.
90 HP at 2800 rpm, 37 seats

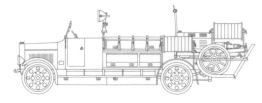

Mercedes-Benz L 2 crew carrier, 1927
6 cylinders · bore/stroke: 100/150 mm · 7.1 lit.
70 HP at 1500 rpm

Mercedes-Benz O 319 D, 1956
4 cylinders · bore: 75 mm · stroke: 100 mm · 1.767 lit.
43 HP at 3500 rpm, 80 km/h, 18 seats

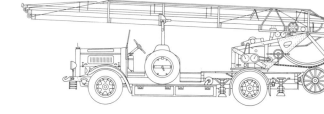

Mercedes-Benz LF 5 fire engine, 1928
6 cylinders · bore/stroke: 105/150 mm · 7.8 lit.
100 HP at 2000 rpm

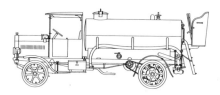

Benz K 5 sprinkler truck, 1920
4 cylinders · bore/stroke: 125/150 mm · 7.4 lit.
50 HP at 1000 rpm · 5000 lit. capacity

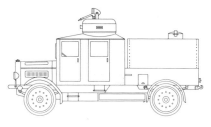

Mercedes-Benz L 5 water gun, 1930
6 cylinders · bore/stroke: 110/150 mm · 7.8 lit.
100 HP at 2000 rpm

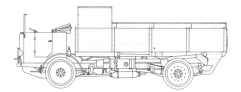

Benz low-frame refuse tipper, 1924
4 cylinders · bore/stroke: 110/165 mm · 6.3 lit.
45 HP at 1000 rpm, 3 tons payload

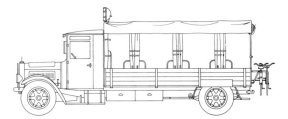

Mercedes-Benz O 4000 crew carrier, 1931
6 cylinders · bore/stroke: 105/150 mm · 7.8 lit.
100 HP at 2000 rpm

Mercedes-Benz L 5 sprinkler truck, 1927
4 cylinders · bore/stroke: 120/180 mm · 8.2 lit.
70 HP at 1300 rpm

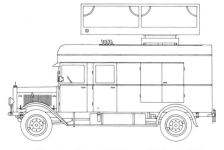

Mercedes-Benz L 2500 turntable truck, 1931
6 cylinders · bore/stroke: 80/130 mm · 3.9 lit.
50 HP at 2000 rpm

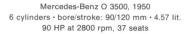

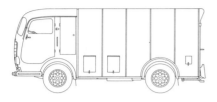

Mercedes-Benz LKO 3000 refuse collecting truck, 1935
4 cylinders · bore/stroke: 110/130 mm · 4.9 lit.
65 HP at 2000 rpm

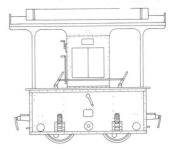

Narrow-gauge locomotive with Daimler 2-cylinder V engine, 1893
4 HP at 580 rpm

Mercedes-Benz LKO 3000 gully-cleaning truck, 1937
4 cylinders · bore/stroke: 110/130 mm · 4.9 lit.
75 HP at 2000 rpm

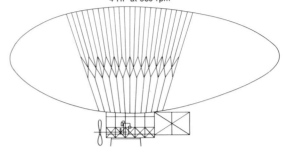

Steered balloon *Deutschland,* with Daimler PL/D aero engine, 1896
2 cylinders · bore/stroke: 104/160 mm · 2.7 lit.
7.1 HP at 535 rpm

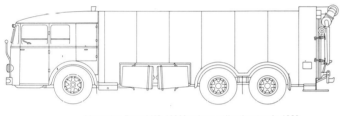

Mercedes-Benz LKO 10000 refuse-collecting truck, 1939
6 cylinders · bore/stroke: 110/165 mm · 9.4 lit.
110 HP at 1600 rpm, gas generator operation

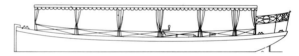

Motorboat with Benz 2-cylinder twin engine, 1895
bore/stroke: 97/97 mm · 1.43 lit.
5 HP at 700 rpm

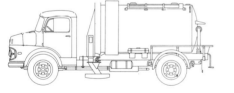

Mercedes-Benz LKO 322/44 gravel spreader, 1959
6 cylinders · bore/stroke: 95/120 mm · 5.1 lit.
110 HP at 3000 rpm

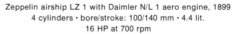

Zeppelin airship LZ 1 with Daimler N/L 1 aero engine, 1899
4 cylinders · bore/stroke: 100/140 mm · 4.4 lit.
16 HP at 700 rpm

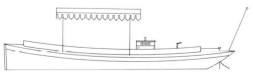
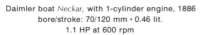

Daimler boat *Neckar,* with 1-cylinder engine, 1886
bore/stroke: 70/120 mm · 0.46 lit.
1.1 HP at 600 rpm

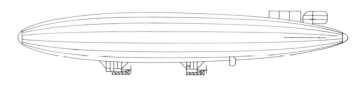

Schütte-Lanz Airship SL 1 with Daimler J 8 airship engine, 1910
8 cylinders · bore/stroke: 175/165 mm · 31.7 lit.
360 HP at 1200 rpm

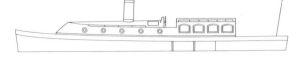

SMS *Kaiser,* with Daimler marine engine, 1911
4 cylinders · bore/stroke: 200/270 mm · 33.91 lit.
100 HP at 500 rpm

Albatros triplane DR II with Benz Bz III aero engine, 1917
8 cylinders · bore/stroke: 125/140 mm · 13.75 lit.
235 HP at 1200 rpm

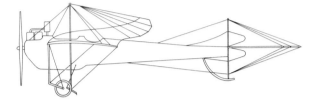

Rumpler airplane *Taube,* with Daimler Kathreiner Prize E 4 F aero engine, 1911
4 cylinders · bore/stroke: 120/140 mm · 6.35 lit.
70 HP at 1300 rpm

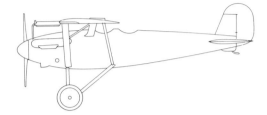

Airplane L 14 with Daimler D III b aero engine, 1917
8 cylinders · bore/stroke: 106/170 mm · 12.0 lit.
200 HP at 1950 rpm

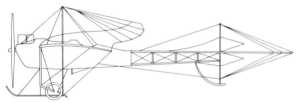

Albatros Airplant *Taube,* with Benz Kaiser Prize FX aero engine, 1912
4 cylinders · bore/stroke: 130/180 · 9.55 lit.
102.7 HP at 1288 rpm

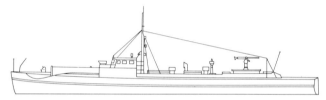

Speedboat with MB 502 engines, 1935
16 cylinders · bore/stroke: 175/230 mm · 88.5 lit.
1320 HP at 1620 rpm

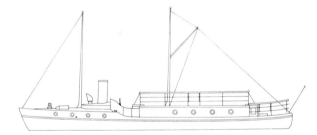

Motor cruiser *Mária Márka,* with Daimler LS 10854 marine engine, 1914
4 cylinders · bore/stroke: 108/150 mm · 5.49 lit.
35 HP at 850 rpm

LZ 130 *Graf Zeppelin II,* with 4 engines Daimler-Benz DB 602, 1938
16 cylinders · bore/stroke: 175/230 mm · 88.5 lit.
1200 HP at 1600 rpm

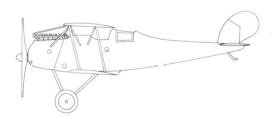

Halberstadt biplane CL IV with Daimler DF 170, DIIIa aero engine, 1917
6 cylinders · bore/stroke: 140/160 mm · 14.8 lit.
180 HP at 1450 rpm

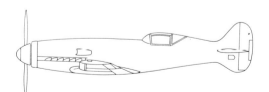

Record airplane Messerschmidt Me 209, with Daimler-Benz DB 601 record engine, 1939
12 cylinders · bore/stroke: 150/160 mm · 33.9 lit.
2770 HP at 3100 rpm

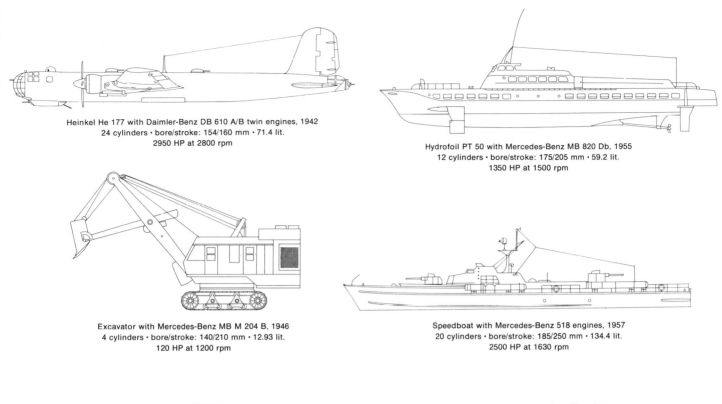

Heinkel He 177 with Daimler-Benz DB 610 A/B twin engines, 1942
24 cylinders · bore/stroke: 154/160 mm · 71.4 lit.
2950 HP at 2800 rpm

Hydrofoil PT 50 with Mercedes-Benz MB 820 Db, 1955
12 cylinders · bore/stroke: 175/205 mm · 59.2 lit.
1350 HP at 1500 rpm

Excavator with Mercedes-Benz MB M 204 B, 1946
4 cylinders · bore/stroke: 140/210 mm · 12.93 lit.
120 HP at 1200 rpm

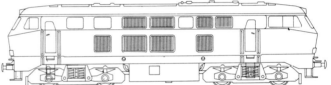

Speedboat with Mercedes-Benz 518 engines, 1957
20 cylinders · bore/stroke: 185/250 mm · 134.4 lit.
2500 HP at 1630 rpm

Diesel locomotive V 80, with Mercedes-Benz MD 820 Db, 1953
12 cylinders · bore/stroke: 175/205 mm · 59.2 lit.
1100 HP at 1500 rpm

Diesel locomotive V 160, with Mercedes-Benz MB 839 Bb, 1959
16 cylinders · bore/stroke: 190/230 mm · 104.3 lit.
2100 HP at 1500 rpm

1. Benz Comfortable. Built in 1897, this model improved the Velo model by the addition of a canopy. The engine has 2 cylinders and develops 3 horsepower. This car, owned by Max Rauck, is kept at the Auto and Motorrad Museum, in Bad Oeynhausen. Photographed at a sixteenth-century farmhouse in Hessingen-Olendorf, Germany, 1978.

2. Daimler Phaeton, equipped with a Daimler Phoenix engine, was built at Coventry. The British Daimler Company was founded in 1869, dedicated from the very beginning to the manufacture of luxury cars. Fitted with "hot tube" ignition, four forward gears, and four reverse gears, it has a 2-cylinder, 4-horsepower engine capable of delivering up to 24 miles per hour. The Phaeton shown, built in 1897, is the oldest British car still running today, owned by Commander E. D. Wooley. England, 1978.

3. Mercedes 70-horsepower race car, 1904. In British terminology, automobiles manufactured before December 31, 1904, are referred to as "veteran" cars. The owner restorers, Paul Foulkes-Halbaro and Bernard W. Garrett, took approximately thirty-five hundred hours to restore the car. England, 1978.

4. 1903 Mercedes Simplex Tonneau with an 18/22-horsepower, 4-cylinder, 3-liter engine, owned by Raffay Company, Hamburg, 1978. The Tonneau, a design that was popular until about 1904, is an open four-seat touring car in which access to the rear seats is by a door at the back. Baron Louis de Cartier ordered this carrosserie but later canceled the order in favor of another model with a larger engine. Jellinek then purchased the body and put it onto this chassis.

5. Detail, 1909 Benz.

6. 1909 Benz 14/30-horsepower, 4-cylinder six-seat tourer. Hohenzollern, Germany, 1978. It was restored by its owner, Peter Oelschlager, Stuttgart.

7. 1925 Benz 35-horsepower truck, owned by Daimler-Benz. Hamburg, Germany, 1978. Benz built his first Diesel-powered truck in 1923. A more complicated system of Daimler's was phased out of production in favor of the Benz system when the companies merged, in 1926.

8. 1910 Mercedes 14/30-horsepower, 4-cylinder (replica bodied) two-seat sports car designed by Paul Daimler. The orange color was favored in the early cars. Owned by the Raffay Company Hamburg, 1978.

9. 1908 Maja, owned by the Raffay Company, photographed at Ahrensburg, Germany, 1978. This model is fitted with a 24/28-horsepower, 4-cylinder, 4.52 liter engine which will accelerate the car to 46 miles an hour. The Laundaulet body is by Bergeon, France. The Maja (my-yah) was named after Jellinek's second daughter and was produced under the auspices of the Austro-Daimler Company, Wiener-Neustadt. Jellinek ordered for his own Austrian Automobile Company six hundred Maja chassis from the Austrian DMG. Despite extensive advertising, the car failed to sell because of outdated design and construction deficiencies. Jellinek's company went bankrupt and was liquidated by 1909. But the model was carried on (with conventional gearbox) as the Austro-Daimler 28/32-horsepower, which later became the successful Prince-Henry-Type (86-hp) of 1910.

10. 1925 Mercedes Type 400, 15/70/100 (short-wheelbase version), driven by a 6-cylinder, 4-liter 70-horsepower engine (100 with supercharger engaged), Wilhelmshöhe, Germany, 1978. This model was produced from 1924 to 1926 by the DMG and from 1926 to 1929 by Daimler-Benz AG. It was a forerunner of the Mercedes-Benz Type 600 K model, which was similarly bodied and manufactured only as a short-wheelbase car from 1927 to 1929. The car shown was ordered by Richard Tauber, the opera singer in 1927. It is owned today by Paul-Heinz Röhll.

11. 1928 Mercedes-Benz Type 710, Model SS, 27/160/200 (W 1156 II), Bryn Athyn, Pennsylvania, 1978. The engines of this period were identified by three numbers

as in this case 27/160/200). The first number was the amount of tax the customer had to pay. In Germany the tax was computed according to the volume of the engine. (This engine is named 38/250 in England, in America, by another system of calculation, and in France there is yet another.) The second number tells the horsepower of the engine at normal speed, and the third the horsepower with supercharger engaged. This car was one of the 141 SS cars manufactured between 1927 and 1935. It cost between eleven and thirteen thousand dollars, and it had a top speed of 120 miles per hour. The car was shipped to the United States in 1929 without a body and displayed as a show chassis in New York City. Tie rods, spring shackles, etc., were chrome plated for the display. The car was later purchased and shipped to Switzerland for the addition of a body built by Graber. When the car was returned to the United States, the pontoon-type fenders were fabricated by the New York City Rolls-Royce distributor.

12. Mercedes-Benz Type 600, 24/100/140, (W 9456), produced from 1924 to 1929, Luxembourg, 1978. This car was ordered as a tourer on November 2, 1926, by Oscar Henschel, of Kassel. The body was later redesigned in the more sportive style, with jump seat, shown here. It is kept in the Daimler-Benz museum.

13. 1928 Mercedes-Benz Type 700, Model S, 27/140/200, (W 11565), a 6-cylinder, four-seat open tourer with factory body. The car was bought in 1928 by E. J. Simmons, Jr., of Greenwich, Connecticut, who traded in a Packard and a Ford on the car. This photograph was taken in 1975 by its owner, Berthold Rückwarth, who restored the machine after bringing it to his home in Bielefeld, Germany, in 1974.

14. 1929 Mercedes-Benz Type 710, Model SS, 27/170/225 (W 06), with a 7-litre engine capable of up to 119 miles per hour, owned by Werner Ehret Rottach-Eegern, Germany, 1978. This car was originally built for royal-family member Prince Hohenlohe Bartenstein and was converted into an SS by Daimler-Benz for Eric Spandel, owner of the *Nürburger News*, in 1929 (the current body is a two-seater by Armbruster, of Vienna, Austria). This car is often misrepresented as an SSK.

15. Mercedes-Benz town cars were produced from 1926 to 1930. The left and middle cars are the type 200 Stuttgart 8/38 hp, (W 02) 6-cylinder car and the type 260 Stuttgart 10/50 hp, (W 11) 6-cylinder car, both of 1930. At right is the Type 460 Nürburg 18/80 hp, (W 08) 6-cylinder car of 1929. The Nürburg model is the largest of the line (named after the Nürburg castle) and was assembled in Mannheim, as were the long wheelbase Stuttgart and Mannheim models. The short wheel-base Stuttgart models were assembled in Stuttgart. Photographed near Mulhouse, France, 1978.

16. 1938 Mercedes-Benz Type 540 K (W 29) 8-cylinder, 115/180-horsepower Cabriolet B with Sindelfingen body. Maryland, 1977. K, denotes that the engine is supercharged. This straight-eight K line began with the 380 K (1933–34), was followed by the 500 K (1933–36)

and the 540 K (1936–39), and ended with the 580 K (1939–40).

17. 1935 Mercedes-Benz Type 290 (W 18) Limousine fitted with a 320 (M 142) engine, owned by Captain Harry Rosensweig, San Antonio, Texas, 1978. The white stripe on the side indicates these cars were used as taxis in Germany.

18. 1937 Mercedes-Benz Type 540 K (W 29) Cabriolet A, left, and 1935 Mercedes-Benz Type 500 K (W 29) roadster, both with Sindelfingen body. The early-thirties, lean-looking body style typifies this roadster, and the rounded-out shape of the late thirties marks this 540 K Cabriolet A. Owned by Robert Friggens, Albuquerque, New Mexico, 1978.

19. 1935 Mercedes-Benz Type 500 K (W 29) supercharged roadster, Georgia, 1978. The roadster body style is closely related to the Cabriolet A. Like the Cabriolet A, it is a two-seater with two doors; unlike the Cabriolet, it has a soft top, which folds into a recessed compartment covered by canvas or leather. Both the roadster and the special roadster models were fitted with a jumpseat.

20. Airbrush painting of 1955 Mercedes-Benz Gullwing by Harold James Cleworth, San Francisco, California. 1977. The Gullwing evolved from Daimler-Benz's need to get back into racing after World War II and reestablished the Mercedes-Benz name. Ordering one thousand, an American importer inspired the company to build a 300 SL production coupe. The doors open upward in order to accommodate the framework of welded steel tubing.

21. 1968 280 SL two-seater sports car and 1955 300 SL Gullwing coupe, California, circa 1975. The 300 SL, introduced in 1954 as the first of the SL line, was followed a year later by a succession of lighter versions for the sportsman driver. S symbolizes a powerful, ultra-comfortable car sometimes with sportive character; L retains its prewar meaning: *Leicht* (light).

22. 1977 Mercedes-Benz 450 SL, Palm Springs, California, 1977.

23. C111 test cars on the Daimler-Benz test track. These machines were originally used in the development of the Wankel engine in 1969 (left and right) and 1970 (center).

24. 1929 Mercedes-Benz Type 710, Model SSK 27/180/250 (WS 06), driven by its owner, Berthold Rückwarth, Germany, 1978. One of seven of its kind still in existence (a total of forty-two SSK cars were manufactured), this extremely strong car, nicknamed the white jumbo, will do up to eighty miles per hour (130 kph) in second gear. These cars were originally raced without fenders and lights. The red racing stripe was used with red fenders only once, at the German Grand Prix for sports cars in 1929.

With the exception of numbers 13, 20, 21, and 23, all the color photographs are by Wendy Grad.

# INDEX